JAKE

An American Original

Volume II

CLIFF GALLANT

JAKE

Volume Two. Copyright 2020 by Cliff Gallant
All rights reserved.

This is a work of memoir and reportage. Facts have been preserved and related truthfully to the best of the author's knowledge.

Unless otherwise credited, photos are the property and copyright of Jake Sawyer.

ISBN: 978-1-950381-34-0

Published by Piscataqua Press
32 Daniel St., Portsmouth NH 03801

www.ppressbooks.com

Printed in the United States of America

JAKE

AN AMERICAN ORIGINAL
VOLUME TWO

**The Astonishing, Shockingly Violent,
Sex-filled, Often Hilarious
Life Story of Jake Sawyer:**

★An Early Hell's Angel Nomad
★U.S. Army Paratrooper
★Legendary Health and Fitness Trainer to
the Elite and Not So Elite
★Trainer of Award-winning Bodybuilders
and Power Lifters
★Arm Wrestling Champion
★Prep School Sports Star
★High Profile Inmate of Notorious State
and Federal Prisons
★Ferocious Fighter and Expert Knife Thrower
★Scoundrel
★A Friend to the End.

THE MEN THAT DON'T FIT IN

There's a race of men that don't fit in,
A race that can't stay still;
So they break the hearts of kith and kin,
And they roam the world at will.
They range the field and they rove the flood,
And they climb the mountain's crest;
Theirs is the curse of the gypsy blood,
And they don't know how to rest.

If they just went straight they might go far;
They are strong and brave and true;
But they're always tired of the things that are,
And they want the strange and new.

-Robert Service

**Dedicated to
Ralph "Sonny" Barger**

TWELVE

When I arrived at Jake's place for our interview this time, Jake was raring to go, as usual. Never known him to be otherwise, actually. He's also always extremely well organized and attentive to the matter at hand, whether it's tending to the maintenance of the very cool vintage Lincoln Town Car he recently acquired, or telling his life story. As has been his practice throughout the interview process, when I arrived he had pictures of the time period we're currently covering laid out very neatly for me to choose from. My eye immediately went to the one taken of some men moving a rug and some exercise equipment into Martin's Health Club, which for years was a very popular physical fitness center, not to mention a few other not so healthy things, in what is today the center of the Old Port, Portland's high-scale waterfront shopping and entertainment district.

When Jake saw me looking at the picture and grinning, he laughed loudly and said, "I thought you'd go for that one! That picture captures a significant part of Portland history! You better believe it! The last time we spoke I was headed back to Portland after my brief but pleasant visit to the Combat Zone and the emergency room of Massachusetts General Hospital, and today we're going to talk about what life was like for ol' Jakie boy when he got back to his home town of Portland, Maine!

"The opening of Martin's Health Club in 1970, under the ownership of my friend, Al Martin, and under the managerial expertise of yours truly, lifted Portland out of the Dark Ages and catapulted the city into

the dynamic and fun-filled place it is today!"
Who knew?

HOME SWEET HOME

"After my rude reception by the Devil's Disciples at The Novelty Bar, and my subsequent visit to the emergency room of Massachusetts General Hospital, that hundred-mile drive up the Maine Turnpike to Portland was the longest trip I'd ever made. My right hand was throbbing so bad with pain that I thought I was going to pass out. I actually did stop and puke a few times. And all this time I had been so looking forward to my return home. To have it marred by something so beyond my control was extremely disconcerting. All I did was make a pit stop in Boston to catch up with some old friends, and look what I got for my trouble.

"When I reported to my parole officer on July 1, not only was I seven days late, but I also had my hand wrapped in a half-cast, with wires sticking out from every knuckle in a grotesque way, obviously the result of having been in a fight, so he was not very happy with me. I told him that I had come across an elderly lady in Pennsylvania with a flat tire and while I was fixing it for her the jack slipped and my hand was cut by the ragged edge of the fender, and she kindly offered to put me up for a few days while my wounds healed. When he heard that, he didn't even change his expression. You know, like when you tell someone something that you both know is a lie, but you have to say something. He gave me that "yeah, yeah" look parole officers become very good at, leaned forward onto his desk with his hands folded in front of him, looked me straight in the eye, and informed me in a very stern manner that being a week late for my appointment, and showing up in the highly suspicious physical condition I was in, were matters of grave concern to him, and that another parole violation, no matter how minor, would leave him no choice but to recommend my immediate return to San Quentin."

So there Jake was, in the Fall of 1968, thirty-years old, back in Portland after three highly eventful years away. He'd been around a bit, to say the least. He said that one of the conditions of his parole from San Quentin was that he had to live somewhere in Greater Portland, and I chuckled a bit at that and asked him how he felt about being confined to the farm at having seen the big city lights.

"I was absolutely elated to be back in Portland! I've always loved Portland!" he yelled. "When I was out on the West Coast I used to call San Francisco 'The Portland of the West,' by which they thought I meant Portland, Oregon, of course, but little did they know that illustrious city was actually named after my hometown of Portland, Maine, which is the most interesting and exciting city in the world! Why the hell do you think I was born here and still live here?!"

"Yea, Portland!" I yelled.

"You better believe it!" he roared, then we settled down and got into his telling me about returning home to the city we both love.

"So there I was, home again, home again," he began, "but there were some very restrictive conditions I had to live under. Keep in mind that the warden at San Quentin had communicated to my parole officer in Portland that I was to be regarded as a very violent,

unrepentant career criminal who had an almost uncanny ability to break the rules and avoid detection.
The warden was even kind enough to share with him
that at San Quentin I was known as "The Ghost," a
nickname I acquired for my uncanny ability to be involved in questionable activity in the prison, but
somehow avoid detection. Suffice it to say that there
were high-placed people in the national prison system, and in California state government, including
Governor Ronald Reagan, I'm sure, who were very eager for me to return to their custody and receive what
they saw as my just desserts. My parole officer went
out of his way to make me understand that I was being watched more closely than any parolee he had
ever known of. Well, that's too bad, I was thinking,
but I did kind of enjoy the recognition.

"As a law-abiding member of the general public
who has no first-hand experience of the criminal justice system, my friend, you'd have no way of knowing
the significance of it but, to my knowledge, I am the
only parolee anywhere who has never been accepted
at a half-way house. That's huge in the criminal justice world, believe me. It is normally a prerequisite of
being released from jail, but none of them would have
me. Even the hardest, most violent criminals can find
a half-way house somewhere that will accept them,
but I was a glaring exception to the rule, as I have
often been throughout my life. I was known as a rab-
ble rouser who could get a group of men to do whatever I wanted them to do, and that's exactly the kind
of individual they don't want at a half-way house full
of men looking for a legitimate way to live their lives.
Damn, after being sentenced to prison after the suicide charge, I organized and instigated riots at two
prison before I even got to San Quentin, where I

pulled more of the same shit. How the hell was some house manager down on such and such a street in Portland going to keep me corralled and under his control?"

Jake in the fall of 1968 at his family's summer cottage on the coast of Maine with a young relative and her dog. Jake's right hand was still in a half-cast from his injury a few weeks earlier at The Novelty Bar.

VOLUME TWO

DOCTOR TAYLOR'S SPA AND COUNTRY CLUB

"My parole officer informed me that one of the conditions of my parole was that I receive some form of life counseling that would lead me to be the person I ought to be, therefore I was to spend the next three months residing with Dr. Paul Taylor, a psychiatrist who lived on a farm in Kittery, about thirty-five miles south of Portland. Dr. Taylor's farm is quite a well-known landmark, actually. You can see it coming up from Boston on the turnpike shortly after you get to Kittery, just on the right. It's the one with the big Hell's Angels big red barn next to it. Guess who painted the barn that color?"

"Jake Sawyer! What a piece of trivia!" I answered.

"Trivia? Now you're saying I'm a piece of trivia?" he said, in a low, menacing voice.

I just looked over at him and gave him a quick smile, like I knew, of course, that he was joking, but, ah, I didn't quite know that for sure.

"I spent three months with Dr. Taylor on his farm and had a very pleasurable and relaxing time with him," Jake said, after chuckling a little to himself. "He was an intelligent, good-hearted guy, and he engaged me in conversation about myself on a regular basis. I enjoyed that, of course, and was more than willing to cooperate. I don't know if the good doctor came to any definite conclusions about me, but he evidently was impressed enough with me to give glowing reports to my parole officer, so I was sitting pretty.

"Sometimes I don't know how I luck into these things. The time at Dr. Taylor's turned out to be a great salve to my spirit. I spent the majority of my time painting his barn, and I truly enjoyed doing it.

For some reason it centered me to have a definite project to focus on.

"And it also tickled the hell out of me that I was painting a huge barn Hell's Angels red right there at the main entrance to the State of Maine, where the millions of tourists who visit the state every year can easily see it. I erected a sign out next to the highway that said: BARN PAINTED HELL'S ANGELS RED BY JAKE SAWYER, THE FIRST HELL'S ANGEL FROM MAINE."

"You did-d-d ...?" I looked up at him wide-eyed and asked incredulously.

"Of course I did."

At that point I started laughing like hell at myself, and after I calmed down I grinned over at him, like I was finally starting to get him.

"Dr. Taylor was a very cultured fellow," Jake continued, "with refined tastes, and almost every night of the week he took me to a different high-end restaurant in the area. Dining out at fancy restaurants had never been my thing. In fact, about the only other time I had ever eaten at a high-end restaurant was when Terry the Tramp and I went to that five-star place in Santa Monica with Bob Dylan and his two lady friends. Man, that seemed like a hundred years ago, considering all I had been through since.

"Yes, that time with Dr. Taylor was very good for me. When I got back to Portland after three months in Kittery under the care and tutelage of the good doctor, I right away started studying to get my state insurance license so I could sell life insurance to members of the community, marry the girl of my dreams and get active in the Jaycees a-gain."

"Ha!" I said.

"Aw, c'mon," he said, "you sound just like my parole officer, doubting everything I say!"

"Well I, ah ..."

"Okay, okay, I'm yankin' your chain," he said, "but I really did become a model citizen upon my return to Portland, though. Everyone with any knowledge of my activities at the time will certainly tell you that. Well, I guess it does depend on who you talk to, but you know how that goes."

THE GRIFFIN CLUB

"The first thing I had to do after I got back from Dr. Taylor's, was find a place to live. I didn't have a job or much money, but, as it has often been in my life, a friend came to my rescue. This time it was Eddie Griffin, the legendary owner of The Griffin Club, a very popular local tavern across the bridge in South Portland, the city I grew up in. Eddie and I had been friends for years, and as soon as he found out I was looking for a place to live and didn't have a lot of money to make it happen, my problem was his problem. Eddie was one hell of a man, one of the best people I've ever known. He did a lot for a lot of people. He lived in a room up over the tavern himself, and we got to be closer than ever. There were three of us living up there, actually, each with our own room, the third being a man named Bill Hoadley, who had been an outstanding athlete for Cape Elizabeth High, and had just returned from serving a stint with the Peace Corps in South America. The interesting thing is that Bill lived in Sacramento at the time I was in the news for leading my Hell's Angels brothers on the suicide charge that got me sent to prison, and of course the incident was big news in all the media. Bill and I didn't know one another at the time, but he knew me very well by reputation around Portland, and he followed the news accounts of the suicide charge and the subsequent events very closely. The last he heard, he said, was that I was in prison and probably was never going to get out, and he said he just couldn't believe it when he saw me walk into The Griffin Club. Turns out that Bill was raised not far from my boyhood home, and was a lifelong friend of Harold Pachios, my lawyer friend who got me liberated from San Quentin. So, there we were, by pure coincidence, living across the hall from each other up over Eddie Griffins tavern. Ain't life grand!"

B&M BAKED BEANS

"Besides having to live locally, one of my other parole conditions was that I had to be steadily employed by a reputable company, which was a pain because me and steady employment were rarely to be found on the same page. Anything was better than being sent back to San Quentin, though, so I got a job at B&M Baked Beans. You never put me and B&M Baked Beans together, did you?!"

"Ah, no," I replied, without looking up from my notebook.

"I worked on the top floor of the factory screwing tops onto jars of beans, which made me almost long for San Quentin. B&M was prison without all the interesting people, and with the constant smell of beans to boot. I had to wear one of those white mesh caps over my hair. I was thoroughly humiliated and felt miserable. I had a fantastic view of the beautiful waters of Casco Bay, but that didn't quite make up for everything else I was going through. Just like having a great view of San Francisco Bay didn't make up for being in San Quentin, you know?"

"Yeah, I can understand that," I said.

"I worked furiously at B&M for eight straight hours, trying to keep up so the very hot and wet jars wouldn't fall off the end of the conveyor belt onto the floor. I had a bloody red circle the exact size of the jar top worn into the palm of my left hand. I had to use my left hand because the right one was still out of commission from its rendezvous with the broken beer bottle at the Novelty Bar, so I had to cradle the jar against my side with my right forearm and screw the cap on with my left hand. It was very awkward and tedious. I was working twice as hard as anyone else just to keep up with them. I thought my shift would never get over.

"My mother always said that my sense of humor would get me through a lot, though, and she was right. One afternoon when jars started falling off the end of the conveyor belt all I could think of was the scene where Lucille Ball is working at a candy factory or something and ends up stuffing candy into her mouth to keep up, and that was it. I started laughing my ass off at my predicament, whipped off my friggin' hair net, and headed for the office.

"I was polite about it, though. I resigned in the proper manner, said good-byes all-around, that kind of thing.

"You thought I was going to tell you about some violent, outrageous, crazy-assed thing I did at B&M, right?"

JAKE

"Right," I said, "now why would I think that?"

MARTIN'S HEALTH CLUB

"As I have told you, no matter what circumstance I was in, in or out of jail, no matter where I've lived, or what I've done," Jake continued, "I've always fit working out into my daily routine, and this period of time was no exception. Fortunately, Eddie had set up an exercise room and boxing gym in the basement of the bar, and I had the use of that, and appreciated Eddie's hospitality very much, but it wasn't adequate for a dedicated weightlifter like me.

"I had been told that there was a guy by the name of Al Martin in town who was interested in expanding the weight-training room he had in the back of his building on Federal Street, which was located in what was then a run-down section of town, but would shortly thereafter become the trendy Old Port, which is Portland's version of Faneuil Hall in Boston, and Greenwich village, in New York.

"I got my first hint about Al Martin when I arrived at this place and saw the sign the sign over the door saying that his locksmithing company was founded in 1829! What?!

"As I stepped through the door, there he was, wearing a cowboy hat, happy as a lark, sittin' behind a desk strumming away (very badly) on a guitar, entertaining a couple of girls with a medley of cowboy songs.

"When he saw me, Al immediately set the guitar aside and said, 'What can I do for you, sir?' very respectfully.

"He could see, of course, that I was a serious weightlifter by the size of my chest and arms, and he saw the glint in my eye when I spotted all the serious weight training equipment he had set up in the large room behind him. Wow! I was salivating!

"Well, we went into the weight training room and sat across from each other on work-out benches and had a chat, where we discovered that we saw eye-to-eye on all of the important things in life, and that was it.

"The upshot of it was that Al bought the oldest brick building on Fore St. for cheap money, and we opened 'Martin's Health Club.'

Photo taken on Higgins Beach, Scarborough, Maine in 1964. Left to right: John DiCola, Mr. America 1969; Jake, shortly after his motorcycle; a friend of one of the guys; Ronnie Damon, decorated veteran and long-time South Portland police lieutenant; and Tom Ellison, one of the Boston owners of Portland Health and Fitness Salon. Jakes crutches can be seen close to John DiCola's right foot.

JAKE

Jake and Al Marti at Martin's Health Club with Paul Anderson, the Olympic weightlifter then billed as "The World's Strongest Man."

From bottom to top, clowning around at Martin's Health Club in 1970: John Hadlock, a world class mountain climber and part-time male stripper; Pete Erskine, a highly decorated military veteran and three-time winner of the Mr. Maine Bodybuilder title; and, of course, Jake, their highly inspirational health and fitness instructor.

Jake and Skip Robinson pose on Higgins Beach in Scarborough, Maine. Skip was affectionately known to the men from Martin's Health Club as "Skippy Cup."

"That day was the beginning of a long and mutually rewarding friendship that ended only with Al's recent passing, and I miss my old pal very much.

Martin's health club was quite the operation. Al operated his locksmith shop on the ground floor, and I managed the gym in the basement and on the second and third floors. You will remember, my friend, that before I went to the Combat Zone, in Boston, and opened up the Mid-City Health Club there, I operated the Portland Health and Fitness studio in Portland back in 1961, so I had something of a local following and there were many people who were very happy to hear that I had returned to Portland and was back at it again."

JAKE'S TRAINING PHILOSOPHY

"As soon as they walked through the door, I hit them with my approach to training right straight on.

"'So here you are in my life,' I said, 'because you have decided that you want to be the best you can be in body and spirit! At least that's what I hope you've got in your head, because that's sure as hell what this place is all about!'

"Of course, they'd look at me wide-eyed, kind of asking themselves what the hell they had gotten themselves into, but then I'd calmly explain a few things to them.

"I am not a 'soft trainer' I would tell them. A soft trainer sets people up with a set of lifts that they can come in and do on their own, thereby giving the trainer time to hide in the office with their feet up watching TV talk shows or Beverly Hillbillies reruns. No, I told them, I am a hard trainer, meaning that I instruct you how much to lift and how to lift it. With me, you do not look around and socialize with your friends between sets, and the resting time between sets is never more than two minutes. I told them to beware of training programs designed to keep you interested, you know, nice and easy so you won't quit. You don't work very hard, see some progress, and then ease off. No, I told them. If you want that, this is not the place for you. I focus intently on you and your goals. I know how to motivate you to bust your ass to get where you want to go in the shortest period of time, and that's what I do.

"Just like everything else in life, I told them, you have to have goals and work hard to succeed. Fifteen minutes of 'intense' training on a very expensive piece of work-out equipment is not going to do it, no matter what the brochure of the company says, or what some money-hungry, ego-tripping, wanna be Arnold Schwarzenegger movie star type dude leads you to believe!

"Martin's Health Club was a fantastic success all around. Al was a highly skilled locksmith and an astute businessman, and I was very good at training people and recruiting clients, so before long things were humming along very nicely.

"One of the major innovations I brought to health and fitness training in Miami Beach, California and Portland was that I made it appealing for women to come and work out in a safe, non-judgmental environment. I used to get them laughing about all of the fat on their hips, and I just loved to see how happy they were when it started to disappear. Women also knew they didn't have to deal with soupy-eyed starers at my place. Glancing was only normal, but if I saw a guy ogling, I'd lead him out the door by the ear, and the women were all for that.

We created an atmosphere that was very appealing to the up-and-coming young professionals of both genders who were flocking to live and work in the Old Port. The area was exploding with activity and we were sitting pretty right in the middle of it.

JAKE

THE ANIMAL PIT

""I also acted upon my knowledge that over ninety-percent of health-conscious men and women were not dedicated weight-lifters and didn't want to spend their time in sweaty gyms alongside grunting muscle-men. I therefore made a place in the basement of the club we called the 'Animal Pit,' where only guys who wanted to lift heavy weights were allowed. A lot of very dedicated body builders worked out in the Animal Pit, including Marty Joyce, Bob Penney, Bruce Chambers and Danny Hamblet, all of whom went on to set numerous regional and world weightlifting records. The place still lives in the hearts and minds of many men from around the Greater Portland area today, believe me. I'm friends with most of those men to this day. What we have in common is that our lives have been devoted to health and physical fitness. I'm proud to say that Martin's Health Club is where most of those guys first experienced the natural high one gets from a vigorous, well-planned and executed work-out, and it made an immense difference in their lives."

I asked Jake who might be a good one for me to talk to out of the group of weight-lifters, and right away he rattled off a half dozen names – but said that the easiest one to get in touch with would probably be his friend Bob Penney, who won a number of state and national body-builder titles and owns Abbey Road Taxi, a long-time and very successful Portland taxi company, and is also known far and wide for his photographic memory.

Bob turned out to be a very friendly, well-spoken guy with a seasoned taxi driver's encyclopedic knowledge of local lore and legend, and it didn't take him too long to warm up to the subject of Martin's Health Club and Jake Sawyer's part in it.

"I think it was in the Spring of 1969," Bob said, "when I started going to Martin's Health Club. I had started working out on my own, but had kind of hit a wall, and Jake gave me some much-needed instruction. He turned out to be a fitness guru to a lot of people, actually, particularly us serious weightlifters.

Jake with well-known professional wrestler Victor Rivera. Jake helped train many big names in that sport over the years.

JAKE

"Giving us a place of our own in the basement, which was called the Animal Pit, was a stroke of genius. Not only did the move spare the men and women who were not dedicated weightlifters from having to put up with our company, but it also brought about a bonding between us heavy weight-lifters that has lasted all of our lives.

"Believe it or not, there's still a bunch of us Animal Pit alumni who meet at Marty Joyce's house for a reunion once a year. We've been doing it for over forty years. Hey, the attendees make for an interesting line-up of local luminaries: Marty Joyce, our congenial host, is a retired bank president; "Skippy Cup" Robinson is a longtime local teacher; Vinnie Bruni is a well-known local musician; John Fairweather is a former firefighter; and Bruce Chambers, who's one of the biggest and most ferocious guys anybody's ever met, does what he wants to do pretty much any time he wants to do it. Last year, another one of our four old lifting buddies, Steve Sawtelle, showed up at Marty's get-together and he had some good stories of the old days that got us all laughing and remembering when. Sadly, though, I have to say our good friend, Ronnie Damon, a much-decorated lieutenant in the South Portland Police Department, and an honored military veteran, has recently passed away and is sorely missed.

"To tell you the truth, there were so many outstanding people who trained at Martin's Health Club that it's hard to single out just a few. There were so many Mr. Maine and Mr. USA trophies won by people Jake trained at Martin's Health Club that I don't dare to try to list them. I know I'd probably omit some very deserving people, and I don't want to slight anyone. Let's just say that what we learned from Jake about bodybuilding, and health practices in general, has stayed with us all of our lives, and we all benefited immensely from the experience.

"Just being around Martin's Health Club was a lot of fun, actually. You never knew what was going to happen, or who would show up. As the word spread about the place, the nationally known wrestlers who were wrestling at the Portland Exposition Building got in the habit of working out with us, for instance. Jake introduced us to Victor Rivera, Antonio Puolase, Chief Jay Strongbow, Superstar Billy Graham, Greg "The Hammer" Valentine, and the Valiant Brothers. Those names might not mean much to your readers today, but in that era they were all very well known nationally. Here I was, a skinny nineteen-year-old kid, just looking to put on a little muscle, and I found myself hobnobbing with guys who were some of the most well-built and athletic men in the world. You really do gain a new appreciation of the athletic ability of these guys when you see close up how big they are and how hard they work to achieve the agility necessary to be a professional wrestler."

When I told Jake all the good things Bob said about him and how fondly he looked back on those days, Jake wasn't very surprised — he's long been one of the attendees at Marty Joyce's yearly get-together, after all, so he's heard it before — but I could tell that he was pleased nonetheless.

Bob Penney

"Skippy Cup" Robinson left, and Marty Joyce getting ready to work out in the "Animal Pit" at Martin's Health Club

VOLUME TWO

LADIES WELCOME

"I didn't know of any health clubs anywhere in that time period that even allowed women to lift weights to become stronger, as added muscle was not considered to be lady-like at that time, but I changed all that. Jack LaLanne had created what became known as "Muscle Beach" in Venice, California, where he had a beautiful blonde woman who did weight training with him showing off her stuff but, of course, that was all for show and was mostly for attracting male clients to his club.

"I managed a number of health and fitness clubs for Vic Tanney at that time –1961– in Riverside, San Gabriel, Arcadia and in Pasedena, and one day Vic and Jack came into my office in Acadia, where most of what I was doing was helping jockeys from Santa Anita Racetrack keep their weight down. I was very tired of training guys to get smaller and lighter, as you might imagine, so when Vic and Jack asked me if I had any interest in managing a new health club they were opening in Pasadena, I was all over it.

"The new Pasadena health club was a lot of fun. I had two beautiful, well-endowed instructresses in tight-fitting leotards standing in the front window hooked up to vibrating machines, and I would go on the sidewalk and hand out free passes to the people who had formed a crowd out front watching them.

"In order to be a great salesperson, you need to be selling something you are honestly excited talking about, and turning other people onto the benefits of health and fitness has always been something that very much excites me. I've always had to have highly motivated clientele to work with, though. I've trained people for over fifty years, and I've dismissed my share of trainees who I found did not have what it takes mentally and emotionally be successful. I've tacked this little motto up with up on the wall of every club I've ever owned or managed, and the trainees who read it and took it to heart experienced great success under my training:

GOOD, BETTER, BEST
NEVER LET IT REST
'TIL THE GOOD IS BETTER
AND THE BETTER IS BEST

This is a direct quote from a Lowell Hell's Angel named Riverboat Ed."

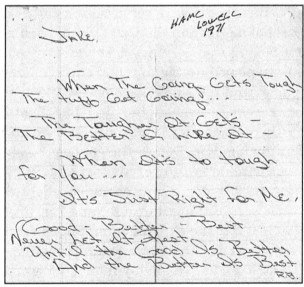

"Riverboat Ed, a legendary member of the Hell's Angels Lowell Chapter spoke these words to me," Jake says. I asked him to please write it all down for me. I relate very strongly to these words as do my brothers. Ed took the time to print it all in his handwriting, which makes what you see here priceless to me."

VOLUME TWO

TRAINING FEMALE BOXERS

"One of my proudest achievements at Martin's Health Club was training two female boxing legends, Kathy Russo and Margie Dunson. Kathy was a beautiful, blond, muscular woman who trained very hard under my instruction and was decking all-comers at the Friday night fights at the Portland Exposition Building. Her only real competition was a tough black woman by the name of Margie Dunson, who had come up to Maine from Alabama to take part in one of Lyndon Johnson' Job Corps work training programs. Margie was not only tough, she was smart, fast, and had a lot of heart. She and Kathy had similar fighting styles, so their bouts were very exciting and elicited a great deal of interest on the part of local boxing fans. Women boxing was very novel at the time, so their bouts were played up big in the sports section of the local paper, and the whole town was wacky over it.

"Kathy beat Margie in the first two fights they fought, then Margie won the third one, which motivated Kathy big time. Before she got beaten, she had been a little reluctant to get into serious lifting. She had been mostly doing arm curls with light dumbbells, that sort of thing, but after she lost to Margie she marched into the club and announced to me that she wanted to start on a power-lifting program. I had long wanted to find a highly-motivated woman to train as a power lifter, so I very enthusiastically told her that if she followed my instructions and worked very hard, I could guarantee that she would increase her overall strength by fifty percent in six months' time, and she did just that.

"The training program I put her on didn't consist

of just heavy weight lifting, of course. I started her out running a half-mile a day after her power lifting routine, and she steadily worked up to at least two, sometimes three miles a day. I also put her on a very high protein diet, which is necessary to achieve maximum body strength. The power lifting routine I had her on was the most important part of the program, though. I had her doing squats with weight on her shoulders that would be extremely challenging to males who outweighed her by fifty pounds. She started out doing ten reps of squats with ninety-pound weights on her shoulders. Within ninety days she increased the weight to one hundred and forty pounds, and after six months she was up to one hundred and ninety pounds!

"Needless to say, Kathy became the fiercest female fighting machine of all time. When she and Margie fought again, Kathy pushed Margie around the ring due to her new body strength, and Margie was worn out by the third round. Kathy completely dominated her in the fourth and fifth rounds and won the fight by a TKO. Margie was completely exhausted and just couldn't go on.

"Okay, so a few days later Margie shows up at Martin's Health Club looking somewhat depressed and sporting a mean-looking black eye, and tells me in a low, deadly serious voice that she's there to train as hard as she had to to beat hell out of Kathy the next time they fight. Well, it turned out that she did work very hard at it, and, to my surprise actually, she sure as hell did beat Kathy the next time they fought.

"So now I had two very dedicated, very experienced, highly motivated women boxers working out at the club, and I worried a little about how that was going to work out on a daily basis. I didn't want any serious bouts to take place on the spur of the moment right there in the club, of course. After a while, though, Kathy and Margie became very friendly training partners, and I was very pleased with that. I have found over the years that working out in proximity to one another bonds two people like nothing else does, and Kathy and Margie proved that to be the case. In spite of all the brutal fights they had fought, after a while neither one of them had any desire to face one another in the ring again because they had become such good friends.

"I had had a fantastic time turning two women I liked and respected into fierce fighting animals! I knew I was breaking new ground by training women so hard, and I was loving every minute of it! Imagine my delight when Margie ended up traveling to Japan to fight for the world championship! She lost, got beaten by some huge Russian she-bear, as I remember, but she fought damn hard, and I knew without any question that she wouldn't even have been there in Japan if it hadn't been for the extreme training program I put her on at Martin's Health Club."

THE LOWELL, MASSACHUSETTS, HELL'S ANGELS

"So, Jake," I said to him, "does all this mean that you had finally found your groove in life? Now that you were back in Portland, after being out there in the world a bit, and had become a very central part of a very successful business venture, were you ready to settle down and lead what might be called a normal life?"

JAKE

"Normal life?!", he exploded. "I've never even come close to living a normal life! I was born to raise hell and that's exactly what I've done every day of my life!

"I desperately needed some diversion from all the wholesome, good work I was doing at the health club," he said, "something to remind myself of who I really am, so what better than to travel down to Lowell, Massachusetts, and spend time with my brothers in the Hell's Angels chapter there?

"Of course, one of my major parole restrictions was that I not travel outside the Portland area, so I had to be very creative as to how I went about getting down to Lowell."

Okay, let's keep in mind that detection in this instance meant a swift return to San Quentin for Jake, possibly for life, no questions asked.

"I'd get on my orange souped-up chopper in the wee hours of Friday or Saturday morning and get out on the Rte 295 South and average about 110 MPH down to Lowell. I really think that the reason I never got stopped by the State Police in the years I traveled down there was that the police, almost literally, didn't see me. If they did, they didn't have any interest in stopping me to find out what the hell I was all about."

What a feeling that would be, I thought. That blue light comes on behind you and the chances are very good that you're going back to prison, most likely for the rest of your life. But then I thought again and realized that I'd stop for a blue light coming on behind me, and Jake most likely wouldn't, so there you go.

A two block long old "row house" on Bridge St. in Lowell, Mass. where all the Hell's Angels and their families lived in the 1970s. Jake is on his "chopper" and his brother, the notorious Hawkeye, has his arm around him.

Jake says his orange chopper had a rare electric starter and an equally rare magnesium front wheel, and that at the time this picture was taken he was on his third engine obtained from Skeets Picard, a wizard Hell's Angel mechanic, having blown the first two engines racing against his Hell's Angels brothers and anyone else who was man enough to take him on.

JAKE

TIGER BELLY

"It isn't as though I didn't have some fun around Portland as well, though. Especially down on the waterfront.

Today the section of Portland known as the Old Port is the ritzy, upscale, touristy part of the town, but fifty years ago, when I arrived back in town, the area was rundown and deserted. The only sign of life down around the waterfront was on the wharfs, where hard-working fishermen tied up their boats after a day's haul, then trouped off to the bars together to spend their day's earnings. They sure as hell carried the smell of fish with them, but they referred to it as the smell of money, and everybody was happy.

"There was a lot of local color in the Old Port in those days, no question. A guy by the name of Zeke Carver and a few other hard-core drunks were holed-up in a neglected and abandoned part of one of the wharfs, living in a very crudely made lean-to, made up of old planks torn up from the wharf, with a worn out tarp draped over it. Zeke was the alpha male of the group, like I was used to being, so right away we bonded.

"Okay, so one hot summer day Zeke is smoking a joint and downing a few beers with me and some of my other waterfront buddies when he announces that it's his birthday. It probably wasn't, but nobody cared, it provided the occasion for celebration, and celebrate we did.

"I had recently made a few thousand bucks on a marijuana sale, so the first thing I did was give a $100 bill to Zeke. Man, did his face light up, as did the faces of his drinking buddies, of course, because they knew that they all now had plenty of drinking money. I also gave a pretty young woman named Cindy, who was a friend of Zeke's gang, some money to go buy him a birthday cake. I knew the other crazy drunk bastards in Zeke's gang were going to go wild when they saw that birthday cake for their leader, with his name on it and everything, so I was really looking forward to Cindy's return. She didn't return, though. The dimwit bitch came back three days later with a new boyfriend in tow, after she had been out on a bender with the money I gave her for Zeke's cake. Needless to say, I was not pleased. It's not a good idea to screw with ol' Jakie boy, especially when he is trying to be nice to you and your friends.

"Okay, so a few days later I'm revving up my Harley to go down and visit my brothers in Lowell, when I spot Cindy hanging around with nothing constructive to do, as usual, so I smile to myself and tell her to hop on. She was delighted with the idea, of course, got all giggly about it actually, and off we went. The young lady had no idea, of course, what a young lady might experience hanging around a bunch of Hell's Angels at party time, but she was definitely going to find out.

"Cindy was very content perched behind me on the reasonably comfortable four-inch square leather-covered seat on the snub-nosed rear fender of the bike. Generally, when someone is new to riding on an outlaw-biker machine you can feel the tension in their body as they grab onto your jacket with both hands for dear life, but that wasn't the case with Cindy. She showed no fear as we roared through the pitch-black night as fast as that souped-up shovelhead Harley engine would go, which was well in excess of 100 mph.

JAKE

"Okay, so at about 2a.m. we rolled up to this old, dilapidated, two-story row house in a rundown area of Lowell. The entire block was rented by Hell's Angels, so you get the picture.

"So, there we were at two in the morning, knocking on my brother Hawkeye's door, because Hawkeye and I loved raising hell together. We woke him up out of a sound sleep, but he didn't mind because Hawkeye and I were very close.

"Alright, so right away we're smoking fine weed and downing many beers, and before long Whiskey George and Riverboat Ed showed up and things started to heat up real good. Then, when Banker Frank appeared with some powdered "crank" things got really rolling. It's called 'The Breakfast of Champions,' otherwise known as speed, which I rarely did, but what the hell, we had a special occasion going on.

"Right in the middle of it all, somehow or other the subject of tattoos was raised, and Cindy remarked that she'd always wanted to get a very small, very cute, tattoo of a tiger on her belly.

"At that point, my man Hawkeye spoke up and told Cindy that he was just the man to make her dream come true. I told Cindy to hurry up and do another line and be very thankful that with Hawkeye on the job her very own little tiger tattoo will be the envy of all her women friends, and she'll be irresistible to any man she came into contact with.

"Cindy laid down on the kitchen table, showing no fear, as usual, then Hawkeye did another line, took out his tattoo equipment, and the great creation was underway.

"After Hawkeye was at it for about an hour, Cindy asked why a small tattoo was taking so long, and

Hawkeye patiently explained that the three-dimensional effect of the image he was creating took some time to pull off, but in the end she'd see that the extra time it took was definitely worth it, as he was one of the few 'magical' tattoo artists in the entire world who could create such a visual masterpiece.

"You should have seen Cindy's face when she got off the table and went into the bathroom to look at herself in the full-length mirror! The tattoo of a growling tiger that Hawkeye had put on her belly went from her navel all the way up to her breasts! And she knew she'd have it on her belly for the rest of her life!

"The moral here is that it's not a good idea to screw over ol' Jakie boy in any way, like Cindy did with the birthday cake, because whatever you put out there is gonna come back at you multiplied many times over. Like, for instance, your name is Cindy, then all of a sudden everybody entirely forgets that, and you're known by the name of 'Tiger Belly' for the rest of your life, you know?"

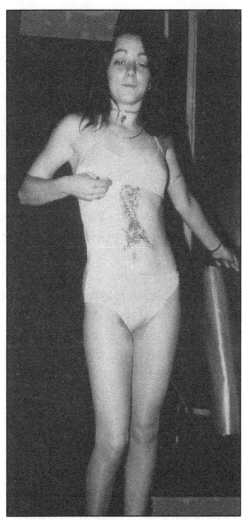

Cindy lived happily ever after, known far and wide as "Tiger Belly."

VOLUME TWO

A PLUME OF DARK SMOKE

"Jake," I said, "you once mentioned a plume of dark smoke that appeared over the local skyline shortly after your return to Portland, and you swore you knew nothing about it. C'mon, what was that all about?"

"You do understand that everything I tell you about that incident *allegedly* happened, of course?"

I assured him of my non-judgmental attitude, and he let loose.

"Well, absolutely out of nowhere, I somehow made the acquaintance of a group of fellows who were allegedly stealing cars in Hartford, Connecticut, and selling them up here in Maine. Because I'm such an impressionable guy, I guess, I ended up accompanying them on one of their shopping trips, and when all was said and done, I somehow ended up as the proud owner of a new two-toned gold Porsche 911S.

"It was one of the finest cars I've ever owned, and I've owned some beauties in my time. I had been driving it for a couple months, then one fine afternoon I was barreling down Route 302, thirty-five or so miles west of Portland, having been up to Fryeburg to visit a comely lass of my acquaintance, when out of nowhere, a blue light comes on behind me. I've always taken action at the first sign of trouble, of course, so all I could think to do was stomp my foot down on the gas pedal real hard and get the hell out of there. You are aware of what being apprehended driving a stolen vehicle would mean for someone on parole, of course.

"My sudden increase in speed worked for ten minutes or so, because there was no way one of those heavy Chevies the police drove then was going to keep up with a new Porsche, especially with a Hell's Angel at the wheel, but police have this annoying habit of radioing ahead for assistance, and it wasn't long before police cars began to emerge from side streets and a long parade of police cars with their blue lights flashing had formed behind me. There was a virtual squadron of them, and their numbers grew at every intersection I passed. They even nosed two cruisers together ahead of me at one point, but I managed to squirm through them. I think they knew that if they didn't leave me room to get through, I would've rammed my way through, and that wouldn't have been pretty.

"By the time our little parade reached Portland I must have had a dozen police cruisers behind me flashing their blue lights, with their sirens screaming. I knew for an absolute certainty that if I stopped for them I was going back to San Quentin, most likely for life, having been apprehended driving an allegedly stolen vehicle at a very high rate of speed, resisting arrest, and assorted other charges they might come up with. Needless to say, I had all the incentive I needed to get away from them.

"Out of nowhere, I came up with an evasive maneuver that proved to be quite effective. It took the form of taking a high-speed, abrupt left-hand turn onto a one-way street, which caused my pursuers to lose visual contact, and I ended up at the on-ramp of the bridge going over to South Portland. I'd managed to lose the State Police and the Portland Police, but when I got across the bridge, I found that the South Portland police had been duly alerted and had picked up the chase, so I decided to make a run for the Griffin Club parking lot, where I could execute my plan.

"When I got to the Griffin Club parking lot, I knew the South Portland police would soon be pulling in behind me, so all I could do was destroy the evidence and remove myself from the scene. Luckily, I kept a can of gas in the back seat for just such an occasion. I hated to do it, but I grabbed the can and poured gas all over the plush interior of my beautiful Porsche, opened the windows to create a crosswind, and threw a match in. I looked back as I was entering the Griffin Club just in time to see that wonderful Porsche 911S blow up like a bomb. What a sight! I could hear sirens in the distance.

"I knew that the South Portland police would become very excited when they saw that black plume of smoke rising up into the air, and indeed they were. A half-dozen police cars pulled into the lot in a matter of moments, and immediately came into the tavern looking for me, where they spotted me casually sitting at the bar, engrossed in a friendly conversation with my friend Bill Hoadley, who just happened to be there. When I first arrived, I reminded Bill and the bartender that I'd been there for over an hour or so, in case they hadn't noticed.

"So, when a group of three or four highly energized officers of the law came bursting through the door, I immediately yelled, 'Wow! We're so happy to see you! That car outside all of a sudden burst into flames and we were just getting ready to call you and the fire department!'

"The cops were so mad they were sputtering, but the evidence they needed to haul me in was burning up outside, and they knew it. I also had two corroborating witnesses who readily and enthusiastically assured them that I had been there chatting with them for over an hour.

"I regretted the loss of that Porsche, but all in all, I made out okay. At least I avoided going back to prison, so that was nice. Score: Jake 1, Cops 0"

THE EAST COAST ARM WRESTLING CHAMPIONSHIPS

"Things at Martin's Health club were humming along just fine at the time. I was signing up a lot of people for memberships, and the guys in the Animal Pit were great to work out with. As you might suppose, we were training hard in the gym cellar, getting stronger and stronger. Then one day, I read in the newspaper about the East Coast Arm Wrestling Championships that were being held in Holyoke, Massachusetts, and a couple of weeks later Bruce Chambers and I were down there right in the middle of it.

"Arm wrestling competition was very popular with the public at the time. There were over three thousand spectators looking on and cheering like mad. I became the sentimental favorite after I won my first few matches because I was so small compared to all the others. Hell, a lot of the strong guys who showed up with the idea of maybe competing rolled their sleeves back down after they saw how big and strong the guys they'd be competing against were. They didn't want to be embarrassed, I guess, but I saw the size of those guys as a tremendous challenge. I was firing on all cylinders as soon as I walked through the door and saw what I was up against.

"I weighed 210 pounds at the time, so I was in the heavy-weight class, which started at 200 pounds, and I was the lightest guy in my class. Some of the men I competed against were well over 300 pounds. I entered the competition in both 1969 and 1970, actually, and each time I arm wrestled twenty-eight district champions from all up and down the East Coast. I was the district champion for Maine, by default, I guess, because no one challenged me for the honor. Anyway, I beat every other district champion in the competition twice in a row, in two out of three bouts. In case you need help with the arithmetic, that's fifty-six straight wins. Then, both years, I lost in the final championship match to a man named Mo Baker, who went on from the East Coast Championships to become the world champion arm-wrestler in both 1969 and 1970.

Jake at the 1969 East Coast Arm Wrestling Championships, with two-time world arm wrestling champion Mo Baker in the center and Jake's good friend and workout partner Bruce Chambers on the left.

JAKE

WRIST BREAKER — Jake Sawyer exhibits the biceps and technique that won him the trophy, rear, for placing second in the U.S. East Coast Arm. Wrestling Championships last week. This is the first time anyone from Maine has placed in the competition. (By Staff Photographer Morrison) *RUNNER UP TO WORLD CHAMP, 2 YR.*

Arm Of Steel, *69 & 70*
Will Of Iron
Garner Trophy

By WILLIAM LANGLEY

Arm wrestling isn't on the Olympic Games agenda yet, but it does occupy a unique place in the world of sports.

It is usually confined to such informal sites as saloons, clubs and other arenas of vague masculine cheer. It doesn't require uniforms, playing fields, special equipment, teams, coaches or elaborate financing.

There are really only two essentials — an arm of steel and an iron will to win.

Utilizing both, Jake Sawyer, ▬▬▬▬▬ manager and instructor at Martin's Health Club here, last week surprised everyone, including himself. He placed second in the 30th annual U.S. East Coast Arm Wrestling Championships.

Sawyer won his runner-up trophy by beating 24 other competitors from all over the East Coast. He lost only to Maurice Baker of Hartford, Conn., two-time world champion.

From the Portland Press Herald, 1969

"All in all, the arm wrestling championships was one of the most intense and challenging experiences of my life. The headline of the story the *Press Herald* ran about me finishing as runner-up in the competition twice was "Arm of Steel, Will of Iron," and that said it pretty well. Arm strength mattered, of course, and I had always had naturally strong arms, but it was determination, focus, and a certain insanity that really made the difference.

"The way it went was that the judge put his hand over the hands of the competitors and when he lifted his hand the struggle began. The difference between me and the guys across from me was that as soon as the judge lifted his hand every bit of my physiological and psychological being exploded, and before my opponent knew what was happening his arm was half-way down. All of the anger that had been in me since I was a child had risen to the surface, and that was it.

"Those guys across the table from me had no idea of the fury they were up against. They saw it as a friendly sporting competition, but I saw it as a fight to the death. Maybe they should have taken the fact that I have KILL OR BE KILLED tattooed on the inside of my right wrist as some sort of warning, know what I mean?"

"My longest match on the way to going up against Mo was with a guy from Philadelphia who weighed 310 pounds and was so strong that it took me almost four minutes to put his arm all the way down after I got it half-way down the instant we started. He was damn rugged, but he wasn't as strong as Mo, who worked throwing large steel plates around in a foundry in Hartford, Connecticut, and outweighed me by sixty-five pounds.

"Mo immediately kicked my ass. No excuses. I was exhausted after winning fifty-six straight matches against some of the strongest men on the planet, but he had fought and won fifty-six straight matches too, so we were even there. He was just a lot stronger than I was. Case closed. When he went on both years to win the world championship after he won the East Coast championship I was not at all surprised.

"C'mon, it was the first time in the thirty-year history of the competition that anyone from Maine had even placed, and I finished runner-up to the eventual world champion both times I competed! And I was the lightest guy in the class I competed in both times!

"An interesting sidelight to it all was that the bodybuilding event that the arm wrestling champion-ship was part of was the first event Arnold Schwarzenegger had attended in America. He had just gotten off the plane from Austria, and he was very impressed with the size and intensity of the bodybuilders he encountered here. He was there to guest-pose in the physique portion of the event. When I asked him if he'd also be competing in the arm wrestling competition, he looked around the room at all the hairy beasts he'd be up against and went into a little act, like he was very afraid. Then he began laughing and talking in that famous accent of his and said: "I might be a little slow, but I'm not crazy!" Everybody around us cracked up when he said that, and right then you knew this guy had a lot of natural charisma and was going places.

"I would also like to add that one of my best friends from Martin's Health club, Bruce Chambers, finished fifth in the arm wrestling competition both years we took part. Bruce had incredible brute strength and all the heart in the world. So, there you go, no one from Maine had ever even placed in the thirty years the championships were held, and now two guys from Portland finished in the top five. Ain't life grand?!"

JAKE'S GUARDIAN ANGEL AT THE
NUCLEAR POWER PLANT

In most instances, I didn't have to solicit stories about Jake, people just came forward with one story after another, but at this point Jake told me about an experience he had working on the construction of the atomic power plant up in Wiscasset, Maine in the early 1970s that was so unbelievable that I really wanted to get it corroborated.

Because the incident occurred some fifty years ago, I was concerned that I wouldn't be able to locate an eyewitness, but after a day or two of thought, Jake came up with the name Leon Dudley. After an online search, I ascertained that a man by that name was currently living in Old Orchard Beach, a town about a dozen miles down the coast from Portland, and I gave him a call.

Leon was breathless when I told him what I was calling about. Here he was, pushing eighty years old, being asked about something he witnessed when he was in his early twenties, and has been raving to family and friends about all these years

"You better believe I remember what happened!" he exploded. "Jake and some other guys and myself were working on the fourth floor of the atomic power plant, and were getting ready to lower some machinery down into a six-yard-wide hole in the center of the structure. Jake was walking backwards, guiding a forklift with machinery on it, and he fell over backwards into the hole!

"We were all horrified as hell! We all knew that Jake was this wild character that had been in all kind of scrapes and made it out alive, of course, but we also knew that no human being could possibly survive that fall, especially because there were tall steel rods sticking up from the bottom!

"We were all frozen in place," Leon continued. "We were all very fond of Jake by that time, but we knew, beyond any doubt, that this was the end of the line for him. I definitely did not want to see what I knew I would see when I looked down into that hole, but somehow or other I managed to get myself over to the edge and look down, and there he was! Alive! Hanging onto the first floor railing by one hand! That he managed to catch onto the railing was amazing itself, but that he was able to do it with one hand and was strong enough to hang on and pull himself up is absolutely astounding! I've thought about it many times over the years! Believe me! I have!"

Leon and the others didn't see what transpired after Jake fell into the hole, but Jake described it for me.

"When I fell over backwards into the hole," he told me, "I remember grabbing a railing that I hadn't even known was there and holding onto it for dear life! My guardian angel had saved me again!"

I sat there thinking about what he had told me about his guardian angel in his experience with the forces of good and evil fighting for his soul when he was freezing to death in Death Valley, and how he said his guardian angel had led him to choose life. It was at this point that I realized that this damn violence-obsessed, ex-con, outlaw-biker ends up having a good deal of mountaintop mystic in him after all, as we shall discover in an upcoming chapter.

Sawyer Gets 1-5 Years On Stolen Property Charge

A Portland bail bondsman was sentenced this morning in Cumberland County Superior Court to 1-5 years at the Maine State Prison after pleading guilty to a charge of receiving stolen property.

Jonathan ("Jake") Sawyer, 36, of Munjoy Street, told presiding Justice Edward Stern that he "spent years trying to get a decent job and finally said to heck with it," paying $600 for a 1971 car which he said he knew to have been stolen.

Cumberland County Attorney Henry N. Berry III, who recommended the 1-5-year sentence, explained that the car was stolen on May 18, 1972, in Concord, Mass., and was bought by Sawyer a short time later.

Berry said that he probably would have requested a sentence of 2½-5 years if Sawyer has been found guilty after a jury trial, but he conceded that "there's always the chance that we might have had a few weaknesses in the case" and that he wanted to be certain that "we have Jake on a string for a while."

The sentence is contingent on Sawyer being placed on parole for the remainder of the term if he is released before five years of incarceration.

Berry said that the charge against Sawyer was made possible after "a long and difficult investigation of stolen automobiles in southern Maine," an investigation which involved the FBI and a number of community police departments.

Citing the fact that Sawyer has previously served jail terms for felonious assault and burglary, Berry expressed amazement at his status as a bail bondsman.

THIRTEEN

When Jake and I agreed over the phone that we'd be talking about the various activities he was involved in here in Portland during this time period, it occurred to me that it might be fun to meet down on the waterfront somewhere, where we'd have an overview of the city, so he could point out this and that locale where these various episodes took place.

"Sure!" he yelled over the phone when I asked him. "In fact, as you will see, the pile of stories I'm about to relate to you, that took place in our little 'City By the Sea,' as it was described by our best known native son, Henry Wadsworth Longfellow, all come together in a very interesting and exciting way with an incident that took place down on the Portland waterfront.

So there we were, sitting down on one of the docks on a log with our backs to the water, enjoying a panoramic view of the peninsula, and drinking Schmidt's Tiger Head Ale.

"So, Jake," I began, "all you did to make ends meet when you got out of San Quentin in 1968 was train people at Martin's Health Club and work side jobs now and then, right? That was about it for the late sixties, early seventies, huh? Sounds pretty calm for you!"

As time went on, I was learning how to get him fired up, not that it ever took very much.

"Oh, really?!" he roared. "You are a fucking riot! How about I take a moment to fill in some glaring gaps in your knowledge of my activities at the time, okay?"

VOLUME TWO

WEED, INDEED

"As to the financial end of things, I was doing very well. One of the things that hasn't occurred to me to tell you is that when I first arrived back in Portland, I immediately started making a great deal of money supplying marijuana to a cadre of local health care providers I had put together. Well, we didn't know at the time that pot dealers would someday come to be known as health care providers but, to tell you the truth, we did feel at the time that we were providing a much needed service to deserving people, including, of course, a lot of people with cancer and other dreaded diseases, so there you go.

"As I have mentioned to you on more than one occasion, I have never done anything in my life with the sole purpose of making money, and the marijuana business I operated at that time was no exception. Truthfully, though, providing people with a much-needed medicinal product was not my primary motivation. Setting deserving people up in a small business operation without them having to come up with the capital that is normally necessary was actually the most satisfying aspect of it for me. All I asked of my care providers was that they deal with me straight up. Their reputation with me was their capital, and, in most instances, everything turned out very well. For those who didn't keep their word and tried to take advantage of my good nature in some way, things didn't turn out so well. There weren't too many of that kind, though. Pot dealing was an honorable business between cool people in those days, and I'm very proud to have facilitated it in my humble way.

JAKE

A REAL ESTATE TYCOON

"As I said, my financial situation at the time was very secure due to my involvement in the marijuana trade, but I needed a place to invest all that money, since it wouldn't do at all for a felon on parole to be depositing large sums of money in a bank. Parole people pick up on that sort of thing pretty quickly. Fortunately, though, multi-unit income properties could be had for a song in Portland at that time, and for one reason or another, there were certain income-property owners who preferred to deal with private individuals than involve a lending institution. Consequently, it wasn't long before I was the proud owner of three very lucrative multi-unit income properties on Munjoy Hill at the eastern end of the peninsula of Portland. Munjoy Hill has now has been yuppyfied beyond belief, but was then a very working class, friendly, know your neighbor part of town.

"I was very pleased to find that ol' time feeling in our friend Stan's Munjoy Hill Tavern," Jake boomed, shooting his arm up and pointing to where the tavern sits about halfway up Munjoy Hill.

"The apartment buildings I owned were lucrative in themselves," he continued, pulling off the caps of another bottle of Schmidt's Ale for each of us, "but they also facilitated my becoming involved in another activity which proved to be very profitable as well. Knowing that I was accruing a good amount of equity in my buildings, my fun-loving lawyer, Dan Lilley, who was the best defense attorney of all time, recommended to me the sideline activity I'm going to tell you about, and I've always been very grateful to him for that."

VOLUME TWO

DANCER'S BAILBONDSMAN SERVICE

"In light of what he knew about my background and abilities, as well as my general outlook on life, Dan suggested that I become a bail bondsman. At first I scoffed at the idea, given the fact that I was an unrepentant convicted felon still on parole from San Quentin, for starters. But the more Dan pushed the idea, the more sense it made to me. Honestly, I was astonished that getting my bail bondsman license would be so easy. All you had to do was fill out a form stating that you were a resident of the state of Maine, and had the financial means to pay someone's bail amount if they skipped out on it, and you were in. The equity I had in my buildings was really all I needed. So, hey, I signed on the dotted line, went home and designed my business card, and I was in business. 'Dancer's Bail Bonds' my business card said, in embossed gold letters on a brilliant white background.

"By the way, now that the subject has come up, I don't know if I've mentioned to you that before the district attorney hung the name Bonecrusher on me at my trial for the suicide charge, I was called 'Jake from Maine' by my Hell's Angels brothers. After they got to know me better, though, they started calling me 'Jake the Dancer', and I became known by that nickname by many people in Portland and elsewhere as well. I've always loved to dance. When I was at a bar I would do so for very long periods of time, whether with a lovely lady out on the dance floor, or off by myself in a far corner, lost in a private reverie. I guess my fondness for dancing stems from my taking classical dance lessons at the Dorothy Mason School of Dance in my youth."

JAKE

I had thought Dorothy Mason School of Dance was for sissies. We boys scoffed at the very idea of taking classical dance lessons, you know? But now I find out that Jake Sawyer took classical dance lessons and loved them. Ah, life.

"Okay," he continued, "this is how the bail bondsman business worked: I'd get a call from the county jail down on Federal Street that some unfortunate individual needed the services of a bail bondsman, and I'd go to the jail and interview them. If I decided that there was a reasonable chance they'd show up for trial, I'd bail them out. The thing I looked for was whether or not they had local ties. If they did, I'd bail them out because I knew if they lived locally, they knew people I knew, which meant that I could locate them if they reneged on our deal. If I decided that they were an acceptable risk and bailed them out, I made it very clear to them that the deal was a matter of honor between us, and they knew very well what the consequences of disrespecting me were.

"Let me provide an overview of what my life was like at the time, if I may, as it may increase your understanding of how this whole bail bondsman thing fit into the larger picture.

"Believe it or not, I was a very rowdy fellow in those days. The various major activities I told you about the last time we spoke, and the ones I'm telling you about today, all took place pretty much simultaneously.

"I felt like I was king of the world. Portland was small beans to me after managing a health club in the middle of the Combat Zone, running with the Hell's Angels in Oakland, and doing time in San Quentin. I strode the peninsula of Portland like a humongously strong madman on steroids, constantly looking for action, and opportunities for having wildly crazy sex, and I got plenty of both, often right in the middle of the fucking street or some other public place!

"So, there I'd be whenever the mood struck, which was often, drunk as a bastard, raising holy hell in some honky-tonk saloon like Joe and Neno's Circus Room or Sloppy Joe's, out on the dance floor, bare-assed naked, dancing my brains out, with some equally as bare-assed young lady performing oral sex on me between tunes! Right out there in front of everyone!

"Sometimes," he continued, "other men would try to do the same thing, you know, trying to be like me, but that kind of thing can be very hazardous if you don't go about it in the right way. I made it look more of a natural occurrence than it actually was, so a lot of men were somewhat misled. Some guy would get beat to a fuck by the bouncer for hauling his dick out in the middle of the dance floor, and I'd be across the room naked as a jaybird, laughing my ass off and getting a blowjob. Hey, there's a certain way to go about things, you know?

"Sometimes, in the middle of one of my grand shows, the bartender would yell over that I had a call from County Jail about someone needing my bail bondsman services, like I'd instructed him to do, you know, for promotional purposes, in case someone in attendance found themselves in need of my services at some future time. People would cheer as they watched me get dressed, give whatever woman I had in tow at the time a little kiss on the cheek goodbye, then run out the door, jump on the very cool orange Harley chopper I had parked at the curb outside, and ride to the rescue of some sorry-assed lad locked in a lonely cell down at County Jail, then I'd often return to the bar shortly after with a protective arm around the grateful looking fellow and the crowd would friggin' explode with cheering!"

Allow me to interject here that I serve as a witness to Jake's activities at Joe and Neno's and Sloppy Joe's, as do many Portlanders of a certain age. Everyone had at least heard of Jake Sawyer, and many of us saw all there was to see of him and his female friends at said establishments, or maybe on board a Casco Bay Lines ferry out in Portland Harbor, like I did. Interestingly enough, that was around the time "streaking" was in fashion. Society seemed to be saying it was okay to be out in public naked, as long as you were quick about it, but evidently all Jake heard was the "it's okay to be out in public naked" part of it, I guess, and then added the sex part on his own.

"The bail bondsman gig was going pretty well all around," Jake continued. "I was able to help a lot of guys get out of jail, and I was making good commission money for my efforts. What you have to understand is that a lot of these guys didn't even have the ten percent of their bail amount to pay a bail bondsman, and I was the only one who would trust them for it. The deal was that they were to pay me my fee on or before the day of their trial, and every one of them swore up and down that they'd have no trouble with that.

"My fee was a secondary consideration, though. What was more important was that I was liable for their bail amount. If they didn't show up on their court date, which happened a few times, I had ten days to produce them before the court placed liens on my buildings for the amount of their bail.

"During those ten days is when I'd become a friggin' fiery-eyed, ruthless bounty hunter. I'd stalk around town looking for the low-life son of a bitch and I'd tell everyone in town who I was looking for. I'd put out the word that if he turned himself in to me, all would be forgiven, which it would have been. I don't lie. If he didn't turn himself in to me, though, and he was still in town, he was mine, and everyone knew it. The night I bailed them out I looked every one of them straight in the eye and told them that if they couldn't come up with my fee, to just come discuss it with me but, no matter what, to make sure they showed up for the trial because I was liable for their bail. I made sure that things were very clear between us.

"The money part of it didn't mean all that much to me, to tell you the truth. What really mattered to me was that the friggin' bail-jumper had disrespected me. They gave me their word, and anyone who doesn't keep their word is a piece of shit. End of fucking discussion.

"As it turned out, I was successful at apprehending every low-life bail-jumper I had to hunt down but, as it turned out, I ended up not having to hurt any of them too much. They had suffered a great deal already just knowing I was after them, so generally it wasn't necessary to do any more than give them a black eye so their friends would know not to fuck with me should the occasion arise that they might need my services. I'm not some kind of vicious animal who enjoys inflicting pain on others unnecessarily, after all.

"The basic problem was that the other bail bondsmen saw that I was getting a lot more business than any of them were. The reason for that was that I had the privately developed enforcement system in place, which I have told you about in annoying detail. The upshot of it is that my system allowed me to more readily take a chance on someone. My success was also due to the astute marketing program I employed, which mainly consisted of advertising my services by handing out my business cards in bars all over town. The other bail bondsmen were also free to do this, of course, but they chose not to for reasons of their own.

"By the way, the qualifications one needs to become a bail bondsman were tightened up considerably as a direct result of my three-year stint on the job. You now have to undergo an extensive background check and only law-abiding, upright citizens get their license. I'm very proud to have played a part in bringing about needed reform to a critical facet of the criminal justice system, actually. As far as I'm concerned, there can never be enough law and order.

"Oh! The Jake the Dancer stuff reminds me of another important part of this period of my life that I haven't told you about, my friend!

"I can't believe I haven't told you about Dancer's Variety yet!" he roared.

DANCER'S VARIETY

"For some reason I'd always wanted to own a variety store, so when I spotted a vacant storefront on Spring Street, just west of the center of town," he said, pointing the area out from our vantage point down on the waterfront. "I was all over it. I called it Dancer's Variety and ran it for three years, from 1971 to 1974, along with operating my marijuana enterprise and continuing with my bail bondsman activities."

It struck me that 1974 seemed to be the stop date for the great variety of activities and enterprises that Jake was involved in at the time, and I wrote "1974?" in big letters at the top of my notebook page to remind myself to ask him about it.

"Dancer's Variety was a very efficiently and imaginatively run place. We always kept the shelves fully stocked with a nice variety of canned goods and the like, and we had a great selection of beer and wine. Our take-out foods couldn't be beat. Travelers who came in to the store from the Greyhound Bus station across the street said our hamburgers were the best they had ever had anywhere. We gave people a generously proportioned patty of well-seasoned hamburg on a steamed roll, topped with a generous slice of tomato, some crispy fresh lettuce, and a side order of fried onions, which customers especially loved. I believe in giving the people the best possible product at the lowest possible price, which is exactly the way my family had run the Sawyer-Barker clothing company for generations.

"We had an extensive and enticing accessories section at Dancer's Variety as well, featuring my own personally designed brand of water pipes. I named them Dancer's Water Pipes, of course, and came up with the catchy slogan: 'More Bounce to the Ounce', written in cursive underneath the name. This was at a time when pot was still very illegal, remember. People were doing five years for simple possession of any amount, and here I was selling pot pipes and allegedly selling weed across the counter at my variety store in the middle of town.

"I also had a good supply of my Dancer's Bail Bondsman business cards on hand, so, with our food inventory, very popular sandwich counter, great selection of beer and wine, our accessories department, and our under-the-counter pot business, Dancer's Variety was a hubbub of activity, without even considering the occasional sale of an unbelievably discounted, previously owned vehicle, which I had acquired through the no-money-invested-by-me business plan I had developed years before."

After he'd finished telling me about Dancer's Variety, I couldn't hold back any longer and asked him why the year 1974 seemed to be the year each of his various activities came to an end.

"That's something we'll get to," he said, waving me off. "I'd definitely feel remiss if I didn't tell you about another most interesting and profitable business I owned and operated from about 1971 to 1974 first, though. You're really gonna like this one!"

I was sure he didn't have time for another major activity, considering everything else he had going on at the time, but he seemed to want to tell me about one more thing, so I humored him.

MYSTIQUE FIGURE WRAP

"I really didn't want to get into anything else, I was out straight as it was, but yet another business opportunity was flashed before my eyes, and it turned out to be one I just couldn't turn down.

"John DiCola, a friend of mine who had won the Mr. America title in 1969, and was one of the bodybuilders who worked out at Mid-City Health Club in the Combat Zone when I managed it years before, gave me a call one day out of the blue. He was all excited about a very successful business he had started by way of capitalizing on his fame as Mr. America, and he wanted to talk to me about opening a franchise in Portland. He was absolutely certain that I could cash in on my golden boy reputation in the health and

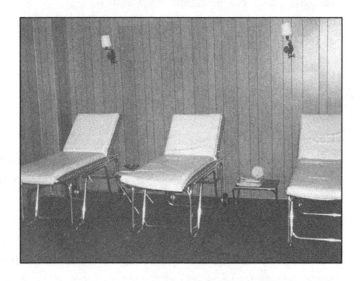

*Jake says: "God bless America and the freedoms we all en-
joy, women included! The ladies have just as much right to
enjoy orgasms on a regular basis as men do! I run into ladies
all the time who ask me when I'm going to open up another
Mystique Figure Wrap, and, you know, that just might happen after we get this damn book done, so let's get it done as
soon as possible for the ladies' sake!"*

bodybuilding world in the same way he had capital-
ized on his Mr. America title. He was so confident that
I'd be a success that he even offered to take the cost
of my opening a franchise in Portland out of the profits
he was sure I'd be making, so what could I do?

"Mystique Figure Wrap was the name of the franchise and I operated it from 1971 to 1974. It was located on Preble Street, right in the middle of downtown Portland," he said, pointing a finger directly at
the center point of the downtown.

"Mystique Figure Wrap was a wonderful gift to all
of the 'full figured' upper-income women of Greater
Portland. Our services were especially popular with
women from ritzy places like Falmouth Foreside and
Cape Elizabeth who wished to trim off a few pounds
for an upcoming special social event, or maybe for
some grand tropical island vacation. We ran a series
of very classy ads highlighting my qualifications as a
health and fitness expert, and included in the ads was
my personal guarantee that the ladies would lose a
minimum of six inches around their entire body and
drop a full dress size after just one two-hour treatment.

"Before we go any further, my friend, I'd like to
make it clear that in no way am I making a judgment
about, or snickering about, anyone's body size. Some
of the most marvelous and sexiest women I've known
in my life have been a little more rounded than curvy,
let us say, but I've loved them just the same, and I just
want to be sure that that gets included here."

I gave him a reassuring nod and just kept scrib-
bling away.

"The Mystique Figure Wrap experience started as
soon as the client stepped through the door. Cindy,
my very sophisticated and friendly special assistant,

made them feel completely at ease right from the beginning, and after she had taken 'before' measurements of their arms, breasts, stomachs, waist, legs
and calves, she'd lead them to my office, where I would
work my boyish charm on them.

"I dressed in a Ben Casey smock, like the one the
young handsome doctor wore in the TV program all
the women were into at the time, and I had my office
in a room off to the side, where I conducted an initial
interview with the clients in order to better familiarize
myself with their special needs and desires. I looked
very professional in my doctor's smock, and I had
framed documents all over the wall behind me, including my Kents Hill prep school diploma, my Paratrooper
School graduation certificate, and a penmanship
award I was given in the third grade. Hey, there was
some stiff competition in that third grade class, believe
me. Anyway, the ladies were all very impressed with
my credentials and my general appearance. They were
all very pleased when I told them that, in my professional opinion they could, without a doubt, benefit
from the services of Mystique Figure Wrap.

"The first step of the Mystique Figure Wrap program
entailed getting a great massage by one of the two full-
time lady masseuses we had on duty at all times. I had
learned some things about how to give a fantastic
massage during my time in California, and it was very
satisfying to pass on what I had learned to my Mystique Figure Wrap employees, who became quite
skilled at putting our clients in a very pleasant and
agreeable frame of mind.

"Let me say here, my friend, that our clientele were
often of the sort that were quite inexperienced in the
realm of carnal gratification, and our masseuses, most
of them being bi-sexual and extremely skilled in their

craft, were often able to bring the ladies to a point of sexual gratification that they hadn't reached prior to their Mystique Figure Wrap experience. I trust that you get my meaning?"

"Yeah, Jake," I said, nodding my head "I get it, I get it."

"After giving them their 'special' massage," he continued, "the masseuses wrapped the ladies from their necks to their ankles in wide gauze bandages that had been soaked in very warm water that, we informed them, had been treated with mineral salts harvested from the Dead Sea and laid out on the shore for a week on a bed of dried sea weed to absorb the vitalizing rays of the Mediterranean sun.

"The ladies would lie for an hour or so on one of our therapeutically designed tables listening to enchanting music being played softly in the background, while basking in the gentle aroma of special incense we had imported from India, or maybe the incense and mineral salts were from a head shop located down the street from us, I'm not exactly sure how that went, but the ladies liked it, and that's all that mattered.

"When their period of meditative relaxation was up, the masseuse would unwrap the ladies and Cindy would come in and take the 'after' measurements of their arms, breasts, stomachs, waists, legs and calves, and – what do you know! - the 'after' measurements would invariably total at least six inches less than the 'before' measurements, just like we told them would be the case!

"The ladies were, of course, very pleased, all considered, and they'd be giggling back and forth with each other as they went out the door, all excited to get home and try on that special dress. We had a great deal of repeat business. Some women had three to four 'treatments' a week, which cost $100 each and the rich ladies did not mind that in the slightest.

"We were anxious for them to get home as soon as possible too, of course, because we knew that the effect of having virtually all their external body parts tightly wrapped for an hour would wear off in a relatively short period of time.

"You know what, though? In the three years I ran Mystique Body Wrap I never had one woman call us and complain that she had gained the weight back. I think that's because they enjoyed the illusion while it lasted. And they might also have enjoyed the 'special massage,' I guess. Whatever, I really don't know. All I can say is that as time went on we had all we could do to accommodate the large number of repeat customers we had. God bless America, all women deserve to have orgasms all the time. I have many friends and acquaintances today who want me to re-open Mystique Figure Wrap and, you never know, I might just do that some day!"

1974 ARRIVES

"Whew!" I said, tossing my pen down onto my notebook. "You sure you didn't have any other activities going on at the time?!"

"Well, maybe a few other things, but nothing worth mentioning, I guess, unless ..."

"Enough!" I yelled, much to his amusement, "but I would really like to know about this 1974 thing. What happened at that time that put a halt to all your activities?"

"I went back to prison, what else?" he said.

JAKE

"For what?" I asked incredulously.

"As you obviously know," he began, "the late sixties and early seventies, which was the time period immediately following my release from San Quentin, was a very busy time for me. My paratrooper training stressed the need to hit the ground running, and that's just what I did when I got back to Portland. Running concurrently along with all the other activities I have told you about, though, was my involvement in a New England-wide stolen automobile and motorcycle ring, and it was that activity that led to my return to prison in the year 1974, just after I had gotten off parole from San Quentin."

I looked down at the floor, shaking my head in disbelief. Just a few years earlier, Jake had been unexpectedly paroled from San Quentin, having been somewhat miraculously delivered from either spending the rest of his life in prison, or dying violently at the hands of his fellow inmates. Now here he was, five years later, back behind bars. I was genuinely perplexed at how an obviously intelligent and well-educated guy from a solid family background could have allowed that to happen, especially because the other activities he was involved in at the time provided him with a more than adequate income.

"Why did you even get involved in the stolen vehicles racket again, Jake?" I asked him, a little exasperated. "Obviously you didn't need the money with everything else you had going on, and you had to know that you'd get caught sooner rather than later. C'mon, there were so many people involved. Not only were there your partners in crime, but all the people who were driving stolen vehicles around. Police from six states were on the outlook for those vehicles. You had to know that the whole operation would come crashing down before very long. Didn't the probability of being a convicted felon facing multiple counts of Grand Theft Auto sometime in the near future concern you at all?"

"What you have to understand," he answered, taking pains to be patient with me, "is that I didn't have any choice in the matter. I was just being who I am, right to the friggin' core. Every day of my life has been lived straight out, completely without regard to consequences. I've always gone for the gusto, mainly because nothing else interests me. I get bored very easily, and I absolutely hate boredom, so there you go. I'd rather die than live a watered-down, average kind of life. That attitude has been both a curse and a blessing all through my life, but it's who I am and I can't do a thing about it. I didn't give a rat's ass about the money I was making. I did what I did because I was excited as hell about being in the stolen car business, and that completely overrode any dread I might have had about going back to prison."

"Okay" I said, shrugging my shoulders.

"Now that we've got that settled, let's get to the nitty gritty," he said.

DANCER'S DISCOUNT AUTO AND MOTORCYCLE

"My favorite thing to do was to drive my three-quarter-ton former U.S. Mail delivery van down to Boston and collect BMWs and high-end motorcycles from the Harvard and M.I.T. parking lots, like I did when I managed the Mid-City Health Club in the Combat Zone. I knew some extremely useful things about the ignition switches of both vehicles, and I also knew that both BMWs and high-end motorcycles went very readily on the re-sale market. It eased my conscience to know that their current owners didn't care that much either way. Their daddy would just buy them another one. He'd have it to them in time for this weekend's skiing trip to the White Mountains, for sure, then he'd collect more than the vehicle was worth from his insurance company.

"Another form the recycled, no-money-invested-by-me vehicle acquisition enterprise took involved a familiar scam, but with a couple of personally developed twists. Here's how it normally went: a guy is making payments on a vehicle he's grown tired of, so he has someone dispose of the vehicle, reports it as stolen, collects the insurance, pays off the balance of the loan, and has enough left for a good down payment on another car.

"Well, it happened in a slightly different way with me. To begin with, instead of waiting for them to tire of their present vehicle on their own, I'd nudge things along a bit by flashing a snappy looking car, van, motorcycle, whatever, in front of their eyes, then casually make them aware that it could be theirs for far less than they thought. I'd pull up to a bunch of guys and look around for the one who had that special glint in his eye. When I spotted him I'd take him aside and explain to him how we could make his present car, along with the payments on it, disappear, and how he could own the gem in front of him outright, with no payments to be made, and maybe end up with a little extra cash in his pocket, to boot. When his eyes widened and his mouth dropped open, I knew he was mine. "Ain't life grand!" I'd say to him as I patted him on the back.

"What made this all possible, of course, was that I was able to acquire the high-end vehicles in question at no cost to me, thereby allowing me to make them available to special buyers at stunningly low prices and still make a nice profit for myself.

"Another little twist was that I'd dispose of the individual's original vehicle in a different way than is customary in the underworld. The way a vehicle is usually disposed of is by hauling it to some remote area and burning it beyond recognition, and I could very well have done it that way, but chose not to, just on general principles. I sometimes like to do things just to see the sparks fly, you know, but they're not always sparks from an actual fire, know what I mean?

"There were times when I actually went out of my way to take unnecessary chances just to keep myself entertained. I didn't really know that at the time, I guess, but looking back on it, I know that's what was going on. Why the hell should I go through all the bother of hauling some damn vehicle up to Tall Pines, Maine, and torch it in an abandoned gravel pit, for instance, when I could just push it off the end of a pier into Portland Harbor instead?

"Yeah, why not?" I said. "It's a deep ocean."

"Well, I'll tell you why not!" he yelled, laughing. "Portland Harbor is tidal water, that's why!" He yelled, jumping up and gesturing to the harbor behind us.

"When the ocean tide goes out, whatever has been dumped into the water tends to get pushed down the harbor to the mouth of the Fore River. So, before long, there was a bunch of my cars plainly visible at low tide sitting down there just past the bridge. Cianbro Construction was working on a project on the shore down there, so their workers were the first to see all those cars sitting there at low tide, and when they did, all hell broke loose!"

When he read the story in the *Bollard* about Jake pushing cars off the end of the Maine State Pier, a friend of mine by the name of Tony Caterina, who enjoys talking about local history, and is a fan of the Jake Sawyer saga, offered some corroborating evidence.

"I didn't see Jake doing his thing at the Maine State Pier myself," Tony told me, "I was told about it by Pete Riccetelli, the well-known Portland boxer of the late 60s and early 70s. Pete told me that he went with Jake one night down to the Maine State Pier to help him push stolen cars into Portland Harbor, but Pete got very alarmed when one of the cars wouldn't sink and remained highly visible as it floated down the harbor. It was one of those Nash Ramblers that people said looked like an upside down bathtub. To make matters much worse, Jake had neglected to turn the ignition off and the red brake lights and directionals were flashing! The police had to see it, and they did! Pete said he started to high-tail it when he heard the police sirens, but Jake just stood there and yelled after him: "I guess I should've turned the ignition off, huh?" Pete said he was amazed that Jake didn't seem to be alarmed in the slightest way about what was happening. After Pete had made his getaway, he said he looked back and saw Jake casually strolling off the pier and stopping to take one more look at the blinking red lights floating down the harbor. Apparently, the police didn't recognize him because it was night, and who would expect whoever was responsible for it to be still around?"

When I asked Jake about what Tony said about Pete Riccetelli, he immediately confirmed the story, but was quick to add that his pushing cars off the end of the Maine State Pier wasn't the only thing that drew the attention of the authorities.

"There were so many cool looking cars being driven around town by individuals who the police knew were not able to afford them, they knew something was up," he said. "One time I was stopped at a light in Morrill's Corner and looked around and saw two of my cars and one of my motorcycles sitting at the other three lights around the four-way intersection!"

A VERY FADED METALLIC BLUE
LINCOLN TOWN CAR

"There's one particular vehicular transaction that took place at that time that kind of sticks in my mind, and I still chuckle when I think about it today. It involved the owner of a very well-known and successful local business, who shall go unnamed.

"He was one of these guys who gets their jollies by hanging around with ruffians like me now and then. He was at the Griffin Club one night when a bunch of us were shooting our mouths off about this and that, and when I said that I had a beautiful, late-model, metallic blue Lincoln Town Car loaded with accessories that I was selling for only $1500, the guy laughed and said he'd take it because he knew that a car like that should sell for around $5000 more than that amount.

"'Can't turn down a deal like that!' he said.

"I didn't have any further conversation with him on the matter until about a week later, when I went up to him on the street and announced that I had his Lincoln Town Car around the corner waiting for him.

"Right away his jaw dropped and he said that gee,

he was only fooling around. I told him that gee, that was just great, but that I wasn't. That riveted him to the spot. He had no desire to be in possession of what he knew to be a stolen automobile, but he also knew what disrespecting me would mean, prominent businessman or not, so he ran to the bank and got my money. All he asked was that I deliver the car to his house in the middle of a dark night and leave it in his garage with the overhead door closed and locked.

"Here's the funny part: about ten years later, a friend of his told me that the guy was so paranoid about being seen driving that stolen Lincoln Town Car around town that he had never taken it out of his garage! It's been almost fifty years now and I wouldn't be surprised if it's still there!"

THE INEVITABLE

"Well, skipping over the boring details, what with the police finding so many vehicles piled up in Portland Harbor, and one thing or another, one fine inevitable day I was arrested on multiple charges of Grand Theft Auto and receiving stolen property, and shortly thereafter I was put on trial.

"My lawyer was Dan Lilley, who was, without a doubt, the best criminal trial lawyer anywhere, and seemed to be attracted to high-profile, long-shot cases. Everybody knew I was guilty, of course, but if anybody could get me off, Dan could.

"I had all I could do to keep a straight face when the judge asked me how I pleaded and I answered 'not guilty.' Apparently, I did it very well at it because that's when Dan started calling me "The Iceman." We've been joking about it ever since. Hey, he had warned me that I could be facing ten years or more, considering the current charges and past felonies, and that was enough to get my attention. I added my current age of thirty-six to ten and come up with the age I'd be the next time I'd able to ride my motorcycle up onto the sidewalk and gather up a young lady to take up to the East End Beach for some fun, and saw that that was a long time to wait, know what I mean?"

"Yeah..." I said, shaking my head and looking up from my notebook. "C'mon, Jake, from what you're telling me, you just about volunteered for this stuff! You knew enough about the legal system to know that what you had been doing and how you were doing it could very well end up with you spending a number of years locked up in prison, but you did it anyway! For fun?! What the hell?!"

"I did it because it's who I am, man!" he yelled back at me. "Sometimes I do things just for the adrenalin rush! It occurs to me to do some foolish fucking thing, and at first I scoff at actually doing it, but I know deep down that I'm going to do it. What a marvelous ride on the merry-go-round I get, though! The fun never stops as long as you keep going for the gusto!"

"Yeah, alright, Jake," I said, shaking my head, "let's get to the trial."

"Dan did very well at putting some kind of case together for me," he resumed. "He told the jury that they didn't have enough evidence to convict me because everybody in town has a Jake Sawyer story, some true, some not, and that it was hard to tell fact from fiction, so maybe these outrageous stories about me dropping stolen cars off Maine State Pier weren't true at all. He also managed to get across to them that even if I did do what I was accused of doing, I didn't do it for the money, I did it to spread the wealth around a little more evenly. His object, of course, was to make them predisposed to like me when he put me on the stand, and from there my winning ways would carry the day.

"Sure enough, when Dan put me on the stand there was an elderly black lady on the jury who took a liking to me. She was the lone holdout for conviction, and the proceedings ended up with a hung jury. The lady and I had caught one another's eye early on and connected in a good way. I think she respected the fact that I didn't rat out any of my accomplices in exchange for being tried on lesser charges. And I also think she was very impressed with what Dan said about my primary motivation being that I wanted to help people own a vehicle that they might not otherwise be able to afford. When I was going by the jury box on our way out of court after the verdict was announced, she leaned over to me and laid her hand on my arm and whispered: 'Don't you be taking those folk's nice cars and fancy motorcycles no more, son.' I'd smiled my biggest and best smile at her and said 'Thank you, darlin'!'

"After the hung jury was announced, Henry Berry, the hard-assed District Attorney who prosecuted my case, sat in his chair after the verdict was read with his head buried in his hands, moaning to himself like he just couldn't believe what had happened. I genuinely felt bad for him. He was a decent man who had worked very hard on the case, and he desperately wanted to see justice done. That sure as hell wasn't the way things worked out, though.

"The hung jury resulted in my avoiding the long sentence I was facing, but the DA's office knew that they had enough additional evidence to try me again, so Dan recommended that I agree to plead guilty to lesser charges in order to avoid a second trial. Basically, the State didn't want to take me to trial again, so Dan told them that I would plead guilty to any sentence that started with the number 1. So, instead of going to trial again and receiving a sentence that would almost certainly keep me incarcerated for ten years or so, maybe the rest of my life, given my history, in a federal penitentiary somewhere, I received a sentence of from only one to five years in Maine State Prison."

"*Only* one to five years?" I muttered to myself.

FOURTEEN

Meeting down on the waterfront turned out to be a good change of pace, but Jake's apartment was still our preferred venue. With the memorabilia from Jake's life all over the walls, the great view of downtown out his window, the comfortable chairs, and the cans of bottles of Schmidt's Tiger Head Ale he always had in his reefer, we had it made.

"I don't drink much now," he said, "years ago I did my share. I've grown to know better over the years, I guess. Alcohol tends to take you over, if you let it, so now I'm happy to stay home and occasionally have just one or two, but no more than that. Today I mostly work out, read history or other things I'm interested in, or watch the History Channel during the winter months, and sometimes I go raise hell for the hell of it. HELL'S ANGELS FOREVER!

"Security means a lot to me at this point. After you've flown around by the seat of your pants all your life, heading off to here and there after whatever opportunity for stimulation presented itself, like I have, you get so you yearn for that feeling of security, you know, a home port to pull into."

I had difficulty thinking of the individual in front of me - brimming with energy and enthusiasm - calmly cruising into any port, but there you have it.

"Jake," I began, "I was going to ask you to talk about what you experienced at Maine State Prison today, but I guess not much happened there, right? I mean, after San Quentin, Maine State Prison must have been pretty boring and uneventful, right? Small potatoes, huh?"

VOLUME TWO

MAINE STATE PRISON

"Well, my friend," he began, calmly this time, having become aware of my tactics to fire him up, "one must be very careful not to presume. What you are unaware of here is that in the other houses of incarceration I was in, notably San Quentin, horrible things were happening almost every day. There are things I did not tell you about when we were on the subject of San Quentin because recalling them is painful for me and could get me in trouble. I'm afraid I have presented prisons and jails to you in a somewhat rosy light, considering all the high times and exciting activities I have described for you, but the reality is that I was very concerned at things I saw and experienced firsthand in those places. Men were burned alive in their cells by other prisoners for violating some aspect of the prison code. Each and every one of us guests of the government were entirely focused at all times in making sure that we were not the next guest of honor at the next friggin' barbecue.

"Yes, as you have surmised," he continued, "Maine State Prison was a kind of country club to me after the other houses of incarceration I had been in. When they found out that I was a former Hell's Angel and had done time in Folsom Prison and San Quentin, even the guards looked up to me.

"I kind of appreciated the regularity and predictability of life at the prison. There were times I missed things like my midnight runs down the Maine Turnpike on my Harley to spend time with my Hell's Angels brothers in Lowell, or partying all night in some honkey-tonk Portland bar, of course but, all in all, state prison was a much-needed break from it all. The

Jake and a friend at Maine State Prison, serving refreshments during an inmate walk-a-thon around the prison exercise track to benefit a local charity. Jake says his one-fingered salute to the prison authorities and to the rest of the civilized world was heartfelt.

Jake with Portland artist Denny Boudreau at Maine State Prison. "Denny Boudreau is a very brave, severely injured, highly decorated Vietnam super war hero veteran. He got sent to prison because he would not rat me out like many others, and we had many laughs anyway," says Jake. "We are 'Men that don't fit in.' I love Denny Boudreau!"

frenzied running around and assorted criminal activities I had been engaged in in Portland after my release from San Quentin had created a sort of tension inside me. I came to regard my stay at Maine State Prison as a kind of holistic retreat, to tell you the truth."

I didn't hear that, I said to myself.

"At Folsom and San Quentin, the convicts were mostly vicious criminals who would as soon drive a shank into your side as not, so the fellows at Maine State Prison were kind of quaint in comparison. Oh, from time to time the inmates would shank or firebomb someone who had ratted someone out or something of that nature, but that sort of thing is to be expected in any house of incarceration.

"There was a prison guard that was a special friend to me when I was in Maine State Prison, who I can now talk about since he has long ago gone to his reward. In the 1950s, my family had a very nice summer cottage on the coast near Rockland, and the guard's father was the caretaker of the garden and extensive grounds. His son and I got to know each other very well, both being energetic fifteen year olds, and we chased girls together in my 1946 ford coupe.

"I had a job as a dishwasher at the historic Samoset Hotel, and every day a chef who liked us gave us the choice of a pint of ice cream or two cans of Tiger Head Ale, and we chose the ale and saved it for our Saturday night girl chasing. Late Saturday afternoon we would jump into my Ford, which had a lowered rear-end and a dual-exhaust system, and roar down what was called the 'River Road' which had a lot of dangerous twists and turns. It's very surprising that I never crashed on that road, because the suspension system in that old Ford was not designed to be driven like a sports car.

Jake with fellow inmates at the Maine State Prison barbershop. The camera used to take this photo was considered contraband, as was the cigar he is smoking, but Jake acquired them from a prison guard he had been friends with since they were teenagers.

Anyway, we never even got close to getting laid, even with the beer and the cool car, but I did learn how to take a young ladies' bra off, after a number of clumsy attempts, which I found to be extremely exhilarating at the time.

"The next summer, which was the summer of '54, when I was not-so-sweet sixteen, I got a job driving a pie truck for Table Talk pie and didn't go back to my family's summer home in Rockland, so I lost contact with my good buddy who I had partied with the summer before. But there he was in 1974, a prison guard at the Maine State Prison!

"It should come as no surprise to you, sir, as familiar as you have become with my talent for getting other men to do my bidding, that my long-lost good buddy supplied me with anything I wanted from the outside, things like pints of Crown Royal whiskey, Henry Morgan Rum, and very high grade marijuana.

"My prison guard friend also brought me a camera that would take twenty-four color pictures, and I made good use of that baby. Cameras, of course, are contraband in prisons, but as you can see by the pictures I took that are displayed on these pages, I got around that little restriction, no problem at all. In one picture you see here I am shown sitting in the chair in the prison barbershop, smoking a big cigar, with some of my 'Regulators' crowded around me. In another picture included here, me and the notorious outlaw Denny Boudreau are walking past the dining hall on our right, and Denny is informing me that there were some guards coming up the hill behind us, and I'm saying to him: "No sweat, smile for the picture, handsome!' Then there's a third picture taken with my favorite camera showing me and my friend Jim sitting on comfortable chairs in front of East Cell Block, with me flashing a big smile and that gesture that says: 'Fuck you, you feminized sissies, I'll be back on the outside before you know it, and I'll be free and wilder than ever!'

"There were some characters at Maine State Prison, I have to say that. One friend of mine, by the name of Gary, was so addicted to burglarizing that he became obsessed with breaking into the inmates' canteen, just because it was the only place available to him to burglarize. He was a very small man, so he was able to squirm through the air conditioning system that went to the canteen. When they discovered a box of Baby Ruth candy bars in his cell the next day, they knew they had their man, but he didn't care. He had three years tacked onto his sentence, but he had gotten his burglarizing fix!

VOLUME TWO

"Then there was Honey Fitz, who was the operator of the prison honey-bucket wagon. You know what the 'honey' actually was, I'm sure. We looked out our cell windows every morning and watched Honey Fitz pulling the wagon around the prison yard, going from guard tower to guard tower collecting the contents of the buckets that were lowered down on a rope from each tower, just the way it had taken place since the founding of the prison in the early 1800s. The honey-bucket wagon in use when I was there was made by convicts in the 1880's, which made it about ninety years old. It was beautifully crafted and ornamented all around with gold leaf trimming, with very high sides made of highly polished oak wood slats, and had very tall, sturdy steel wheels with hand-crafted red spokes.

"The name Honey Fitz was given to every operator of the honey wagon in honor of Brian Honey Fitz Plourde, who was the operator for thirty-two years, starting in the early 1900s. He was a world-famous opera singer who robbed a bank because the Italian opera singer he fell in love with said that the bravest men she knew robbed banks. Well, she might have been impressed by him robbing a bank, but evidently his being apprehended and sent to prison kind of took the sheen off the affair for her, because he never heard from her again after the prison walls closed behind him. So there was Honey Fitz every morning for thirty-two years, pulling the wonderfully crafted and beautifully ornamented honey bucket cart around the yard, going from tower to tower at Maine State Prison, all the time singing the finest of classical opera. All the inmates had to do was open their windows in the morning to hear one of the best opera singers in the world singing his heart out!"

JAKE

DOING TIME WITH MY OL' PAL
DICKIE WEYMOUTH

"As I rounded the corner coming back from chow one morning, headed for my cell in the East Block, there he was, sitting in his wheelchair, my ol' pal Dickie Weymouth!

"Dickie had been one of a breed of men in Portland in the 1960s who were notorious as street fighters. Small neighborhood bars were all over the city at the time, and many of them had men hanging around in them who had the reputation of being the toughest street fighters in the neighborhood. Dickie frequented a number of them and claimed the turf around them as his domain. I kind of got into that sort of thing myself now and then, as you might suspect, but I respected Dickie for his street fighting prowess and I kind of admired his spunk, so even though I might have been able to get the best of him on a good day, I never tangled with him because I liked him.

"Well, Dickie's winning streak was eventually ended by another real tough guy named Dickie, oddly enough. Dickie Weymouth had attacked my old friend Dickie Stewart, a black guy, twice before, over something having to do with a woman, and both times Dickie Stewart had kicked the shit out of him. Hey, Dickie Stewart knew that the only way he was going to see an end to it all was to kill the guy, and he didn't want to do that, but Dickie Weymouth blew right through a restraining order and attacked Dickie Stewart again one fine evening. Dickie Stewart pulled out a shiny new pistol he had purchased for just such an eventuality and shot him. The wound wasn't fatal, but did result in Dickie Weymouth being paralyzed from the waist down. Less than six months after the shooting, though, Dickie was back in the barroom in his brand new wheelchair, raising hell just as if nothing had happened.

"Now here I am, a couple of years later, encountering none other than Dickie Weymouth sitting in his wheelchair at Maine State Prison.

"'Dickie,' I said, 'how the hell did you manage to do something that got you sent to prison when you're in a wheelchair?!'

"'They gave me two years for strong-armed robbery,' he said. 'The crazy thing, though, is that I'm innocent, believe it or not. I was out on bail on a trumped-up robbery charge when they picked me up and charged me with the same robbery again! It was some kind of a paperwork fuck-up! It's confusing as hell! I don't even know why I'm here! Those friggin' low down pigs charged me with the same crime twice and I wasn't even guilty the first time!'

"I was laughing so hard the tears were running down my face and I had to lean against the wall. But Dickie was serious, and he looked at me with such a long, sad face, that I just had to cheer him up.

"'You were born guilty, just like me and every other asshole in this place,' I said to him, 'but you make me laugh, damn you, and I'm going to make your stay at this little out-of-the-way resort just as fun-filled and delightful as if you were living at friggin' Disney World!'

"Well, I sure as hell kept my promise to Dickie. I sent a lot of prison contraband his way, and nobody but nobody fucked with him, because everyone knew he had been my buddy on the outside and I was taking care of him on the inside. Dickie had his responsibilities to fulfill for me, of course, just like various other individuals I was protecting did. He had to be housed in the prison hospital because of being in a wheel-chair, and I had him pilfering cans of my beloved tuna fish every day as a great source of protein, which was an important part of my health regimen, so everything balanced out very well.

"Dickie didn't like being incarcerated, no matter what the conditions were like, though, and he always said that if he got caught again committing some crime, he'd go down in a blaze of glory because he'd rather die than go back to prison. Being in a wheel-chair was prison enough, he said, so he wasn't about to allow anyone or anything to add further to his mis-ery. Well, sure enough, shortly after he was released, I saw a piece in the paper about Dickie being in a bar talking about killing cops if they ever bothered him again, and after some patron called the cops on him for talking like that, they appeared and began to ques-tion him. Sure enough, just like he said he would, he pulled out a gun and started shooting at them, and was killed by their return fire. 'Suicide by cop,' I think it's called today.

"Dickie was one problem child, that's for sure, and he led a life that a lot of people looked down on, but at least he had integrity. He damn well did what he said he would do, and that is what gains a man respect in the world we inhabited."

THE WAY LIFE SHOULD BE

"All in all, I had a hell of a time at Maine State Prison. I know how sick that sounds, but I did. I was friggin' stoned on weed, tripping on LSD, or drunk out of my mind most of the time, and the fun just kept coming.

"I also lifted weights and ran three miles every day, spurred on by the huge amounts of steroids I was consuming.

"What facilitated all this hilarity for me was that shortly after I arrived on the scene I became the mailman in the notorious East Cell Block, which meant that after all the other inmates got locked up after evening chow, I was on the loose for three hours, going from cell to cell, or 'houses', as we called them, delivering inmates' mail and other miscellaneous items. After the honey bucket operator position, which I wasn't about to apply for, the mailman position was the most sought after position in the prison, so almost immediately after my arrival I informed the current holder of the position that I'd be taking over for him, no questions asked. There I was every night, going from house to house, delivering not only the mail, but also a wide variety of prison contraband, for which I was justly compensated. Hey, getting a piece of the action every time something went down in the prison wasn't half bad.

"I wasn't entirely dependent on my fellow prisoners for subsistence, though. Along with the guard who I had been friends with as a teenager, I had this other guard, who owed me big time for a favor I had done him on the outside long ago. He would bring me anything he could fit into his lunch box. Drugs were the main thing I had him procure for me of course, mainly because I rather enjoyed them myself, but also because they were the number one medium of exchange within the prison. Window Pane acid was the rage at the time. It came in small dark squares and it always sold well. It got so I controlled the jail population quite well by passing those little babies around.

"As for the drunk part, that's where pruno came in.

JAKE

Anyone who's done prison time knows that pruno is a home brew made from prunes, yeast, and sugar, which are smuggled out of the kitchen and made into a very smooth, great tasting alcoholic drink. I've never understood why pruno has never been marketed on the outside. Maybe it's because of the name, I don't know, but it would make a million if it were prepared by the right ex-con. It tasted a lot better than the local high-priced craft beers brewed locally today, that I can tell you for sure."

THE MAINE STATE
PRISON "REGULATORS"

"As I have told you, my friend, I have long considered exercise to be the secret of having a happy and rewarding life. No matter what was going on with me, I've always fit vigorous exercise into my routine. Maine State Prison had a fully equipped weight room, and I was in heaven. I got to be in the best shape of my life. I weighed 210 pounds and I could curl 100 lbs in each hand ten times. Anyone who knows weightlifting knows how extraordinary that is. I was very pleased to discover that as long as I could pay for it, I could order a case of tuna fish through the prison commissary containing forty-eight cans of the finest muscle-building food on the planet earth.

"By the way, weightlifting is banned in most prisons today, and that's because of people like me who spend our time in prison working out like animals, so we can be ready for whatever comes down when we hit the streets again."

Yes, I thought to myself, that makes a lot of sense.

Jake and some friends at Maine State Prison, 1975

THE TUNNEL TO NOWHERE

"I was getting bigger and stronger, and was making a lot of money through my various sidelines, but boredom started to set in anyway, the way it always does with me, but out of nowhere some excitement developed.

"I was fortunate enough to be asked by a couple of my fellow 'residents' if I would kindly help them with a project they had underway. They were cell mates and they had a large piece of plywood covered by a colorful rug in the center of their cell floor. They invited me to their cell to take a look at something, and when they moved the plywood aside, there it was: a hole about two feet in diameter. They were digging a tunnel out of the prison!

"So what I did was smuggle dirt from the tunnel – which the two cell mates had dug with a claw hammer and a piece of crowbar – out of the cell block and had some other friends spread it evenly around the dirt basketball court.

"Well, the two cell mates kept at their digging, and I continued to do my part, but when the tunnel reached the middle of the lawn out in front of the prison, disaster struck ... they hit a solid rock formation and could proceed no further.

"Well, the next day, the two cell mates decided to exhibit their uncompleted tunnel to the warden, just because they were so proud of it. Hey, they were both doing life without parole, so what could they lose? The warden, of course, threw them in solitary confinement for a month, but they had had six months of great fun digging the tunnel and co-ordinating their efforts with me and my friends, so it was well worth it."

A CALL TO ARMS

"One day out on the yard, I asked the warden if he would allow me to put up sign-up sheets for any convict willing to volunteer to fight for their country in the war that was going on in Vietnam. I knew he had spent twenty years in the Marines, and I also knew he respected the fact that I was an honorably discharged Paratrooper, so I assumed that he would take my idea very seriously. I told him that a number of convicts were released from prison to fight in both World Wars, and they acquitted themselves very well. And we know that Maine boys make good soldiers, I told him. Just look at how Joshua Chamberlain and the 20th Maine mounted the charge at Little Round Top that led to the North winning of the Battle of Gettysburg, which, of course, was the decisive battle of the Civil War.

"Actually, the warden laughed at the very idea of enlisting convicted felons in the military and sending them to Vietnam to fight the enemies of America. He thought the whole idea was completely ludicrous. But that's not what he said after he stopped laughing. I have gone over it many times in my head and I remember exactly what he said: "What the hell, go ahead! Hang up all the signs you want to! Those North Viet Cong won't know what hit 'em!"

"After the warden's rousing words, I immediately got right into my little project. Before long, prisoners began signing up in droves to volunteer to go to Vietnam! Keep in mind that most of them were grossly out of shape, had little or no education, and couldn't pass the physical test required to be admitted into the military. The majority of them were confirmed alcoholics or drug addicts, as well. But they got all fired up when I told them that not only would they get out of prison by signing up to fight in Vietnam, they'd also get all the alcohol and drugs they wanted, not only in Vietnam, but also when they returned home as war heroes. They were so excited they wrote long letters home to their friends and loved ones informing them that they had decided to make amends for their wrongdoings by serving their country in combat, and if they survived they'd be coming home as heroes and free men ready to live happy and successful lives.

"The letters the guys sent home got the warden in a lot of trouble, actually. He was besieged with calls

and letters, most of them being from wives and girlfriends who were very upset at the prospect of their
man being sent to fight and maybe be killed in Vietnam. They said things like their loved one had only
robbed a gas station or something and didn't deserve
to die for it. They also informed the warden that they
were contacting their elected representatives on both
the state and national level, and that they'd been assured that he'd be hearing from them soon.

"Very early one morning, at about 4 a.m., as I remember, a guard came to my cell and said he had orders to take me to the warden's office immediately. I
knew that this wasn't going to be a very good day in
the 'joint' for Jake. When we got to his office, I saw
that the warden was looking very tired and distraught.
At first he didn't even notice me standing there. He
was just standing silently behind his large oak desk
looking down at a pile of letters spread across it,
steaming and muttering to himself. Then after a while
he slowly looked up at me and said: "I want you to see
all the anguish and alarm you've caused, Sawyer.
These letters are from the families and friends of men
in this prison who wrote home and told them that they
soon would be going to war to fight for their country
and might not return. Do you have any idea about the
amount of hurt and confusion the people who wrote
these letters are going through?"

"He went on to say that he didn't have any idea that
what he had considered to be a ridiculous request by
me would turn out to be such a gigantic embarrass-
ment for him and the entire Maine State Department
of Corrections. The Governor of the State of Maine had
been on the line to him, he said, because the prisoners' relatives and friends had also written to him and

to their representatives in Washington looking for an-
swers. He said that he had no idea that I had taken
him seriously when he said it was okay for me to put
the sign-up sheets all around the prison, and that I
had misled and disillusioned the prisoners who signed
up, had unnecessarily alarmed their loved ones, and
had caused great harm to him personally.

"I didn't say much in response. There was really
nothing to be said. A number of prisoners, along with
a couple of guards, had heard him say what he said. I
wouldn't have any problem getting first-hand witnesses to testify at any hearing board he might con-
vene, and he knew it. Everyone present obviously
knew he was joking, but, hey, the man said what he
said.

"So, there was no way he could penalize me, but,
needless to say, the warden and I weren't on very good
terms after that. His dim view of me was made even
darker by the fact that I had become a hero to my fellow prisoners. When I told them about my visit to the
warden's office, they all cracked up big time and had
me tell the story over and over. The more intelligent
prisoners knew from the git-go that the whole thing
was a sham, of course. Contrary to common opinion,
lawbreakers are not always stupid, and those guys
certainly weren't. I'll bet some of them are still talking
about how they signed up to fight in Vietnam while
they were in prison. Hey, a good story goes a long
ways, you know?"

FIRE IN THE EAST BLOCK!

I commented to Jake that a lot seemed to have gone
on in the relatively short time he spent at Maine State

Prison and I asked him if he had anything else about his stay there worth relating.

"No, I guess not," he said, after giving it a little thought, but then he very casually said: "Oh, wait. What about the time I set a huge fire in my cell block? Is that something you might want to hear about?"

"Yeah, yeah," I chuckled, shaking my head. "Let's hear it."

"Okay, here we go," he began. "I was housed in a single cell on B Corridor, on the ground floor of the East Block during my stay at Maine State Prison, and the day I moved in I noticed that there was a cell down in the far corner of the corridor on the side opposite my cell chock-full of dust-covered furniture that had been stored there for years. Wow! I could not believe my good fortune! I immediately knew that there would sure as hell come a day when I would set that whole pile of old dusty furniture on fire! I just had to bide my time and wait for the proper moment! It gave me something to look forward to, you know?"

"Yeah, yeah, of course," I said.

"The day arrived about two months after my arrival," he continued. "It was the birthday of one of my favorite pals, by the name of Keith "Tank" Parkinson, and I promised him the biggest birthday bash he'd ever had. He was a very funny, very tough, nineteen-year-old wildcat. He had done a stretch some years before for beating a snitch half to death, and this time he was doing seven years on a strong-arm robbery charge. What a piece of work he was! The best part of his robbery story is that when the police came after him, he jumped on his Harley and led them on a high-speed chase up, down, and around the streets of Biddeford and Old Orchard Beach. He ended up riding his bike the length of Old Orchard Beach Amusement

Pier at an estimated speed of ninety miles per hour, crashing through a construction site at the end of the pier, and zooming off into the ocean. He tried to swim away, of course, but that wasn't working out, especially with his leather jacket and boots on, so he just bobbed around in the water shouting obscenities at his pursuers on shore until they got a police boat and rowed out and subdued him.

"Now here we were, Tank and me, doing time together at Maine State Prison, close neighbors no less. What with all the access I had to prison contraband, we were drinking Crown Royal, straight-up, smoking high-grade pot, and tripping on Window Pane acid at the same time! Man, we had some conversations! And he was a very loyal and effective pal to boot! I just had to do something special for my buddy Tank on his birthday!

"Keep in mind that as mailman I got to be out of my cell and on the loose until eight in the evening, so I was able to get in a lot of mischief. Sometime before I had reached into the cell where the furniture was stored and stashed a can of paint thinner behind a table that was lying on its side, so the scene was set for Tank's birthday celebration, and when the big night came I sprinkled the paint thinner all over the furniture and reached through the bars and threw in a match!

"Whoosh! That whole pile of old dust-covered furniture instantaneously burst into flames and then the CELLabration was on!"

Yes, Jake did emphasize the 'CELL'.

"What you have to understand here is that, due to the location of the fire, at no time was any prisoner in danger," he continued. "I told them all beforehand that some smoke might drift their way, but not to worry because my plan was to immediately alert the guards to the spontaneous combustion that had taken place with that old furniture, and I knew that the first thing they'd do is free the prisoners from their cells which, of course, they did. Every one of those prisoners told me it was the most exciting night they'd experienced in prison. Tank, of course, was especially happy. We adjourned to my cell after the smoke had abated a bit to get high on our usual assortment of mind-altering substances, and we very much enjoyed watching the firemen with their hoses dousing the furniture and grumbling to each other about how stupid the prison authorities were to store old furniture like that for so long. I laugh to myself thinking of how Tank and I kept yelling 'CELLebration!' over and over through it all. Hey, you have to consider the circumstances and our state of mind, you know? Sometimes it doesn't take much. Tank said that without question it was the best birthday he had ever had, though, and that's all that mattered."

CAMELOT COMES TO MAINE STATE PRISON

"Even though I was quite content in Maine State Prison, after a while I started thinking a lot about getting out of there. As I've said, I missed spending time with my Hell's Angels brothers down in Lowell, and I could also hear the streets of Portland calling me. Not having women in my life became kind of a drag too, if you know what I mean."

"The thought had occurred to me," I said, nodding my head.

"When I began advocating for myself in earnest it

wasn't long before my release. The first step of my plan was to request a meeting with the warden, and he agreed to see me, in spite of the fact that I had embarrassed him by recruiting prisoners to fight in Vietnam. He was grateful that I was johnny-on-the-spot when that furniture his staff let sit there for so long burst into flames, so he was willing to let bygones be bygones as far as the Vietnam thing went.

"So the warden and I were back to being buddies, and I told him what I wanted to talk to him about. It was a rehabilitation activity I had in mind for myself and other convicts that would serve to relieve some of the tension I saw building up in the prison. He leaned forward on his desk, all ears. I'll never forget how the blood drained out of his face, though, when I told him that what I wanted to do was send away for life-size blown-up Jackie Kennedy dolls and rent them on a nightly basis to inmates so they would have pleasant company in their cells and experience sexual satisfaction as well. The dolls had three strategically placed holes so as to add variety to the sexual experiences of the prisoners, I told him. I also assured him that I would issue severe warnings to each prisoner about what the consequences of not returning their doll in absolutely clean condition would be, so there was no reason for him to worry about sanitary issues of any kind.

"As I had anticipated, the warden was totally freaked out!

"Oh, my God!" he yelled, "I've never heard anything so sick! You are absolutely out of your mind!"

"Sure enough, just as I knew he would, the good warden made an appointment for me to see the prison psychiatrist, and I was on my way to better mental health.

JAKE

DR. DAVID HASSON

"I've always enjoyed visiting with psychiatrists because, well, we talk about me, and also because they are so easily manipulated. I've learned that the way to get along with psychiatric counselors is to act as though their diagnosis is spot-on correct, and that they have given me a whole new way of looking at myself. I've always told them very sincerely that I now had a new lease on life, thanks to them. That's absolute bullshit, of course. I always had known everything they said about me to be dead wrong, but what the hell, I've had everything to be gained by cooperating with them and nothing to lose, so thanks a lot guys.

"When I knocked on his door, the prison psychiatrist said, "Yes, come in" very meekly, like he always did with prisoners, in order to make them feel more relaxed in his presence, he later told me. When he saw me walk through the door with my tremendous physique and a big smile on my face, he knew immediately that he wasn't dealing with some guy from up in Mangy Moose, Maine, who got drunk on hard cider one snowy night and shoplifted a bag of Freetos from the general store. I could immediately see the effect my presence had on him, so, wanting to take full advantage of his befuddlement, I walked over to his desk and stood there grinning down at him and said: "Hello there, doc! The warden thinks I'm crazy as hell and he told me that you are a highly trained professional who would certainly be able to cure me, so here I am! I am very excited about getting my head straightened out and becoming a productive law-abiding citizen once again, so let's get started!

"When he read in my records that the U.S. Army

had tested my IQ at a high number, he sort of nodded his head a little, like, okay, here's an interesting case. At first I objected to many of the things he had to say about me, just so he'd have a hill to climb, but after a while I allowed him to think he had won me over, and that he had provided me with some great insights into why I am the way I am.

"Actually, I became very fond of the guy. Dr. David Hasson and I are still friends to this day. I would say, without any hesitation, that he was the most popular and most effective member of the Maine State Prison personnel when I was there. He helped a lot of people work through some very serious personal problems. I also have to acknowledge that he provided me with some insights into my psyche as well.

"After getting to know David through our therapy sessions, though, I realized that he needed my help at least as much as I needed his. In those days he was extremely lean, had a sallow complexion, and was low energy. I asked him about his diet, and he said he lived primarily on fast foods and didn't eat breakfast. As far as exercise, he said that he played basketball and ran track in high school, but hadn't had an exercise routine since that time. I was quite alarmed by that, of course, and I immediately got him on a special high-protein diet and recommended an exercise program for him. I'm happy to say that after a couple of months, he began to look a lot healthier, and there was a renewed confidence about him. No more meek, "Hello, come in" when a prisoner knocked on his door. It was more like: "Yeah, c'mon, get in here!" which had the effect of putting him in charge and, in the end, put him in a better position to help people, which Dr. Hasson is all about.

"I put the good doctor in touch with a bodybuilder

friend of mine who had a gym not far from the prison. Skeet was his name and he was what's called a "hard trainer" like I am. It wasn't long before eating properly and exercising regularly was right at the center of David's life. He was so into his new way of life that he came to my cell even on his off hours to ask me about this and that food supplement or something of that nature. My cell was in the east cell block and it was the oldest, coldest, craziest cell block in the prison, but that didn't deter him.

"So, there he was fairly late one afternoon, sitting on my bunk taking in everything I had to say about proper diet and exercise, when all of a sudden a guard came by and locked all the doors for the night and was gone before Dr. Hasson could make his presence known! Clang! the door went, but I told him not to worry, that the guards came by every few hours, so chances are he'd be out long before morning.

"Dr. Hasson knew I would never hurt him, but there evidently was something about being locked up with 'Bonecrusher' Sawyer that messed with his head, so he immediately yelled for the guard. The guards were used to hearing yelling from somewhere in the prison, though, so it took five or ten minutes for them to respond. The experience left an indelible impression on Dr. Hasson. He later told me that the feeling of being locked in a cell, even for a relatively short time like that, had tattooed on his brain what prisoners went through, and the experience added to the feelings of empathy for which he is so well known.

"At this time, I would like to make it clear that Dr. Hasson is one of the most admirable people I have met in my entire life. He did so much for the inmates at Maine State Prison that he became a hero to me then, and he continues to be my hero today. After his stint at Maine State Prison, Dr. Hasson established a counseling practice in Portland, and his specialty was treating Vietnam vets for Post Traumatic Stress Disorder on a pro bono basis. Damn, I wish I had a dollar for every friend of mine who has told me that Dr. Hasson virtually saved his life. The man has an absolute genius for deflecting attention and recognition away from himself, but it's not going to happen this time, though. We will sing his praises in this book, my friend! I love ya, Doc!"

Jake got no argument from me there. He arranged for me to meet Dr. Hasson and he turned out to be everything Jake said he was. My intention, of course, was to talk about Jake, or maybe about Dr. Hasson himself, for the purpose of better understanding his relationship with Jake, but that wasn't happening. I ended up pouring out my own life story to him and left feeling that a huge weight had been lifted from my shoulders. Ya jes' nev'a know what's gon'na come from what.

"Yes, I became quite fond of my friend Dr. Hasson during my time at Maine State Prison," Jake continued, "but that didn't prevent me from following through on my plan to manipulate him to further my ends. Even though I insisted, with great humility, and with genuine regret for my past wrong doings, that it was important for me to pay my debt to society, and that I wasn't sure that I could be trusted on the outside, he became a committed advocate for my release.

"Those were the days when parole was granted very liberally. The criminal justice system hadn't come upon the realization yet that there is such a thing as career criminals, and that setting certain ones free would only allow us to commit more crimes. Because of people like us, parole from prison is much harder to obtain today, and maybe I should feel guilty about that, but all that mattered to me at the time was getting out.

"The administrative authorities at Maine State Prison were more than happy to accept Dr. Hasson's recommendation, considering the effect I was having on the prison population, and after only nine months and eleven days in Maine State Prison, I was paroled. There I was, back in Portland, eager to resume my former activities.

"I would also like to say at this time that if there are any impressionable young people out there reading this, that they should not get the idea that prison is all fun and games. It isn't. It sure as hell isn't, and it wasn't always that way for me either. I laugh about those days sometimes, but nobody likes being in a cell and not being on the outside. Nobody. I had some very lonely and painful times in prison. I just made the best of a very bad situation. Better not to get in the situation in the first place, know what I mean? Just because I'm a crazy bastard, doesn't mean that anyone else has to be."

I told him that I was gratified to hear him say that, and he just nodded over at me, like he was happy to oblige.

A letter to the editor by Jake. In the late 1990s, the state of Maine decided to tear down the old state prison where Jake had done time in the 70s. Jake tried to convince the state to save the oldest, most historical section of the prison. Not one historian cared and they destroyed a part of the prison that was older than the state itself. The residents of Thomaston voted to completely remove the prison and turn the whole area into a park. (Note the way Jake signed the letter)

VALUABLE HISTORICAL SITE

Save Maine State Prison – reap profits

The state of Wyoming has spent millions of dollars restoring two old unused prisons because they have become two of the leading tourist attractions of that state.

Tourists spend a lot of money every year visiting these infamous prisons, and they spend it on T-shirts, coffee mugs, etc.

I am referring to the old Wyoming Territorial Prison at Laramie and the former state penitentiary at Rawlins, Wyo.

Myself and a growing number of Maine citizens are hoping that our 179-year-old prison can be saved for the same reasons that Wyoming and other states spent millions to save their historical prisons.

This very historic old prison is a potential gold mine! It's right on Route 1.

Tear down some of the newer buildings to greatly enlarge the available parking and have fun making money.

I am trying to help save a lot of very interesting Maine history and I need a lot of help.

Get involved and help save the place where Maine's "baddest and wildest" men did "hard time" for 179 years!

I hope that the people in charge talk to historians in Wyoming, Arizona, etc., before they make a huge mistake and destroy a valuable historic site!

Jake Sawyer
Maine State Prison
Class of '75
Portland

Maine State Prison, a Route 1 landmark that opened 179 years ago, closed this month and the 450 inmates were bused to a new $75 million prison 5 miles away in Warren. Plans call for bulldozing the brick prison next month, though some state lawmakers say the $3.8 million for demolition could be better spent making up for a budget shortfall. Readers say it would make a great tourist attraction.

The Associated Press

This time, when I arrived at Jake's place, I had something I'd been wanting to ask him about. In the course of chronicling his life story in the *Bollard* magazine, I constantly ran into people who had one Jake Sawyer story or another, and I had become accustomed to discounting most of them after checking with Jake, but a persistent story had to do with his having been the founder of a local outlaw-biker club, by the name of the Iron Horsemen, in the late 1960s. When I asked him about it, though, Jake was quick to set me straight.

THE IRON HORSEMEN

"Here's the story: There was a bunch of guys with motorcycles hanging around a bar I haunted for a while, and they got inspired by all my war stories to start their own motorcycle club, so I began providing them with a certain amount of counsel. I told them that if they really wanted to start a motorcycle club, the first thing they had to do was to stop thinking about themselves as individuals and form an intense loyalty to one another. No more one-man shows, I told them. All for one, one for all, and there you go. They bought the idea, of course, and they'd make a big show of hugging each other after they got drunk, but it soon became obvious to me that they had no idea of what I was really talking about.

"The kicker came one night when I went to the bar and saw that one of them was beat to hell, and when I asked them what had happened to the guy they told me that some guys that hung around another bar had beat the crap out of him, but he sure as hell deserved it, so there were no hard feelings.

"What?!" I fucking bellowed at them. "It doesn't matter what he said or did, he's your brother and that makes him right! You fight one member of an outlaw motorcycle club and you fight them all, regardless! I don't give a fuck what your brother did! You guys get on those bikes you've got parked out front and go after those guys who did this to him or I'll fucking pound every one of you myself right now!

"Well, they made a big show of saddling up and cruising around looking for the guys who beat their buddy up, but I knew their heart wasn't in it. When I came across some of them a couple of days later and they told me that they had decided to let the whole thing go after all, I said they were all a fucking bunch of pussies who ought to dump their bikes in Casco Bay and start riding the friggin' bus. They didn't like that, of course, but what could they do?

"The kicker was that a few weeks later I found out that three or four of the members were doing heroin. That's what did it. I fucking hate heroin! Any trust-worthiness anybody might have had about them goes out the window when they start playing with that shit! Get 'em outta my sight!

"So one Friday evening I showed up at Kingswood Apartment Complex in South Portland with my trusty baseball bat in the back seat. There must have been at least ten Harleys parked out in front of the apartment where they were having their meeting. When I went up and knocked on the door, no one answered, so after I knocked a little louder and still no one answered, I went up to bat and smashed a multi-layered glass window. You wouldn't believe the explosive sound that made!

"Still no response from inside, though, so I went around to all sides of the building and smashed in all the windows of the apartment. Then, believe it or not, since there was still no response from inside, I started smashing up all of their motorcycles!

"Still nothing! Even after I screamed some of their names and challenged them all to come out and fight me all at once.

"Well, I had disturbed a lot of the other residents of Kingswood Park, and I had accomplished what I set out to do, so I decided to jump back in my Chevy Blazer and get the hell out of there. I didn't get far before the blue lights of many police cars flashed behind me, though.

"The officer who stopped me wasn't in any hurry to come to my car alone, of course. I saw him through my rearview mirror radioing for back-up, so I had a little time to myself to think the situation through. One of my chief concerns was that I was still on parole from San Quentin, which meant that virtually any infraction, even a speeding ticket, could send me back. Now I had threatened felonious assault on multiple individuals, caused serious property damage, and could easily be identified by many eyewitnesses, including all the neighbors who were hanging out their windows cheering me on.

"You will remember that the warden at San Quentin warned me that if he ever saw me again, I'd never get out. The worst part of sitting there waiting for the officers to come down to my car was remembering the way the warden smirked and said, 'See ya soon!' the last time I saw him.

"The officers were certainly taking their time coming to my car, and with good reason, considering the individual they were dealing with. Come to find out, they were waiting for Lt. Ron Damon to arrive. Ron was one of the guys who worked out at Martin's Health Club with me, and it was known throughout the local law enforcement scene that Ron and I were friends, and had been for many years.

"When Ron arrived on the scene and came down to my car it was definitely an awkward situation. He knew damn well right that I wouldn't have done what I did to those guys without a damn good reason, but he had to do his job, and I understood that.

"When he asked me where I'd been that night, I said that I was just returning from a pleasant drive along the seashore, and now I was headed to pick up my date for the evening. He laughed, of course, because he knew I was lying, but when he spotted the baseball bat in the back seat with shards of glass embedded in it, he got quite serious all of a sudden, and just looked at me and shook his head, then walked back to the other police officers and got into a very intense discussion with them.

"I thought sure as hell I was history, but after a little while Officer Damon walked back to my car and said it I was free to go. Unbelievable! I was sure they were at least going to beat me up!

"I was amazed that they just let me go! Ron told me a couple of years later at the gym that they had been looking for a way to get at those punks themselves, but hadn't been found a way yet, and were very grateful that I had done their work for them. They knew, like I did, that those guys' sorry-assed outlaw motorcycle club was completely done for after the way I had humiliated them, so case closed. Happy to have been of service, I told Ron.

"Can you believe that that original group of losers

didn't even know about the existence of a nationally active outlaw-biker club named the Iron Horsemen? After that original Portland group of pretenders dissolved, a few of the higher-functioning members applied to become the Portland chapter of the national club, and today the Portland chapter of the Iron Horsemen is highly respected in the outlaw-biker world.

"So no, my friend, contrary to persistent rumors, I was far from being the founder of the local Iron Horsemen Motorcycle Club. I do not even have any connection with them, even though I respect the hell out of them."

THE WAYWARD ROAD

Something had been gnawing at me since Jake and I last spoke, and I knew we had to get at it before we could proceed any further. When we talked over the phone to set up the appointment in his apartment for this interview he said he'd be telling me about his being sent to Lewisberg Federal Penitentiary only two years after being released from Maine State Prison, and somehow or other that blew my mind. As we were settling into our chairs across from one another it gushed out of me with a force that surprised both of us.

"C'mon, Jake!" I blurted out, "how the hell did you end up being sentenced to Lewisberg only two years or so after you got out of Maine State Prison?! There you were, an extraordinarily healthy, extremely capable thirty-seven-year-old man with your whole life ahead of you! You were back home in Portland instead of being locked in some cage somewhere! Freedom! You could do whatever you wanted to do! Including hopping on your Harley and ramming down the turnpike to visit the Hell's Angels whenever you wanted to! You couldn't do better than that?! How the hell did you allow that to happen, man?!"

At first he just sat there looking stunned, but then he threw his head his head back and gazed up at the ceiling for a moment, kind of grumbling to himself. I didn't know what to expect, but then a smile crept over his face and he lowered his head and looked over at me with a broad grin and punched his fist in the air and yelled: "Right on, brother!"

I'd never talked to him the way I just did, and he was delighted with my progress. That old tightening of the stomach was gone, and he knew it. I'd gone right straight for it, just the way he says you always have to, and he was proud of me. Wow.

"The last time we spoke, my friend," he said, after we'd chuckled a bit over my growth spurt, "I thought I'd made it clear to you that when I act out in the way I do it's just me being who I am. It's like I don't even have a choice. Consequences don't even enter the picture. I did try to stay out of trouble with the law after I got out of Maine State Prison, man, I did try, but I just couldn't make it happen.

"What the hell, do you think I really wanted to go back to living in a cell? I thought I was going to spend the rest of my life in San Quentin, but by a miracle that I am grateful for to this day, I did not. Believe me, I definitely didn't want to ever go back to any kind of house of incarceration ever again.

"It isn't just about what you're missing by not being on the outside, it's also about how friggin' bad it is on the inside. I tried to make the best of extremely unfortunate situations, but the truth is that it's degrading to be locked up, and it's very dangerous too, no matter what prison you're in, who you are, or how you handle yourself while you're in there. Yes, you can act in certain ways that make things a little safer for yourself, but you're still always in a life or death situation. People who've never been in prison think they'd use their time alone to maybe read or write a lot, but the reality is that when you are alone in your cell you're constantly fretting about what you might've said to this one or that one that might cause you to get a long piece of metal thrust into your lower back some morning on the way to breakfast. It doesn't matter all that much if you're in a state prison or a federal penitentiary, either. The thrill of it all fades away after a while, you know?"

The *thrill* of it?, I thought to myself.

"So, okay, I didn't exactly become a model citizen after I got out of prison, but I was determined not to return," he continued. "I didn't do foolish things, like before. I was still somewhat involved in the auto discount program I've told you about - I liked being able to offer my customary 80% discount offers to worthy buyers - but there was no more doing things like dumping stolen cars into Portland Harbor. Maybe I was growing up? I don't know, but I no longer felt the need to shove what I was doing up law enforcement's ass, and that was progress, I guess.

"I also didn't make any effort to revive the sizable marijuana distribution network I had been running, nor did I reopen Dancer's Variety, because that would have made me more visible in the community than I wanted to be at that time. I had also sold Mystique Figure Wrap when I was sentenced to Maine State

Prison, so I no longer had income from that source either.

"I still owned three apartment buildings on Munjoy Hill, though, and they proved to be a very good safety net. There wasn't a lot of rental income left after I paid all the overhead involved, especially because I developed the bad habit of letting my tenants slide if they couldn't come up with the rent. I did use the equity I had in the buildings to revive my Dancer's Bail Bondsman business, and with all the time I had on my hands to devote to it that activity was soon more lucrative than ever. I was able to provide a much-needed service to a lot of deserving people in the process, which was very important to me, as you know. Most of my clients were low-income, of course, and I've never understood why having less money than the guy in the next cell over means that he can get out of jail and you can't. Everybody knew that if I believed what they said about paying the fee they owed me, and if I thought they'd show up for their trial, I'd help them get out of jail. Their word was their bond. And, of course, they all knew what disrespecting me would mean, just like before, so things always turned out just fine."

"Alright, Jake" I said, "what happened? If you had matured so much and were so determined to go relatively straight, at least by your standards, how the hell did you get sent back to jail, and a damn federal penitentiary, no less?"

"Would you believe I was sent up on a bum rap?" he said, laughing.

"No, you've already told me that you've deserved every punishment you've ever gotten, so what did you do this time?" I said.

JAKE

PARTY TIME

"Well, my friend, you know how they say that the biggest mistake a bar owner can make is to become his own best customer? That's pretty much what happened with me and my buildings. I lived in one of the apartments, and when my tenants came by to pay their rent, or maybe just to visit, I'd end up partying all day and night with them and anyone else who might happen by, and you know how that goes. Before long, there were a whole lot of people running around my place at any given time, many of them being on the unsavory side. You have to keep in mind that even though I was pretty much staying legal myself, I was still a very central figure in the Portland underworld, through my activities as a bail bondsman, and through my knowledge of how the criminal justice system works. Anytime someone was in trouble they'd be rapping at my door for advice. I was a one-man social services agency!

"My apartment was on the first floor, and sometimes there'd be so many people partying I'd completely lose track of who was who. Drugs and alcohol galore, fantastic friggin' orgies, decadence like you wouldn't believe. Neither would you believe, my friend, the number of very well-known and respected people who took part in the debauchery at one time or another. I've never been one to name names, that's for damn sure, so I won't, but when I see them around town today putting on uppity airs I sometimes give 'em a sly little smile and it tickles the hell out of me when their face reddens a little and they scurry away. A boy's gotta have his fun, ya know?"

"Anyway," he continued, after we'd chuckled a bit

over that one, "what ultimately led to my undoing was all the war stories I was telling about my past exploits. Things like my time in the Combat Zone, all the high times I had with my Hell's Angels brothers, the time I had spent in some of the country's most notorious houses of incarceration and at the Maine State Prison. I just couldn't lay off the story telling, man, and after a while it became impossible for me to live up to the image of myself that I had created and stay out of trouble with the law at the same time.

THE GREAT WEED CAPER

"The thing that led to my falling into the arms of the criminal justice system once again started as a kind of joke, really. There had been a major marijuana bust in Portland and the feds had a mountain of the stuff stored at the Coast Guard base over in South Portland. So naturally, a lot of the people who were hanging around my place started to fantasize about how cool it would be to liberate all that weed. I scoffed at the whole idea, mainly because I was far less naive than they were and knew beyond a doubt that there wasn't a chance in hell that anybody could successfully steal all that pot under the noses of the federal government, and that even if anyone did pull it off, they'd be apprehended in no time flat. The feds are not people you want to square off against, because they're very smart and very tough. Chances are real good that they're going to win and you're going to lose. We're not talking the local Sheriff's Department here folks, I assured them.

"We've got a deja vu all over again situation going

here, my friend. I know you are very familiar with the details of my leading my Hell's Angels brothers on the "suicide charge" into the home of some enemies of the club. How I had stood up in a meeting and told my Hell's Angels brothers that it was a very bad plan that would likely result in either death or being sentenced to a long prison term prison for anyone who took part, and yet I ended up leading the charge. Well, sir, that was pretty much the same scenario with the very ill-advised pot heist that I'm about to tell you about. I knew damn well right what a stupid fucking idea it was to steal that weed, but I ended up being the friggin' point man, just like with the Hell's Angels suicide charge. I put the whole damn thing together, knowing all the time what the friggin' end result would be. So I guess I can't blame you for the way you came in here all heated up about me fucking up and going back to prison so soon after my release from Maine State Prison, my friend."

What could I say. I just looked over at him and shrugged my shoulders, like it was still confusing as hell to me, but what happened, happened, so let's just keep going.

"Here's how it all came down," he said. "Two of my long-time tenants, a couple of long-haired hippie-type brothers named Richard and Scott Weeman, somehow or other made the acquaintance of a couple of young Coast Guard guys who were among those who had the responsibility of guarding the weed. The Coast Guard guys were very naive, just out of high school, extremely impressionable, and the Weemans became obsessed with the possibilities that presented. They got the young men into the party scene at my place. When people found out about them guarding the weed they became, like, famous for it. That kind of attention is sometimes hard for a young man to deal with, especially when he's away from home and has made contact with a group of very cool people, a good number of them being extremely delectable and willing females. It soon became apparent to them that all they had to do was agree to look the other way for a very short time some night when they were on duty and all they desired in life at the moment would be theirs.

"I knew the whole idea was absurd and would end up with grave consequences for everyone involved, of course, but with the involvement of the two Coast Guard guys, the Weeman brothers were absolutely certain we could pull it off. I was very resistant at first, I kept poo-pooing the idea all to hell, but what ended up swaying me was a story the *Press Herald* ran on the front page about how well the weed was being guarded by the Coast Guard, and how impossible it would be for anyone to get at the stuff. The big picture they ran on the front page of some Coast Guardsmen carrying machine guns and trying to look real menacing was too much for me to bear. The gauntlet had been thrown to the ground big time, and everyone was watching to see what I would do. So what else could I do but let out a ferocious roar, pick it up, and lead the charge?"

It was a question I chose not to answer.

"There were three of us that took part in the operation," Jake continued. "The Weeman brothers and me. There was a fence that went around the heavily fortified government truck the weed was stored in. Our Coast Guard buddies said they could be away from the gate of the fence for exactly eight minutes, starting at 4:00 am. So everything had to go precisely according to the plan.

JAKE

"The Coast Guard guys had given me critical information about the type of locks that were on the truck, and I had done my homework on them, so I was able to pick both of them in just a few seconds. Then it was a matter of getting about two dozen sacks filled with marijuana from the truck to our truck in the remaining time. I'll never forget the skunky smell of high-quality weed that hit us when we opened the rear door of that truck. The Weemans were completely blown away, and would've just stood there breathing in and getting high if I had let them, but after I yelled that we had to get the fucking job done the three of us began working feverishly and were successful at liberating a lot of pot in the allotted time.

"What an experience it was to drive that truck smelling of skunk weed through the streets of South Portland in the early morning hours. You have to keep in mind that I had grown up not too far from that area and my family has deep roots there. In fact, the street in and out of the Coast Guard base is named Sawyer Street, which, as I've told you, is was named for John Sawyer, who is an ancestor of mine who was licensed by the Town of Falmouth and operated, in the year 1719, the ferry from where the Coast Guard base is now across the Fore River to Portland!"

Oh, please, I said to myself, sometimes this stuff is just too much.

"The weed had a street value of well over a million dollars," Jake continued, "but I knew that getting that much for it would be a long, drawn-out and dangerous process that would likely get us busted, so I made arrangements to sell the whole stash to a single buyer for ninety-thousand dollars, which was a very big chunk of change in the 1970s. The whole idea was to get the stuff out of our lives as quickly as possible and be satisfied with what we could get. One of the major things I had learned from all the jailhouse stories I had heard was that being greedy is often what gets people caught, so I knew it was very important not to make that mistake.

"A couple of days after I had made the sale, I met the Weeman brothers at the St. John Street McDonald's to give them their share of the money. They were all bug-eyed, excited as hell. They couldn't believe that we had actually pulled it off and that I was handing them each $30,000 across the table as they were eating their friggin' unhealthy as hell Big Macs, with French fries and friggin' large cokes. They were completely dazzled and their jaws dropped when I handed them the money, but having my wallet bulging with ill-gotten cash was not at all new to me, of course. I tried to calm them down and get them to realize that just because we'd made away with the weed and had gotten to the part where we'd sold it and had a lot of money, that didn't mean that the movie was over. Not by a long shot.

"I stressed to them above all else that they should not flash their new found wealth around town, and they both solemnly agreed that they would not. But then two days after I gave them their cash, Richard pulls up all smiles in front of one of my apartment buildings in a late-model, very cool looking fire engine red MG sports car!

"'You fucking asshole!' I screamed at him, 'When they pull you in for questioning you'd better forget my fucking name, or I'll haul your ass up the stairs to the top of the Munjoy Hill Observatory Tower and throw you the fuck off it!' Because of my interest in Portland history, I knew the historical tower to be one-hundred and four steps to the top, and knew there wouldn't be much left of Mr. Weeman when he hit the bricks. I've always liked it when my knowledge of local history somehow comes into play relative to my various adventures.

"There wasn't any hint of joking around in my voice, and I could see by the look on Richard's face that he took me very seriously, but I still knew that there was a very good chance that the shit was going to hit the fan sooner rather than later. There were just too many either stupid or hopelessly naive people involved.

"The feds, naturally, immediately grilled our two Coast Guard buddies and they didn't last long at all, of course. The separate interrogating rooms technique works every time. They caught one of them making a statement that was inconsistent with what the other one said, they both got flustered and spilled their guts, and the next morning the feds are knocking at the door of the Weeman's apartment, flashing a warrant and asking who the MG out front belongs to. The Weeman brothers were arrested on the spot, but I'd spent the night elsewhere and wasn't at home at the time. I knew without a doubt that they were hot after me, though. The brazen nature of the operation pointed very clearly in my direction, so even if the Weemans didn't rat me out, which they didn't immediately do, evidently, mainly because of my severe warning to them. I knew that it wouldn't be long before the hounds of justice would catch up to me, though."

ROCKY MOUNTAIN HIGH: WARD, COLORADO,

"I knew I had to get out of town as quickly as possible and find a place where I couldn't be found. So, I looked for advice from one of my other tenants, who I knew had considerable experience in the matter of making oneself scarce. Cameron Bishop was his name, and he had been number one on the FBI's 10 Most Wanted list for eight years or more for his part in trying to bring down the federal government by bombing a series of very tall government electricity towers. He, along with some other politically radical tenants of mine, had appeared quite prominently in the national news at the time, as a matter of fact.

"Cameron said that he had been contemplating a change of scenery at about that same time himself, and had his sights set on a small outlaw hideaway town high in the Rocky mountains by the name of Ward, Colorado, where such luminaries of the Old West as Jesse James, Cole Younger, and many other notorious outlaws had hidden out. Jessie and Cole had both been longtime heroes of mine, so I didn't need more convincing. Shortly thereafter, we jumped in my Chevy Blazer, taking with us a large stash of very potent Thai weed Cameron was in possession of at the time, and were off across America.

"We had a very enjoyable trip across the country, actually. We took a few detours here and there along the way to visit friends I had made on my trip back from California a few years before, and had a lot of good, clean fun wherever we stopped. When we got to Colorado, I dropped Cameron off at a small ranch at the base of a mountain where some radical friends of his were holed up. I continued on my own up a very steep rough and broken trail to the top of a two mile high mountain, where I found the place I was looking for. Ward is 9,253 feet in elevation and actually looks down on Denver, which is about sixty miles away and

The day before this picture was taken, Jake had been riding
all day in a hard rainstorm for over 600 miles as the last leg
of a high-speed trip across America. Longtime bikers are
amazed that his rear wheel did not lock up when his rear
axle gave way.

only about 5000 feet in elevation, so it's quite a place to arrive at.

"I made quite a sensation when I made my appearance in Ward because the population of the town was only a few dozen people, and they went months without seeing anyone new. They all came running and gathered around when I pulled up in front of the only store in town in my new Chevy Blazer. When I stepped out, there I was, this six-foot-two, broad-shouldered giant in a cool leather jacket who looked like he'd dropped in from another planet. They knew no one ever came to Ward without a good reason, of course, and just as a matter of security, they had to know who I was and what I was doing. When I told them that I was a friend of Cameron Bishop, the town sheriff, who was a short guy named Fuzzy, ran off and telephoned Cameron and when he returned and told everyone that Cameron had said the I was a good friend of his and a well-known Hell's Angel, they all started laughing and applauding. They got so excited I thought they might crown me emperor of the town or something. Right away there was something I liked about the place.

"There was a very attractive hippie woman who was the mayor of Ward and she liked me right off. I spent my first night in town at her place and ended up living with her from then on. We had a very open relationship, though. We didn't hawkeye each other's comings and goings in the slightest bit. I've never minded women with unshaven armpits and hairy legs, no matter what the altitude, and there were a number of very attractive women of that type in Ward, along with a good supply of pot and home brew, of course, so life was good.

"There was a spirit in Ward that kind of took me

over, actually. Every one of us was an outsider of some kind and there was tight kinship between us. We kidded around a lot, had some great home-cooked meals together, did a lot of wild dancing out in the fields to great fiddle music, that sort of thing. A lot of the people there were social activists hiding out from the law, so a lot of very stimulating conversation went on. Patty Hearst had holed up with friends at Duck Lake near Ward for a while when she was on the run from the feds. I just missed meeting her, which was too bad, because we had the same kind of family background and probably would've hit it off really well. What did work out very well, though, was that many of the hippies types were into seances, things like that, so I got to be in contact with Jesse James and Cole Younger, and they both said they were thrilled to death to make my acquaintance! Then we smoked another joint."

He rocked back and forth in his chair laughing like hell at that one, while I sat there across the room groaning.

"Unfortunately," he went on, "my time in Ward totaled only about four months. I was entirely content there, and might even have been content to stay there forever, but one day I received some news that put a different light on things. A friend from home wrote and told me that the FBI was putting a great deal of pressure on my parents to cooperate with their search for me, and they were making things uncomfortable for them in many different ways. Of course, I always took great pains to keep knowledge of my activities and whereabouts away from my parents, so they couldn't have helped with the investigation anyway, but the feds knew that I couldn't tolerate my mother suffering because of me, and that's why they were harassing her.

"Anyway, after some long hugs all around with the friends I had made in Ward, I hopped into my Chevy Blazer and drove back down the mountain, headed across the country back to Portland to present myself to the appropriate authorities, knowing full well that the only possible outcome of that would be a lengthy incarceration.

"Hey, I still enjoyed the hell out the ride across the country, though. Stopped here and there, did this and that. Took my time and did it up right. Life is precious and we can't let moments go unappreciated, know what I mean?"

"Yeah, what's to worry," I was thinking.

HOME TO FACE THE MUSIC

"When I got to Portland and turned myself in, Detective Mike Russo took me aside and said I was facing forty years in federal prison, and they were very confident that they could convict me because the Weeman brothers had ratted on me and would testify against me at my trial. They had been given two years at a correctional facility for youthful offenders in Morgantown, Virginia, and after the first year they ratted me out to gain their freedom, knowing that I would do much more serious time than just the one year or so they had left on their sentences.

"At this time I would like to say, sir, that I would very much like to include the Weeman brothers in any profits that might come from the sale of the bestselling book and blockbuster movie we're putting together here, so if they're reading this, Richard and Scott should be sure to get in touch with me. We became good friends over the years when they were my tenants, and I know there are some good stories we'd enjoy recalling. Anything that might have happened subsequent to our previous happy days together has been forgotten, of course. So, if they wish to contact me themselves, or if there is anyone who is interested in a reward that will be paid for information pertaining to the whereabouts of Richard or Scott Weeman, they can contact me through the publisher of our book, correct? I know that at one time, one of them was living in Colorado and the other one was living in California. I have had people watching them..."

"Yeah, sure, Jake," I said, "I'll, ah, talk to the publisher about that."

"Detective Russo and I had become good buddies over the years that I was a bail bondsman," Jake continued, "so he leveled with me right from the start. All I had to do was tell them what I did with the weed after we stole it and I'd do another short stretch up in Maine State prison, instead of serving a long sentence in a federal penitentiary. Yeah, like hell. I hardly knew the guy I sold the pot to, I didn't know if he was a good guy or an asshole, but there was no way I was going to rat him out, regardless. A rat is a gutless coward who deserves to be exterminated, and I am not a rat, end of story.

"After I was indicted, I spent six months in County Jail awaiting trial, which was not my idea of a good time. There I was, locked up down on Federal Street instead of dancing with lovely hippie women high on a mountaintop in Ward, which is sure as hell what I wanted to be doing. My only consolation was the fact that I was a celebrity in the County Jail, both with my fellow prisoners and with the jail personnel. C'mon, I had been a Hell's Angel, done time in San Quentin and

Folsom Prison, and had pulled off the great pot heist the whole town was talking about. Hell, my bail was higher than the bail of all the other inmates put together! You can't believe what a huge ego trip that was for me!"

Yes, he's right, I thought to myself. I couldn't believe it.

"It was boring as hell in County Jail, though, there's no denying it," he continued, "but at least we had a lot of pot. I taught an old biker acquaintance of mine named Homer who was assigned to outside detail how to shove an ounce up his ass in such a way as to adequately secure it there without hurting himself, and how to walk so it wouldn't become dislodged. Homer got to be extremely good at it, and his efforts were appreciated by one and all. We'd stand on our tiptoes looking out the cell windows watching for Homer to return from work, and when we spotted him coming down the sidewalk walking in that special way, everybody would cheer like hell. Hey, everybody needs to be a hero at one time or another, and this was Homer's shining moment. One of the guards proved to be very helpful as well. He was a Jesus freak, and we needed something to roll the weed in, so I told him I was starting to have spiritual feelings, and asked him to bring in a Bible for me. "Sure, Jake!" he said. We were just getting to the end of the Old Testament when my trial date arrived.

THE TRIAL

"With the Weeman brothers testifying against me at my trial, I had absolutely no chance of acquittal, but I had Dan Lilley again as my lawyer, so I was confident that he'd be able to successfully negotiate a favorable sentence. When I arrived in court and saw who the prosecuting attorney was, though, I knew we were in for a dog fight.

"It was George Mitchell! The man who was later to become a powerful United States Senator, respected international diplomat, and one of the most accomplished and respected people in the world!

"He had that special look about him even then. You knew he was going places, and that he wasn't used to losing. He was a great guy, though. He was putting everything he had into getting me put away, and he never wavered from his mission one bit, but as the trial went on it became obvious that he and I liked one another. He knew from my reputation that I was a very colorful character, and he enjoyed joking around with me, kind of on the sly. A little raised eyebrow here and there, that kind of thing.

"George is a quiet, conservative kind of guy, of course, and he has his customary way of dressing — blue blazer, gray slacks, white shirt and red tie — and even though he had the same thing on every day, when I walked by him I'd always say: 'Nice outfit, George!' and he'd laugh every time. Of course, I couldn't leave it at that, though. I got my pal Truman Dongo to get me a blue blazer, gray slacks, white shirt and red tie, and when George saw me being led into court dressed like that it cracked him up so much I didn't know if he could continue. I wasn't trying to soften him up, though, I really wasn't. I just liked him and enjoyed making him laugh.

"George Mitchell wasn't the only rising star in the courtroom, though. When we took our seats on the first day of the trial, Dan nodded in the direction of the judge and whispered to me that they had assembled the A Team in my honor. I didn't know who he was at the time, but the judge turned out to be none other than the legendary Judge Edward T. Gignoux, the man for whom Portland's new federal courthouse was later named. Judge Gignoux was a very stern, wise-looking man, though, and I wasn't at all inclined to attempt to joke with him the way I was with George Mitchell.

"Well, George got his wish, but it didn't quite turn out as he expected. I was convicted of four felonies, and Judge Gignoux gave me ten years on each one, just the way George urged him to, but then, as I was standing there stunned, trying to get my head around the fact that I was probably going to spend the rest of my life in prison, I heard the judge say the wonderful words: 'To be served concurrently.' Man! Ten years when I was facing forty! And then Dan leaned over and said I could possibly get out in less than three! Those were the days as I've mentioned, when parole was granted very liberally.

"Truthfully, I didn't know the reason for Judge Gignoux's leniency until a number of years later, when I ran into a former federal agent at J's Oyster Bar who told me that the judge admired the fact that I absolutely refused to help myself by ratting anyone out, even when it would have been much to my benefit to do so. The former FBI agent told me that the judge had developed a deep disgust for the Weeman brothers after it became apparent from their testimony that they had lassoed me into the whole thing, rather than the other way around, and now, here they were, ratting me out to save their own asses. So, as it turned out, Judge Gignoux truly was a very wise man with a very strong sense of fair play, and I'm happy that he ended up having a beautiful new building named after him.

"As for the Weemans, I'm sure the good judge would enjoy knowing about it if the Weeman bothers and myself were to eventually get together and settled matters in a most congenial and satisfactory way. I look forward to that happening at Richard and Scott's earliest possible convenience. If they don't happen to see this themselves, I would remind any acquaintances of theirs of the previously mentioned monetary award that will be paid for any information leading to their whereabouts."

SIXTEEN

This time Jake had a picture of the grounds of Lewisburg Federal Penitentiary sitting out on his living room table when I arrived at his apartment, and the grim, institutional bleakness of the place gave me the chills.

"So, now you were back in the big house, Jake," I said. "You were looking at San Quentin all over again, man. Lewisburg is a far cry from Maine State Prison, huh?"

LEWISBURG FEDERAL PENITENTIARY

"Damn right it is!" he exploded. "Maine State Prison was play time for me, but life got serious real fast when I arrived at Lewisburg Federal Penitentiary.

"Needless to say, the feds weren't happy about the relatively short sentence I received, after they were certain they'd put together a case that would get me put away for the rest of my life for stealing their pot, so they went out of their way to make sure I did some very hard time at Lewisburg. Most people think of San Quentin and Folsom as being the toughest prisons in the country, but when an inmate hears 'Lewisburg Federal Penitentiary' they take in a quick breath and their stomach tightens. You know that feeling, right?"

"Yes, I do," I said, nodding my head.

"At the time, Lewisburg was the foremost maximum security prison complex in the country," he continued, "the inmate population was mostly made up of mob bosses, Black Muslim extremists, bomb-throwing social activists and big time bank robbers. You know, serious menaces to society, people who were well known on the outside for their extreme anti-social behavior and who had many loyal followers. It really wasn't the kind of place you'd expect a guy to be sent for stealing some pot up in Portland, Maine.

"The reason for the special treatment I received, my friend, was that the FBI wanted to get me killed. Pure and simple. It's the truth whether you or anyone else wants to believe it or not."

He could see by the little shrug I gave that I was somewhat dubious, so he smiled condescendingly and patiently laid out the scenario.

"When the court failed to get me put away for life, the prison authorities, in collusion with the FBI, not only made sure I was sentenced to the most violent prison in the country, they also went a step further and planted the rumor with the inmate population that I got a reduced sentence for ratting out my accomplices, knowing full well that rats are the most hated form of life throughout the entire prison system. Odds were that I'd be sliced up and left to die in a far corner of the prison yard before a month was up, and the authorities sure as hell knew it.

"As I was being processed into the prison, an old cellmate of mine from San Quentin was handing out clothing, and he told me about the dangerous rumor that had spread throughout the prison concerning me being a rat. The first time I stepped out on the prison yard and looked around I knew that every one of those guys hated my guts, just the way I would've hated any one of them if I thought they were a fucking rat.

"My fellow prisoners made things very bad for me

right from the start. Complete shunning, with a constant tension in the air. I knew the attempt on my life could come at any time, and it finally came after about four days. I was damn well ready for it, though. I'd been actively planning since my buddy warned me what was coming. Within an hour of arriving, I had mounted a razor blade on a toothbrush and had myself an easily concealed lethal weapon. Whenever I was alone with any inmate, or out on the yard with them all, I had that homemade weapon of war cupped in my hand, ready for swift and immediate action, and I had hidden three shanks in the ground out in the yard. I also drove shanks into the ground in three strategic areas of the prison yard, as a kind of plan B.

"Then it happened. A guy going by me on the yard made a move to shove a shank into my chest but, fortunately, because I was always hyper-aware of any action going on around me, I was just a little quicker than he was and managed to block his arm and slash his face a number of times before he could react. I gave him a few more slashes than was necessary, just to make my point. Then, while he was standing there bent over, yowling his friggin' head off and bleeding all over the place, I drove the other end of the toothbrush about an inch into his fucking thigh and said: 'Bye-bye-for-now, asshole, come at me again and I'll slit your fuckin' throat!'

"My fellow prisoners made very close note of the fact that when the attempt on my life was made, I didn't act the least bit afraid or respond to the attack in a defensive manner. My impulsive reaction was to respond with a ferocious fucking counterattack of my own that completely overwhelmed and terrorized my attacker. I am happy to relate that after the incident no further attempts were made on my life by him or anyone else in the prison.

"That's not because they were afraid of me, though. Oh no, they could have found a way to get me. They left me alone because they respected the way the whole thing went down. They took note of the fact that I stayed absolutely faithful to the prison code we lived by. They knew very well that I expected to be attacked, but I didn't whine to the prison authorities about it and ask to go into protective custody, or be transferred to another prison. I stood my ground like a man and waited for whatever was going to come my way.

"They were further impressed by how ready I as for the attack when it occurred. Not only did I defend myself against my attacker, I brutalized the fuck out of him. If I had had a polite 'oh I understand, let's be friends after all' attitude, I'd would've been attacked again the next day. This was not a high school football game, after all. My message to them had to be loud and clear: anyone who comes after me again better be ready for the fight of their life, which they are probably going to fucking lose.

"So I had them pretty well on notice, I hoped, but you never know with so many cons around, and with so many of them desperate for recognition, what the hell one of them might do. Putting a Hell's Angel who had done time in San Quentin and fights like a crazed Viking warrior down for the count looks very good to other convicts on your prison resumé.

"Waiting for one of them to have the balls to come after me was no way to live, though, especially when I knew that the whole thing was based on a damn lie! The truth was that the judge gave me a lighter sentence because he respected the fact that I didn't rat out my accomplices, even though they were undeserving low lifes; it sure as hell wasn't because I had ratted out anyone. I knew that just telling my fellow prisoners the truth wasn't going to do it, though. Not even close. Talk is cheap on a prison yard and a lot of people claim a lot of things. Fortunately, though, I came up with the idea of writing to a friend back home and having him mail me the copy of the *Portland Press Herald* that contained the story of my trial. The story made it very clear that I had refused to divulge the names of my accomplices in exchange for a lighter sentence and man, was I elated when I returned from chow one night and saw that a copy of the *Portland Press Herald* had been tossed through the bars and the front page story about my trial was lying face-up on the floor of my cell!

"Okay, here's how I handled it. The most powerful man in the prison yard was Tony Provenzano, who everybody referred to as Tony Pro. He was the Capo, or 'Captain,' in the Genovese crime family that controlled mafia activity in Philadelphia and up and down the East Coast. With that kind of power, whatever Tony said in the Lewisburg prison yard was the last word on the subject, no questions asked. I knew he was the man I had to convince that I wasn't a rat, so I walked up to him in the prison yard as he was playing bocce with his friends, like he always did, and handed him the newspaper story and said: 'Please read this Mr. Provenzano.'

"I'd never be able to tell you how happy I was to see that wide Italian smile come over Tony's face as he read the story. After he finished reading, he looked over at me and actually started laughing.

"Tony was acting like the mafia dons did in *The Godfather* when someone got accepted into the brotherhood. Well, I knew I wasn't the right nationality for full admittance into that particular brotherhood, but there was no question that I was in tight with Tony all the way after he knew the truth about me. Within a half an hour after I gave him the story, everyone on the yard knew that not only was I not a fucking rat, but they also knew I had been sent to Lewisburg because I refused to, no matter how much it would have helped me.

"They also knew that the feds get pissed as hell when they can't turn you into a rat, so they sure as hell would've planted a lie about me that would circulate throughout the prison population and very likely get me killed. The truth about me was right in the damn newspaper story, which I made sure got circulated around the whole friggin' prison then made it back to me. There was no way I was going to part with that little piece of merchandise."

Ah, the power of the written word, I was thinking.

"So now they all knew that they had been wrong about me, but what impressed them even further was that I hadn't tried to change their minds without hard evidence to back my story up. I didn't snivel and beg them to listen to my story, I didn't go into the prison protective custody program, and I didn't ask to be transferred to another prison, even after the attempt on my life was made.

"Okay, so now I was the toast of Broadway and pretty much had the run of the place. The best part of my day got to be playing bocce in the afternoon with Tony Pro and Johnny Dio, and the other mafia guys. It was a real honor to be invited to play with them, especially because I'm not Italian. Bocce is a bonding activity among the brotherhood. It's all very relaxed and friendly. You can take all the time between shooting you want to for casual conversation, so we all got to know one another very well.

"I was amazed when I found out how powerful these guys I was playing with were. Johnny Dio ran operations in the New York garment district from the prison. All the time we were playing, guys would be running up to him with messages. Bocce is a game that requires a lot of skill and precision, though, so those guys knew better than to interrupt Tony Pro or Johnny Dio when they were shooting, no matter what the message was. Guys have been known to take a midnight dip in the East River with tire rims tied around their ankles for a lot less than causing a Don to lose a bocce match.

"After the prison population found out about me and witnessed the way I handled myself around the yard, a kind of fascination about me developed around the place. One day out in the yard a crowd of my fellow prisoners gathered around me and one guy asked if all Hell's Angels were like me, and I yelled: "Hell, yes! Hell's Angels fight to the death! We never retreat! We always attack! I prepared myself for war the moment I knew you guys were out to get me! That's the way we all are! Bring it on! Fuck you! We're either the bravest or the craziest bastards on earth! Maybe both! That's why there's not too many of us! We're the most exclusive club on the planet! Hell's Angels Forever!"

JAKE

Jake in Lewisburg. Jake's training partner at the time was Ralph Gambena, a former NCAA Wrestling Champ turned bank robber. At this time, Jake could bench press 330 for reps and could squat 300 for reps (not bad on a crippled right leg). He had 18" arms, weighed 195 lbs and could run 7 miles after training with Ralph.

*Jake with the men he trained with
at Lewsiburg Prison, 1979*

JAKE

TORTURED BY THE WARDEN

"Alright, so you get the idea. I wasn't the meekest individual to be incarcerated at that particular federal house of detention. I had positioned myself very well within the prison hierarchy, obviously. But let me tell you about an incident that took place at Lewisburg that endeared me to my fellow inmates even more, especially to the mafia bosses.

"You have to understand that after the feds sent me to Lewisburg to have me killed on the yard as a rat, and that didn't happen, they were more aggravated with me than ever, and became obsessed with getting the name of the guy I sold the pot to. To the point where they would do virtually anything to get the information they wanted, including physically torturing me. There are those who are under the impression that a department of the United States government would not be involved in such activities, but let me assure you that those people are quite mistaken in their belief.

"The warden's name at Lewisburg was Charlie Fenton, and he was one cowardly, ruthless motherfucker. Ol' Charlie was well aware that he had to proceed with extreme caution when it came to getting information out of inmates under his charge, because some of those guys had the best lawyers in the country on their side, but he had a self-developed, truth-divulging technique that left no long-lasting physical traces. It had worked admirably for him with a number of other overly stubborn inmates, evidently, so he thought he'd give it a go with me.

"Doesn't seem like much of a deal to someone who

hasn't experienced it, but what the righteous warden did was have four guards hold me down while he beat the bottoms of my feet with a piece of garden hose. Never have I come close to experiencing such pain in my life. The bottoms of your feet are super-sensitive and are full of nerves that can send excruciating pain all throughout your body. Every time good ol' Charlie asked me for the name of my accomplice and I just grinned at him like I had no idea what he was talking about, he grinned back at me and took a whack at the bottom of my feet. The bastard whacked me over and over again, and each time the pain was worse. I actually thought I was going to lose my mind. I sure as hell wasn't going to tell him what he wanted, though. Fenton was telling me over and over again that he wasn't enjoying it, so to please give him the name he was after and he'd stop and give me some nice salve for my feet. Then my head would clear and I'd see that evil fucking little grin of his and I'd hate the bastard even more.

"What you have to understand here is that I was barely acquainted with the individual I was refusing to rat on. Truthfully, I didn't even care what happened to him. I just knew that I wasn't going to rat on *anyone*, no matter who they were, and no matter what the circumstances were. After each whack, Fenton would ask me for the name of the guy I sold the pot to, and I'd give him the name of a movie star or some politician and he'd get more and more pissed off. After a while, though, I told him that I absolutely couldn't take the torture anymore and was ready to cooperate.

"Okay, Sawyer," he said. "I'm not enjoying this anymore than you are. Just give me his name and we'll get you out of here and you'll get deluxe treatment all the rest of the time you're with us. Might even get you paroled a lot sooner than you might have thought.

Okay, just give me his name and we'll all be happy."

"I started kind of sobbing and whimpering, like my spirit was completely broken and I could barely talk, so Fenton leaned over and put his ear close to my mouth, and when he did, I screamed: "I sold the pot to your fucking mother and she turned out to be the best blow job I ever had!"

"That sent him over the edge, of course. He went wild with the friggin' garden hose until there were beads of sweat on his fucking forehead, but after a while he knew that no amount of physical torture was going to get him anywhere with me, so he had the guards drag me off and throw me into solitary.

"Oh yeah, I would like to add here that Warden Fenton tortured a friend of mine, Richard Picarrillo, in the same way he did me, and Picarrillo's lawyer took Warden Fenton to court and he was found guilty! It's a matter of public record in Pennsylvania. Picarrillo was a very high-profile convict because he was associated with my friend, Cameron Bishop, in their efforts to bring down the federal government, but that didn't prevent him from getting shafted by the court. In spite of all that cowardly Warden Fenton did to him, he was awarded only one dollar for the pain and suffering he endured. All this is a matter of public record. Fuck you, Charlie Fenton!

"While I was in solitary after being tortured, one of the guards who had held me down was so impressed by what he had witnessed that he spread the story I have just related to you throughout the inmate population. Consequently, when I got out, I found that I was held in even higher esteem than I had been before, especially in the eyes of the mafia bosses, because they were always looking for guys who would be loyal, no matter what."

VOLUME TWO

LIFE AT LEWISBURG POST-TORTURE

"Life around the prison immediately got rosier than ever for ol' Jakie boy as a result of the grueling incident with dear ol' Warden Fenton, as you might imagine. I was elevated to the top tier of the food chain when it came to obtaining prison contraband, so I had all the drugs and booze I wanted, and life was good.

"When I played bocce with my Italian friends now, they tended to be even more at ease around me than before, and we became closer and closer. Before the torture incident, once in a while when we were playing I could see knowing glances between them when the talk got too close to certain subjects, and they'd all clam up, but after the incident with the warden that didn't happen nearly so often.

"I made some good friends at Lewisburg, and learned first-hand why prisons are the breeding ground for much of the criminal activity in the country. I could have been set up for a life of great adventure and untold riches through the contacts I made at Lewisburg. Tony Pro said I could name my ticket in Philadelphia, or anywhere on the east coast, and Johnnie Dio said he'd be happy to set me up with a very lucrative position in his New York garment district operation. They also said they would be willing to bankroll any enterprise I might want to get involved in up in Portland. That sounded tempting, but, when you get right down to it, I wasn't Italian, and things do tend to get right down to it in certain situations, you know? I've always been very reluctant to form alliances with groups anyway, given my volatile nature, and I thought it best to avoid any future trouble with the Mafia. Bring on the federal government, hell, yes, but spare me the boys in soft felt hats with long cigars hanging out of their mouths."

OVER THESE PRISON WALLS

"There were some memorable moments at Lewisburg with inmates besides the mafia bosses as well, of course. There was the time I helped a guy make a hang-glider in the craft shop for him to glide over the walls. I told him that I'd carry him and his flying apparatus on my back up the tall tower that was in the middle of the yard, and he could take off from there and sail right over the wall, no problem. I might have even talked him into the whole thing, I can't quite remember. Anyway, we got the thing made, but the guy had stuffed some pictures of his family he wanted to take with him in his back pocket, and when a guard saw him walking to the tower with the pictures sticking out of his pockets he knew immediately what was up because he knew how important those pictures were to the guy, and that the only reason he'd have taken them down off his cell wall and stuffed them in his pockets was if he was going to make a break for it. Too bad, all around. I had the whole prison prepped for a fantastic show. Damn that guy and his pictures. Oh well, you just never know what's going to come into play in any given situation, you know?"

"Yes," I said, "another one of life's lessons."

"Well," Jake said, "I wasn't about to let that fizzled affair affect my reputation, I'll tell you that. I managed to provide a decent amount of entertainment otherwise now and then. I even created a large visual guide to the prison – and there it is!" he yelled, pointing to the very creation laying on his tabletop next to the official map of the prison.

"The amusing names I came up with for the various sections of the prison entertained my fellow convicts all to hell, of that you can be sure. They started calling the places by the names I gave them, and I'll bet those names are still used today in Lewisberg Federal Penitentiary! What a legacy!

"Yeah, all in all, I had some memorable experiences at Lewisberg," he went on, shaking his head and smiling to himself. "Tony Pro told me some stories I've never repeated to anyone, because it's not nice or very healthy to retell stories your mafia buddies told you, but so much time has passed that it wouldn't matter a bit now because all the players are gone.

Following page: Jake created this farcical map of Lewisburg Federal Prison for the amusement of his fellow convicts, and it was much enjoyed as it circulated throughout the prison population, he says. He gave the map to a prisoner when he got paroled, and after Jake contacted him, the man, who got paroled a few years later himself, mailed the map to Jake, after all these years, for inclusion in this book.

JAKE

UNITED STATES PENITENTIARY, LEWISBURG, PENNSYLVANIA

A. SWIMMING POOL.
B. HANG-GLIDING SCHOOL + TAKEOFF POINT
C. DANCE HALL
D. LEWISBURG BAR + GRILL!
E. CONVICTS RIFLE RANGE!
F. SELF DEFENCE SCHOOL.
G. ONE OF MANY TOWERS FOR OUR BIRD-WATCHING CLASSES
H. THE WALL THAT KEEPS PEOPLE FROM BREAKING IN
I. INDOOR OLYMIC SWIMMING POOL
J. DROP ZONE FOR OUR SKYDIVING TEAM
K. NOTELL MOTEL
L. LADDER FACTORY
M. GIGANTIC WHORE HOUSE
N. GUN + AMMUNITION STORE!
O. MY TREE

26

"Tony was 'big' in the East Coast mafia, and had been the vice-president of the New Jersey Teamsters union. He had been very close to both Richard Nixon and Jimmy Hoffa over the years. A couple of weeks after Nixon resigned, he made his first public appearance playing golf with Tony, that's how close they were. Tony was always making little jokes about how mafia money got passed to Nixon, even while he was in office, and you knew whatever he said was the truth. What you have to understand here, is that Tony Pro didn't stand out in the middle of the Lewisburg Federal Penitentiary prison yard and tell loud, hair-raising stories that invariably had to do with his amazing valor and undying loyalty to his friends, the way other convicts did. No way. There was an aura around him that wouldn't have allowed that. He was respected in the prison so much that no one in the chow hall took a bite of their food until Mr. Provenzano was seated and had started eating. And we're talking a very large dining room full of criminally insane, pathological killers who'd never respected anyone or anything in their entire lives!

"No, Tony never opened up to anyone but his personal confidants, and I'm very proud to say that I became one of them, especially considering that I had started out as lower than bug shit in his eyes. Anyone who's played bocce the way it's played in Italy knows that easy, friendly conversation between the players is woven into the game. One day Tony stopped short before shooting and looked over at me with a very sincere look on his face and said I must have liked my accomplice a whole lot not to rat on him when they tortured me. When I told him that, no, I didn't even particularly like the guy, that the reason that I wouldn't rat on him was that I wouldn't rat on anyone ever, Tony looked at me like I was his long-lost son and we became tighter than ever."

"Okay, great, Jake," I said, "let's have a good Tony Pro story."

THE LAKE TAHOE SNITCHES MUSEUM

"Awww right, here you go", he laughed: "Once upon a time Tony Pro was playing bocce on the prison yard of Lewisburg Federal Penitentiary, when he began musing about some of the things he missed about the outside, and got to talking about the good times he'd had at Lake Tahoe, which is a beautiful lake more than six-thousand feet up in the Sierra Nevada Mountains, and is the largest freshwater body of water in the country, with the exception of the Great Lakes. I naturally thought Tony was missing Lake Tahoe's great beauty and cooling breezes, but that wasn't it at all. Tony said the Mafia dons and their trusted associates loved Lake Tahoe because of the privacy it afforded them when they were alone out in the middle of the lake on their big, showy yachts. It turns out that a lot of the shorefront property around Lake Tahoe was owned by Mafia figures, and a good deal of the bonding that took place within the organization happened there. A lot of the action that came down on the streets of New York and Chicago had its origins out in the middle of Lake Tahoe. Let's say that logging some Lake Tahoe time looked very good on your resumé.

"It wasn't all work out there in the middle of the lake, though. The dons and their close associates had certain ways of entertaining themselves, Tony told us. The whole line-up of the usual carnal pleasures was available to them, of course, but they were always looking for something new. So one of them came up with the idea of having some fun with some people they didn't like very much. Here's how it went: they'd invite some unsuspecting low-life who had ratted on somebody to come spend some time with them on the lake, all expenses paid to and fro, except that the fro never happened. They'd even wire the guy some money to get new clothes for the occasion. It was right out of *The Godfather*, the scene where Michael Corleone had his brother-in-law strangled to death right after promising him that he was going to spend the rest of his days enjoying the Las Vegas high life.

"Everyone on the yacht would be wearing their classiest suit when the guest of honor arrived. He was given a first-rate meal of his choice, and, all-in-all, was wined, feted, and entertained to the point where he was certain he was in the best of graces of all concerned. Hey, he was even given the seat of honor, which was a beautifully designed heavy oak chair that was placed next to the senior don's place at the head of the table. The mark could hardly believe his good fortune, but suddenly everything changed when the head don gave the nod and two guys came up behind the honored guest, abruptly covered his mouth with duct tape, tied his body very securely to the chair, then lifted the whole nicely wrapped package to the side rail of the yacht, where heavy weights were added to the bottom of the chair before it and its occupant were slowly lowered into the chilly waters of Lake Tahoe, where the whole package sank straight to the bottom.

"What you have to understand here, my friend, is that Lake Tahoe is located some six-thousand feet high in elevation, and is more than sixteen hundred feet deep in some parts, so it's extremely cold on the bottom. Tony said that it's so cold down there that deterioration process doesn't take place at all!

"'Those snitches are still down there!' Tony said, 'they're sitting in their oak chairs, wearing their best suits and ties, and they're all staring straight ahead with their eyes bulging out, just like they were when they were lowered down the side of the yacht!'

"Tony said that there was this one snitch who they hated real bad because he had taken to living large on the money he had been paid by the feds to rat on his accomplices. Cruising around town in his new Cadillac convertible, things like that. After the unsuspecting gentleman had been invited to spend a fabulous weekend at Lake Tahoe, and he was being feted in the way the other special guests had been, imagine his surprise and momentary confusion when, Tony told us, just as he was enjoying the aroma of a fine Sicilian wine and trying to ascertain its vintage, he saw his nice new Cadillac convertible floating into view on the deck of a barge. The picture came together for him, though, when he was taped and tied like the others were, transferred to the deck of the barge, sat up in the front seat and tied to the steering wheel of his new Cadillac convertible, which was then taken out of gear and pushed off the end of the barge!

"Tony assured us that those snitches would always be down there! A bunch of very alarmed looking, very well-dressed guys sitting straight up in oak chairs with their eyes bulging out, just the way they were when they were lowered off the side of the yacht! And they're all sitting around a nice new-looking Cadillac convertible with another guy looking like they do, tied to the steering wheel! Rats frozen in place for all time! *The Lake Tahoe Snitches Museum* Tony called it!"

VOLUME TWO

THE BLOCKBUSTER:
WHERE JIMMY HOFFA IS BURIED

"Okay, Jake," I said, "that one was pretty good, but you said you had a few Tony Pro stories, so let's hear another one."

Jake smiled when I said that. It was what might be called a smile of recognition. That I didn't hesitate to make such requests meant to him that I was becoming more relaxed in his presence, I guess. I got the impression that I was far from being the first person that he had nurtured in such a manner.

"Yeah, man, here we go," he said, gleefully rubbing his hands together.

"What this involves," he began, "is some very explosive insider information revealed to me by Tony Pro on a subject of national interest.

"First let me say, my friend, that the reason I haven't told you the story before is that my instincts are to never, ever, comment on anything involving any acquaintance of mine that might involve them having broken the law. The story I told you about the fun and games at Lake Tahoe isn't that, of course, because rubbing out a snitch isn't against the law as far as I am concerned. It's also true that all the people involved in the story would be well over 100 years old by this time and, even if they are still walking the planet, I know they'll get a big laugh out of the whole thing when they read about it, and they'll swear that every word of it is true.

"What I have to say concerns Tony Pro's famous buddy, Jimmy Hoffa, the head of the Teamsters Union, who mysteriously disappeared without a trace

some years before Tony and I were at Lewisburg together. Tony Pro has always been the FBI's primary
suspect in Hoffa's disappearance, and I'm here to tell
you that they are definitely on the right track. The
word among the mafia dons in the prison was that
Hoffa's elimination occurred because he insisted on
reassuming the presidency of the Teamsters after he
got out of prison, and the mafia preferred Frank Fitzsimmons for the position. Fitzsimmons was in the mafia's pocket 100% and Hoffa was in only 75%, so there
you go.

"Hoffa was last seen at a restaurant outside of De-
troit, and there's never been any doubt that the mafia
had him killed, but the huge question that no one has
been able to answer is where his body is buried. In-
tensive investigations have taken place. Damn, they
even dug up Giant's Stadium once, but no one has
been able find Jimmy Hoffa's remains.

"That is what I have to tell you today, sir! I know
where Jimmy Hoffa's body is buried!"

Right away I'm thinking that maybe I can go online
and find out how to send Geraldo Rivera's people an
email.

"What brought up the subject of Jimmy Hoffa was
when I mentioned to Tony that I had spent the year
before I was sent to Lewisburg hiding out in Ward,
Colorado," Jake continued.

"Right away Tony says 'Hey, that's in the Rocky
Mountains,' all excited like, because he wasn't a guy
anyone would expect to know that kind of thing.

"'Right, Tony!' I said. 'How did you know that?'

"'Because some guy I knew spent some time hiding
out near Ward, Colorado, and we got to talking once
and he said there was a lot of great places in towns
around Ward to hide bodies. I knew they'd be hot after

finding this guy Jimmy's body, of course, so I had a
couple of the boys stuff him into a plaid sleeping bag
I had hanging around my place, and they threw the
sleeping bag with Jimmy in it into their trunk, and
headed for the Rocky Mountains.'

"Right away Tony gave me a big smile and said he
couldn't remember Jimmy's last name, he was just
some guy by the name of Jimmy, he said, laughing. I
didn't want to seem too interested in what he was telling me, so I waited a few days before I asked him very
casually if he could remember the name of the town
they brought Jimmy's body to.

"'Sure!' he said. 'It was Neverland, Colorado! It's a
place full of old gold mines, and my guys dumped the
plaid sleeping bag with this guy Jimmy in it in one of
them! They're NEVER gonna find him there!' he yelled,
laughing. He was pleased with himself over that line.
I almost think that's why he told me the story, actually, so he could use it. I couldn't bring myself to tell
Tony, though, that the name of the town is Nederland,
not Neverland. Nederland is a small mountaintop
town about a dozen miles from Ward. I used to go to
Nederland to lift weights with Chris Chapman, who
had been Bob Seeger's bass player.

"Tony didn't say a thing about how Hoffa was killed,
or what his last words were, or anything like that, so
I can't help anyone there, but I can assure the whole
damn world that Jimmy Hoffa's bones are resting in
an old abandoned gold mine in Nederland, Colorado,
stuffed in a plaid sleeping bag. It's been fifty years, but
that's no problem today, with DNA, you know?"

I decided against contacting Geraldo Rivera. I'm not
a fan of sensationalism, and I might even become an
accessory after the fact. So I decided to let whoever
reads this to run with it or not, as they choose.

JAKE

PAROLED FROM LEWISBURG

"I was out of Lewisburg on parole in about two and a half years, mainly because I behaved myself. I had no problems with the prison authorities after my torture showdown with Warden Fenton, and I pretty much had run of the place after I had risen to the top of the inmate hierarchy, so I had no desire to misbehave and upset the apple cart. All in all, things had gone very well at Lewisburg and I had a lot to be grateful for. One of my mafia friends obtained a small radio for me, and one of my favorite memories of Lewisburg is dancing alone in my cell listening to a favorite song of mine, by Waylon Jennings. I love the line in it that goes: *I've always been crazy, but it's kept me from going insane.* Funny how certain things stick in your mind, ya know?"

"So, Jake, after you got paroled from Lewisburg you had calmed down a lot, and pretty much went straight and had a normal life, right?" I said with a straight face.

"Of course I did!" he yelled, with a big laugh. "Be serious, my friend!" he quickly added, "I'm going to tell you some things the next time we talk that are going to knock your friggin' socks off! When I got out of Lewisburg in 1980 is when my life finally got interesting!"

Oh, my word, I said to myself, oh, my word.

Next page: Poem written about Jake by Mike Parker, of Ward, Colorado, circa 1980, while Jake was in Lewisburg.

VOLUME TWO

POEM TO INVOKE THE GODS OF THE POST OFFICE
POEM TO CONJURE UP LOVE LETTERS FOR OUR
CAGED BROTHER JAKE THE DANCER

tonite he sits in lewisberg Pennsylvania federal prison
        but his spirit has arisen
we work out & gather to braid the possibilities
jake does a series of a hundred in a million push-ups...

he came to town carrying a wooden indian
told fuzzy right off he was an honest criminal
with a recommendation from superstars off the ten
        most wanted list
            he joined ours quick
within 48 hours he was a womens legend
he was too big not to believe
he had big Harley arms   jake the dancer   hells angel
sweet hero of the underground
he'd done his time in prison
but nothing touched his spirit
he's bigger than life   too tall to hide
he's touched our insides picked up lisa &
        sent her running
he settled in became a wildflower in a wild summer
became a town body-god   got folks workin out
        flashin' his grin
then he committed the crime of going home to maine
& they threw him in the Portland federal prison
said he stole a load of pot from the coast guard
        can you imagine that...
they squeezed the guy that ran off at the mouth for im-
munity & he SOLD jake – in jail he organized misfits

JAKE

into a volleyball team, got people jogging
pushing down on the cold concrete floor
he pushed them
>   *out like his momma's prayers*
>   *they say he dabbled in tankerloads*

they say he fed our heros when they
>   *starved underground*
they sentenced him to do a weary 10 in Lewisburg
>   *JAKE SAWYER*
>   *#441149*
>   *Box 1000*
>   *Lewisburg, Pennsylvania*
>   *17837*
>   *8 9 19 2000 three thousand*
drops of
sweat pushing off the prison floor
in a cage that could never be big enough
in a rage of righteousness that won't be silenced
jake the dancer hones the edge of his high
thinks about us as the lights go out
& the touch of a letter against his chest
is what feels best
>   *till the sun comes out*
>   *& the weights come out*
>   *& the mail comes in*

MIKE PARKER -sometime near 1980 – Ward Colorado.

VOLUME TWO

A SPECIAL GOOD-BYE

"One more thing, my friend," he said, "if you don't mind. There is something that happened shortly after my release from Lewisburg in 1980 that I would like to mention at this time.

"You will remember that the reason I turned myself back in Portland when I was hiding out in Ward was that the FBI was making things difficult for my mother back home, and I just couldn't live with that. We were always very close, as you know, and I couldn't bear the thought of her being unhappy on my account.

"We corresponded regularly by mail when I was in Lewisburg, but I'm sorry to say that a short time after I had done my time and returned to Portland, my mother became ill and things were never the same with her. I paid a visit to her in the hospital that I will recall very vividly for the rest of my life.

"I had no idea how sick she was, because I had been in denial all the way, I guess, but my heart sank when I walked into her room and saw how weak and down-hearted she looked. She was a real trooper, though, like she always had been, and at the end of my visit she brightened up and said: 'Always keep your sense of humor, Jonathan, because you're going to need it!'

"That's what she always used to say to me when I was a kid, so it completely cracked both of us up. As I was leaving her room, I did a little can-can dance for her just as I went through the door, and when I looked back at her she was laughing her head off and happily waving good-bye to me. I was filled with joy. It was the last time I saw her.

"My mother was the love of my life and my best friend, and I miss her every day."

SEVENTEEN

When I arrived at his place for our interviews, Jake was always bright and sunny and raring to go, but this time he was kind of holding back, like something was on his mind, so I asked him what was up.

"You have correctly deduced, my friend," he said, "that something is bothering the hell out of me and I need to get it straightened out before we can proceed."

"Okay," I said, "let's have it."

TURNING IN HIS HELL'S ANGELS COLORS

"When I read the last installment of our little story in the current issue of the *Bollard* magazine, it seemed to me that some of my Hell's Angels brothers might get the impression that I represented myself as a member of the Hell's Angels when I was hiding out in Ward, Colorado, and later when I was at Lewisburg Penitentiary, and I want to assure them that that was absolutely not the case. Whenever anyone asked about the Hell's Angels, I'd always say the same thing I do today, which is that I'm proud to be a *former* member of the most exclusive club on the planet – the Hell's Angels Motorcycle Club! Hell's Angels forever!

"I ceased to be an active, dues-paying member of the Hell's Angel in the summer of 1968, when I was paroled from San Quentin and returned home to Portland. Because of the conditions of my parole from San Quentin, I couldn't go down to the Lowell, Massachusetts, chapter of the club and attend meetings on a regular basis, and neither could I go on the required number of motorcycle runs with my brothers. So, out of respect for the club, there was nothing left for me to do but resign my active membership and stop wearing my colors. Shortly after my return home, I neatly folded my colors from the Hell's Angels Nomads and put them in the safe at the Eddie Griffin Club, in South Portland, along with a letter saying that, in the event of my demise, the colors should be returned to the president of the Hell's Angels Motorcycle Club, Oakland, California.

"I did not wear my colors after I got back to Maine, out of respect for the club. When I found the Hell's Angels, I found my true family. I looked up to Sonny Barger as the strong father figure I never had, and when I met my other Hell's Angels brothers I finally found what it was like to be treated with respect just for being who I am, but I never tried to be like anyone, not even them."

"Okay, Jake," I said. "I assumed that your intention was to become an active member of the Hell's Angels again after you got paroled from San Quentin, so how come that didn't happen?"

"Sometimes you ask too many questions!" he roared.

I didn't even look up from my notebook, and he sat there across from me fuming for a while, as if he was deciding whether or not he was going to give me any kind of an answer, then he took a deep breath and blurted it all out.

"Would you believe I was too much of a fucking wild man for even the Hell's Angels?! My brothers loved me as much as I loved them, but I was bringing unwanted attention to the club! Always getting arrested for this and that, getting in scraps with bikers from other clubs you know, that kind of thing.

"Damn! I was everything my Hell's Angels brothers could have wanted in a member! I was intensely loyal, I loved to fight, and I was a highly skilled motorcycle rider who knew every friggin' thing there is to know about motorcycles. Hey, I led the suicide charge into the house of some enemies of the club even though I was against the plan from the very beginning! And please keep in mind that, to my knowledge, I might have become a patch-holding member after maybe the shortest time spent as a prospect in the history of the club! I didn't have to go through the months and sometimes years of initiation that other prospects did! But as it turned out, I was just too fucking hot to handle! Even for the Hell's Angels! I couldn't stay out of trouble, so I was useless to them!

"I told you about all the criminally insane shit I did around Portland immediately after I got out of San Quentin. Having public sex with willing females on numerous occasions, busting up bars just for the hell of it, not to mention running a stolen car ring and managing an extensive marijuana distribution network. And law enforcement was already enraged about me being paroled from San Quentin after only two years, when they thought they had me for life. The FBI was so pissed off that they couldn't get anything on me that they started bringing heat down on my Hell's Angels brothers way over in California about the things I was doing in Portland, and I wasn't even wearing my colors.

"After I got off parole I contacted the president of the Hell's Angels, who at the time was, of course, my brother Sonny Barger, about renewing my membership, and I know it hurt him to do it, but he told me that renewing my membership just wasn't going to happen, he said that my behavior was causing heat to come down on the club, and that I had to turn my Hell's Angel colors in to the Lowell chapter of the club at my earliest opportunity. That was like a drop-kick to the friggin' chest, of course, but I immediately complied. Coming from my brother Sonny, I took it as my duty. I immediately got my colors out of Eddie's safe and brought it down to Lowell and turned them in. Whatever Sonny says is not to be questioned in any way, and I would never ever consider doing so. He is the greatest leader of men who ever existed, and I've always been proud to have him as my brother.

"There is one thing that I want to make clear, though, and that is that I have never been voted out as a member of the Hell's Angels Motorcycle Club. Sonny, being the good friend and fine gentleman that he is, allowed me to turn in my colors on my own and to assume inactive status in the club, which has always meant a great deal to me."

After just about having me write in my blood on his living room wall that the above clarification of his relationship with the Hell's Angels would appear in the book, Jake seemed satisfied and ready to move on.

Right, Jake," I said, "now that we've got that settled, let's get to what happened after you got paroled from Lewisburg Federal Penitentiary in 1980, when you were forty-two years old. I assume you had calmed down a bit from the time you were thirty and got paroled from San Quentin, huh?"

"Well," he said, "you assume correctly, my friend. I wouldn't say I calmed down to the pace of say, a normal human being, but I was definitely not the rampaging whatever the hell I was ten years before. I did occasionally practice the discounted used auto sales business technique I had perfected over the years, and

JAKE

I might have been known to sell a little pot here and there – I've always been a dedicated caregiver – but my life was fairly calm overall and my activities were up-front for the most part.

"As soon as I hit town, I checked in at Martin's Health Club, of course, and connected with my old training buddies. No matter whatever else was going on in my life, working out and training others in the fine art of physical fitness has always been my calling, whether I was in jail or not, and before long I was back working at Martin's Health Club with as much shazam as ever and business was booming."

THE STATE OF MAINE TUG-OF-WAR
CHAMPIONSHIPS

"Some of the most valued friends I've ever had in my life are guys I worked out with and trained at Martin's Health Club: Al Martin, Ronnie Damon, Bob Penney, Sonny Day, Bruce Chambers, and Steve Sawtelle. So right off, life was grand for me at that time, since being in the company of men I respect and admire has always been a prerequisite of a satisfying life for me.

"I can't resist telling you a little story involving those guys that still makes me smile when I think about it. The State of Maine tug-of-war championships for the year 1980 were being held that summer on the sands of Old Orchard Beach, and the guys at Martin's Health Club were all excited about putting together a team. They were absolutely certain that no team in the state would stand a chance against them. They gave a great deal of thought as to who from the club would be on their team, and I assumed I would be the lead puller, of course, but they ended up not even putting me on the team! The reason for that, they told me, was that they thought I was too light, and didn't have the muscle power in my legs they wanted!

"Ha! They kind of forgot, I guess, that I had won the runner-up trophy for the East Coast Arm Wrestling Championship two years in a row not all that long ago, even though I was the lightest guy in the competition, thereby putting to rest any question concerning the effect of my relatively light stature might have had on my performance. But some people have to be shown the same thing over and over until they finally get it, I guess.

"Instead of going off pouting in a corner by myself at having been disrespected, snubbed and doubted, I went on a mission from hell to assemble my own tug-of-war team, with me as the lead puller. I rounded up some very rugged individuals to be on my team, believe me. This one guy named Frank could wrap his arms around a V-8 engine and place it on a work bench by himself, and my pal Crazy Red was in the habit of hauling lobster traps out of the ocean for hours at a time without the use of a trap pulley. When you've been pulling that much weight up from deep in the Atlantic Ocean with muscle power alone for as long as he had been doing, you're not worried about a little tug-of war.

"Our team sponsor was Eight Corner's Market, in Scarborough. We used to practice in the large parking lot behind the store by tying the end of a very strong rope onto the rear-end of a jeep and impeding its forward progress after Jane, the very attractive lady driver and team member, stepped on the gas. Jane said she got the speedometer up to 80 miles per hour before she could budge us!

JAKE

*The Eight Corners Market tug-of-war team,
with Jake at bottom, center.*

"Oh, yeah, when the competition took place, Andela
Ronan was on our tug-of-war team too. The rules
specified that the teams had to be made up of eight
men and one woman, and I went out of my way to find
an attractive woman for our team. The hell with looking around for a rugged one. Inspiration is key, you
know? Anyway, I had a few other guys built along the
lines of those two brutes I mentioned, along with me
pulling for all I was worth and providing a great deal
of vocal encouragement.

"Anyway, the good news is that we ended up dragging my buddies from Martin's Health Club along the
pearly white sands of Old Orchard Beach for a fairly
easy win.

"My team won every match we competed in and won
the trophy, and Martin's Health Club finished second.
It was billed as the State of Maine Championships, but
tug-of-war teams had traveled to Old Orchard Beach

from all over New England for the competition and both Martin's Health Club and my team beat them all. Actually, Eight Corners Market won the tug-of-war championship the next year too. In fact, we didn't lose a match over the two years we competed, ever, to any team. We retired undefeated.

"I was proud of my team, but I was proud of my friends from Martin's Health club, too. Oh, how I enjoyed displaying that trophy at Martin's Health Club, though!

"After the tug-of-war championships, Bob Penney, who later became Mr. Maine, and is still one of my closest friends today, talked me into taking part in the Maine State Arm Wrestling Championship competition that was held in 1982 at the University of Maine in Portland, and I won my weight class hands down, so to speak – even though I was the oldest guy in the competition! I was forty-six years old and I put those twenty and thirty-somethings down like they were babies!

"Of course, it wasn't just a matter of brute strength. Although I still had a good deal of that, it was more a matter of one-hundred per-cent friggin' resolve. The scenario was the same as when I competed in the East Coast Arm Wrestling Championships ten years earlier. The other entrants looked at it as a friendly competition, but I looked at it as an all-or-nothing fight to the friggin' death. When the judge lifted his hand off our fists and yelled 'Go!' I instantaneously turned into an enraged beast and their arm was half-way down before they fully realized we had gotten started. Oh, I guess it wasn't always that easy, you know, I was getting a little older, but I never did happen to get beat, and they did give the trophy to me, so I guess I did quite well, all considered."

JAKE

"Gee, Jake," I said. "All that athletic completion sounds pretty wholesome compared to the things you were doing before you went to Lewisburg. So, I guess you had turned over a new leaf, huh?"

"Yeah, right, and the moon stopped coming up over Casco Bay about that time, too," he said, to his great amusement.

"Oh, I did try to stay out of trouble, I really did," he said, growing serious again. "Going off to one house of correction or another now and then was getting a little old. I was involved in doing some petty shit that I shouldn't have gotten into, though. I just couldn't entirely stifle my base instincts, you know, and my parole officer became very concerned that he might have to revoke my parole. My parole officer was Bill McGlaughlin, and we became good friends, actually. Bill was always very fair with me, and I appreciate all he did for me.

"This might be a good time to talk about how I have always felt about the police and about law enforcement in general.

"I have been a pain in the ass to those in the legal system all of my life. I'm sure that the majority of police personnel think I'm a scumbag, and I don't blame them. But, you know what? I know beyond a doubt that anyone of them would put their life on the line to save my crazy ass if that's what it came down to, like they would for any other citizen. I absolutely cannot think badly about people who are that full of character and are that friggin' brave!

"Another thing: I know I've deserved every day I've been incarcerated, mainly because I was always guilty as charged.

"And here's something else: every young person out there has to know that if they fuck up and get sent to prison, they are likely to suffer a great deal in many different ways, including getting raped, beaten, and raped and beaten again. Prison is pure hell, so don't get misled by any of the rosy stories I tell. I was trying to make the best of an extremely bad situation."

THE WAY MINISTRY SOFTBALL TEAM

"This was around the time that I was asked by a good friend to be the coach of The Way Ministry softball team, and it ended up being one of the most rewarding experiences of my life. Softball can be a highly invigorating and highly competitive game, of course, and the level of competition in the statewide church softball league is very high. Just because they led their lives according to religious principles didn't mean that they weren't one-hundred percent intent on beating another bunch of religious guys from other churches.

"We had a very wide range of talent on our team, from star athletes from local high schools and colleges to mentally challenged people, and I made absolutely sure that everyone got equal playing time. Some of the other teams kept their less able players sitting on the bench for most of the game, but I put them in the line-up right from the first inning. I'd put someone with less ability in center field, for instance, and put two of the more capable players in left and right, where they could cover for the center fielder.

"The team spirit and camaraderie that developed on the team made us a powerhouse of a team, and we ended up winning the state championship! Some of the other teams had more overall talent, but we were one for all, all for one, all the way, and we'd usually end up winning by one way or another, just because we were so into playing together as a team. What you have to understand is that the mentally challenged people on the team had been routinely excluded from this and that activity throughout their lives. Many of them experienced their first moment of victory on the Way Ministry softball team. I can still see the delight on their faces today, and I have no doubt that the memories of our wonderful summer together have stayed with them all of their lives.

"I, of course, had been an outsider my whole life, so I've always been able to relate very strongly to mentally challenged people, or to anyone who has something different about them. When some of the more talented people on the team came up to me after we won the league championship, and said that The Way Ministry softball team had been the best sports experience of their lives, I actually got a little misty-eyed, my friend."

The Way Ministry softball team with manager Jake Sawyer, far left, posing with their 1983 Championship trophy.

JAKE

A QUARTER MILLION CASH OFFER

"Not long after my parole from Lewisburg, at a time when I was trying to get re-established in civilian life and was very low on funds, my parole officer made me an offer that would have solved all of my problems very nicely if I had accepted it. All I had to do, Bill said, was to give the feds a little information concerning the whereabouts of some political activist friends of mine who had allegedly bombed a federal building or two here and there, and as a way of saying thank you for helping my country, the feds would grease my palm with $250,000 cash!

"'They just don't get it!' I screamed at Bill. 'They fucking tortured me at Lewisburg to give them the name of the guy I sold the pot to, and I wouldn't give it to them even though I hardly knew the guy! Now they think they can run a quarter of a million dollars under my nose and I'll rat out my friends?! I told Bill to tell them to shove their quarter million dollars up their friggin' assess!'

"Bill knew when he made me the offer, of course, what my answer would be. He was just passing on the message, and I understood that. I also understood that turning down their offer would most likely result in my parole being revoked sometime in the near future, but Bill said he might have a way of making that not happen, if I was willing to go along with a plan he had come up with."

VOLUME TWO

THE TOGUS VETERANS HOSPITAL PSYCHE WARD

"'Jake,' Bill said, 'would you entertain the thought of being committed to the psych ward at the Veteran's Hospital up in Togus, Maine, for a ninety-day treatment and evaluation period, after which time we would reevaluate the need to revoke your parole?

"Damn! Bill thought I'd be offended by the very idea of going to the VA nuthouse, but I loved the idea! It was a lot better than going to prison, and I had always enjoyed the company of odd characters and I ate psychiatrists for breakfast! Bring on the loony bin! Here we go! I set out for Togus in my 1950, chopped flat black Merc, smiling like a lunatic all the way!

"So there I was in the psychiatric ward at Togus, which ironically is just a pleasant thirty-minute drive from Kents Hill prep school, where I had been an honor student and star athlete in what seemed like the not so very distant past. Oh, my, what a long strange journey I've been on, my friend."

"Yep," I said, without looking up from my notebook.

"The scene on the psych ward was very much to my liking, actually," Jake continued. "There was always soft music floating out of the ceiling, and I got to like the bright and shiny floors, and the warm sun that was always streaming through the windows. But I what I enjoyed most of all was the company of my fellow fruitcakes. Except for when I was with my Hell's Angels brothers, I had never felt such warmth and all-around goodwill. My new buddies were a lot of fun, too. What I looked forward to most was playing poker for pills. We'd get all medicated up and have a hell of lot of fun imagining we were playing for millions in Las Vegas. We were very content until it was time for our next dose, which, of course, had been the attending staff's plan all along.

"The meds were the kick in the ass about the place, though. They had us line up four times a day for our fixes, and by the end of the first month I was dragging myself around the place like a friggin' zombie. Most of the time I didn't know if I was looking out the window at the pretty trees or playing fantasy poker.

"The shrinks were a real hoot too. I agreed my way through all of my therapy sessions. I couldn't have been more agreeable, actually. The meds took the edge off my volatile personality, and the charming self that I had suppressed for so long emerged in a most appealing way. Everybody loved me. The doctors, the nurses, and all the other zombies thought I was the greatest. They would have elected me King Nut of the whole joint if I was interested. For the first time in my life, though, that kind of thing didn't mean a thing to me. I guess the drugs took away my competitive edge and my usual need to dominate other men in any way I could.

"At the end of my ninety days, it was determined that my commitment had been a complete success and I was released to the custody of my parole officer. My friend Bill was overwhelmed by the change in me.

"Well, Jake," he said when I walked meekly into his office for our first get-together after my release, "from all the reports I've had from Togus, you're a changed man and we can forget about revoking your parole."

"Thank you, Bill," I answered. "I feel so rested and am experiencing such inner peace that all I want to do is live a quiet, happy and productive life from now on.

"Well, the quiet, happy, productive life idea lasted for about as long as the time it took me to get from his office to the nearest toilet, where I could flush down my take-home meds.

"Fuck 'em! Society had been trying to subdue me by various means all of my life and the chemical route wasn't going to work any more than anything else had. The point everyone had always missed is that I'm not the fucked up one, they are. They can have their half-lived lives of quiet desperation, I said to myself as the last of my meds gurgled down the toilet. I'd lived every minute of my life right straight friggin' out, goin' for the gusto every minute of every day, and nothing was going to change that about me in any way, least of all a handful of zombie pills every day.

"The next time I reported to Bill I stepped into his office and said: 'Howdy, Bill! How the hell are ya?!' and he said: 'Oh, no ...' He knew damn well I was back to being who I always was, and that it was just a matter of waiting to see what kind of trouble I was going to get into next.

"Actually, though, I managed to stay out of trouble for a considerable length of time after my release from the funny farm. I didn't exactly operate on the good side of the law at all times, you know, but I did manage to avoid the extreme behaviors that had gotten me into so much trouble in the past."

Well, what do you know, we all mellow a bit with age, and apparently Jake's no exception, I thought.

THE COURTROOM EXTERMINATOR

"Everything was sailing along just fine, until one morning I read in the newspaper that a guy named Joey Aceto, who I had done time with, was going to be testifying that day in federal court against a friend of mine who was on trial for bank robbery. You know, of course, how much I hate rats, so, before I even knew what I was doing, I had put on my leather motorcycle jacket and pulled on my boots and was on my Harley cruising down to the Federal Street courthouse to attend the trial. I didn't know what I was going to do there, but I hoped it wouldn't be much, really, because I absolutely did not want to go back to prison. Way down deep I was seriously itching to do something, though. I could tell by the way I was dressed and the way I was revving my engine as I motored down the street, I guess. Somehow, it felt like old times.

"Joey Aceto was on the stand testifying when I walked into the courtroom, and there were armed officers of the law stationed about ten feet apart from one another all around the courtroom. I knew right away that they were anticipating trouble from me when everyone's eyes turned towards the door as my boots hit the floor, boom, boom, one after the other. Aceto stopped testifying and just sat there staring at me like everyone else was. After the judge brought the court back to order by clearing his throat – he didn't want to acknowledge the effect my arrival had on his courtroom by using his gavel, of course – the officers all gave me their best tough cop steely-eyed look, like, try anything Sawyer and you're dog meat.

"I went out of my way to appear peaceful and non-threatening, though. Truthfully, I was still hoping that I'd get out of this fairly cheaply. I knew I was going to do something, of course, but maybe it would just be something like yelling out something about Joey Aceto being a lying fucking rat who will definitely be exterminated soon, and just leave it at that. They'll probably give me thirty days in the County lock-up for it, or something like that, I was thinking, but it would be worth it.

"Rather than take a seat up front, which would have alarmed everybody, I sat somewhere in the middle of the courtroom among the other observers, because being in the midst of innocent bystanders has always been a strong deterrent to extreme behaviors on my part.

"As I sat there listening to Aceto spill his fucking rat guts about the activities of my friend Lex, though, an uncontrollable rage built up in me more and more with every word he spoke, then: 'Arrrggg!' I was on my feet roaring!

"Aceto screamed and fell over backwards in his chair!

"I found myself out in the aisle headed for him, and he was screaming in fear and scrambling on the floor, trying to escape.

"Before I could get very far, a half dozen or so cops tackled me and threw cuffs on me and proceeded to haul me away with my toes dragging on the floor.

"They had closed the heavy mahogany doors of the courtroom after I arrived, and when we got to them the officers of the law used my head as a battering ram to swing them open. Without much further ado we were on our merry way down the courthouse hallway, with the eyes of the notable judges and assorted dignitaries who were pictured on the courthouse walls following us all the way. Then, after our little trek down the hallway, there we went, kerplunk, kerplunk, down a very hard wood staircase to a holding cell in the basement, into which they tossed me in a most ungentle manner.

"So, there I was, in a friggin' cell again. I should have been bummed out, considering how hard I had been trying to be good, but the first thing I did was sit on the edge of the cot chuckling to myself. Why, I'm not exactly sure, but the whole thing tickled the hell out of me for some reason. Maybe because I had sort of watched myself do what I had done, rather than consciously making a decision to do it, or something like that, you know what I mean?"

"Sure, I know what you mean, Jake," I said. "Sure I do, sure I do, I guess."

THE NEW YORK CITY METROPOLITAN CORRECTIONAL CENTER

"After I had been in the holding cell for about forty-five minutes, the same crew of police officers who had escorted me out of the courtroom reappeared and told me that the judge had expressed the desire to see me, and would I please accompany them in a civil manner. I complied, because by that time I had calmed down quite a bit, but when we got to the courtroom I realized that I should have made a run for it after all. After the commotion I had caused, the judge had been forced to clear the courtroom and cancel court for the entire day, and he was not at all happy with me. I think I'd describe his mood as one of seething fury, now that I think of it, and it was very clear to me that he was determined that I was going to pay big time for what I had done.

"The judge gave me what throughout the U.S. penal system is called '90 Days in Hell.' That would be three months in the Manhattan Metropolitan Correctional Center, which was, and still is, not only the most secure, but also the most gruesome correctional facility in the country. Damn, I would wake up in the middle of the night with bedbugs all over me!

"Just to give you an idea of how secure MCC is, consider that El Chapo, the top boss of the Mexican drug smuggling cartel, was held there after his extradition to this country, after having escaped from a maximum security Mexican prison through a mile long tunnel out of the prison his people had dug.

"There's no way El Chapo, or anyone else, was ever going to escape from MCC, though. You are in an eleven story Manhattan skyscraper, and not only is the place extremely secure, it's also exceedingly confining and utterly lacking in any degree of privacy. You are constantly under strict surveillance.

"There were some pretty big fish at MCC when I was there. If anyone is known to have extensive outside connections, MCC is where they put you on ice. It was a common thing to look out the windows and see mafia bosses being shuffled into waiting limousines after being released on bail.

"There was no escaping from the place, that was for damn sure, but it didn't prevent a couple of guys from trying. They were looking at life in prison and had nothing to lose. It was a classic prison escape plan, and I witnessed the whole thing. They threw a chair through a thick Plexiglas window on the seventh floor, then tied a great number of sheets together and lowered them out the window, with the intention of shinnying down to the sidewalk. The chances that they wouldn't be detected were non-existent, of course, but when you're that desperate, you do desperate things.

"First, I saw the string of sheets being lowered out the window, then a skinny guy appeared and threw his leg over the sill. I couldn't believe what I was seeing. I watched as he shinnied his way down the side of the building hanging onto the sheets, and I thought he was going to lose his grip because he was so weak and skinny.

"It actually looked like he was going to make it, and I was cheering for him, but then a fat guy appeared at the window and threw his leg out onto the ledge. When he did that the skinny guy yelled for him to get back in and wait, but the fat guy had obviously lost his patience, and was going for it. He kind of rolled out the window and grabbed onto the sheets, but he wasn't quite as successful at the venture as the skinny guy was. He managed to make about one floor down before the string of sheets broke loose from the window and he went plummeting down the side of the building. The skinny guy hit the sidewalk an instant before the fat guy did, and then, splat!, the fat guy landed on top of him. What a sight that was! I'm sure there are passersby who have nightmares about it to this very day. That's life in the big city, I guess.

"So, there I was, wasting away in the penthouse in the sky that was called Manhattan Metropolitan Correctional Center, when one fine day my keepers rousted me from my reverie and told me I was free to go. That surprised the hell out of me, because my release date was still a number of weeks away, but the system had made a mistake, and I was being released to go back to Maine way early. I didn't feel that it was up to me to set them straight, of course. I mean, who would? As soon as I was out the door, I started running like hell down the street, headed for the airport, paid the People's Express fare of $19 at Newark Airport, and by that afternoon I was back home in Portland, keeping a very low profile.

"I took a job at my pal Craig Johnson's bait company down on the Portland waterfront and pretty much minded my own business and all was well until, one day months later, the foreman told me that there were three shiny-shoe guys in the office who wished to speak to me. I knew running was pointless, and resisting might have reflected badly on my employer for harboring me, so I went to the office and greeted them wearing a big smile, with my wrists together, ready for the prison bracelets I knew at least one of them had hanging out of his back pocket."

Jake working on the Portland waterfront in the mid-1980s, trying to keep a low profile after his unexpected early release from Manhattan Metropolitan Correctional Center.

JAKE

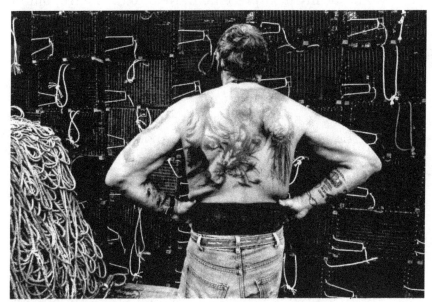

Jake displaying his tattooed back, facing piled lobster traps down on the Portland waterfront, while on the run again in 1984 for a while.

MOON AND HALF MOON

VOLUME TWO

"Next stop, Danbury Federal Prison, in Danbury, Connecticut, for a few weeks stay on the way to what would be my next placement. Next to the Metropolitan Correctional Center facility, Danbury was like a day care center. During my short stay there, I started a weight-lifting program for the benefit of the prison population, the way I have at the various houses of incarceration I've spent time at throughout my life, no matter how short my stay there was.

"The most interesting thing about my stay at Danbury, actually, was that Reverend Moon, of the Unification Church, was there at the time for income tax evasion. He was considered to be the Messiah by his followers, so he didn't mix too much with the prison population, and spent his time with his Korean right-hand man, who we all called 'Half Moon.' I did manage to rattle Reverend Moon's cage now and then, though. I'd say all kinds of wild shit to him and he'd chuckle like a little Buddha or something. I tried to get him to tell his followers that if they believed in him, they should overwhelm the place and free us all. He told me that it was just a matter of time before he took over the world anyway, though, so why bother? I couldn't help but admire the man's positive attitude.

"After Danbury, my home for a year was Ray Brook Federal Penitentiary, in upstate New York. Ray Brook was a piece of cake as well, after the hell holes I had been in. I like to think that the weight-lifting program I started there lifted the spirits of my fellow inmates considerably and set many of them on the road to a more socially responsible life. One does what they can, whenever and wherever they can, you know?"

*Jake, at left, with weightlifting pals inside
the federal prison at Ray Brook, New York.*

EIGHTEEN

On my way to Jake's this time I was smiling to myself thinking about the time earlier when we met at the top of the parking garage and it occurred to me that I might like to try it again. The view we had of the Western Mountain range up there seemed to get his spirit soaring, and I was also curious to see whether our friend the imperious seagull might visit us again.

When I suggested the idea to Jake he was all for it, like he is most things. Truthfully, the whole idea of meeting in places that might inspire him was kind of pointless, anyway, because, no matter where we met, he was always raring to go.

"It actually turns out very well, my friend, that we'll be meeting up here today because it gives us a good view of the location we're going to be talking about. Right over there to the right," he said when we got there and were sitting in his van, pointing across Back Cove to the East Deering section of Portland, "is where a very lucrative enterprise of mine was located for four years, from 1985 to 1989."

JAKE'S AUTO SALES

"When I was released from Ray Brook Federal Penitentiary and returned home, one of the first things I did was open Jake's Auto Sales over in East Deering. Jake's Auto Sales could have been the most honest long-term activity I've been involved with in my entire life. Everything about the business was legitimate and aboveboard. Contrary to what you might be thinking, I didn't deal in stolen vehicles or do anything else of that nature.

JAKE

"Not only was everything about Jake's Auto Sales legitimate, but I also had the great satisfaction of being able to set many worthy people up with safe and reliable transportation at a very low cost. I've never done anything just for the money, and the used car business was no exception. I treated everyone who came through my door as if they were friends of mine. Before long, it got to be quite a status symbol in certain quarters to have that distinctive red and white Jake's Auto Sales bumper sticker on your car.

"The story of how Jake's Auto Sales came to be is the most interesting part, though. It's one of those Portland stories that happen just because of where the city is on the map, and how appealing it is in so many respects. It's also about whatever it is about Portland that produces bizarre individuals like me who attract bizarre people from other places. This is the story of one of those people, and the major part he played in the saga of Jake's Auto Sales.

"A lot of Portland people will remember when a man named John Coffin came to town in the mid-1980s and made a hell of a splash in many different ways. He was about sixty-five years old at the time, and was still filled with piss and vinegar, after having lived an amazing life up to that time.

"John was a big, happy-go-lucky guy who had been a stand-out student and athlete in high school and college, then joined the Army when the Korean War broke out and saw a lot of heavy action before being captured and spending the last year of the war in a North Korean P.O.W. camp. Nothing I, or just about anyone else who's ever lived, went through was half as bad as what he went through. He told me he went from 240 pounds when he was captured, to 152 pounds when he was liberated. He was all skin and bones and could hardly drag himself around. He said he saw and experienced indescribable brutality, but the worst part of it all was spending a year listening to his captors tell him that they were winning the war and that he'd never be released. He knew that could never be true, but after having the same lie hurled at him for so long, it became difficult to hang on to any kind of hope. His love of life and his will to survive got him through all the physical and mental torture, though. He told me that there were times when he didn't know whether he was dead or alive, but then came the day when a group of American GI's came busting into the camp. After having gone through a kind of fucking hell that the rest of us can only imagine, it was over.

John Coffin, multimillionaire and former
P.O.W. in North Korea.

JAKE

"After his discharge, John returned home to Marblehead, Massachusetts, where he married his high school sweetheart and made a huge fortune rehabbing and selling high-end ocean-front properties, so life was good. There was an unsettled, angry and resentful side to him, though. When a person has seen and experienced what he had, they have a tendency to scoff at the ritzy lives they saw people around them leading. So, one fine day, John pretty much flipped off Marblehead, Massachusetts, and did a belly-flop onto Portland, Maine, which he had discovered on a week-end excursion and become intrigued by. He liked the combination of small-town grittiness and urban bustle, he said.

"We're talking a huge, barrel-chested, brash-talking, show-off multi-millionaire looking to make a big impression. Look out, Portland. The first thing he did was buy a business block on the waterfront that included the Commercial Street Tavern, so he'd have a place to hold court. Then he started acquiring more neighboring properties, just so he could stand in his bar and point out buildings he had acquired or was in the process of acquiring.

"Basically, John was having fun ramming it up society's ass, just like yours truly has been known to do from time to time. He rode around town in a big white Cadillac convertible, wearing an Australian bush hat, with a brightly colored silk scarf around his neck. The topper, though, was the silly-looking inflatable dummy sitting across from him on the passenger's side. He was putting on quite a show even before we paired up, but when we did, look the hell out!

"When two loud-talking tough guys meet, they usually either become fight-to-the-death enemies or very tight buddies, and the latter is what ended up happening with John and me. I was in the Commercial Street Pub one night mouthing off about something or other (surprise, surprise), and he yelled out that if I didn't shut my trap he was going to take me outside and beat the fuck out of me. Of course, that put a big smile on my face, even though I could see that he obviously knew how to handle himself and weighed well over 250 pounds.

"I took him up on his challenge, of course, and when we got outside I planted myself in front of him and jutted my jaw out and told him that, in consideration of his advanced age, I'd give him the first punch, but that he should turn and run after that because if he didn't I was going to fuck him up so bad that from then on there would be two friggin' brain-dead dummies riding around in that car of his.

"That cracked him up big time, of course, because he wasn't used to being challenged in any way, so after we traded loud insults back and forth for a while, laughing our guts out all through it, we went back in and spent the night drinking together. High alert time, Portland, it's the duo from Hell.

"John just loved being seen around town with me. We spent our time riding around in his car, with the dummy in the back seat, dreaming up what crazy-assed thing we were going to do next. He had money up the ying-yang, and we were both exploding with energy, enthusiasm, and a deep-seated need to raise hell, so here we go.

"Okay, here's the picture: there I was, fresh out of prison, back in Portland once again, broke as a bastard, riding around town in a new Cadillac convertible with a guy who was easily the most eccentric multi-millionaire in the entire country, with him offering to set me up in any kind of business venture or anything else I wanted to get into, the more bizarre the better.

"When I told him about my long experience in the hot car business, and how my activities in that area had led to fundamental changes in the State of Maine used car title law, that did it. Setting up the universally recognized all-time Grand Theft Auto King in the used car business rang his chimes big time. Then, there it was. One afternoon on one of our joy rides around town we spotted a small office build-ing with all kinds of parking space surrounding it, sitting on the corner of Washington Avenue and Veranda Street, and Jake's Auto Sales was born.

"I wanted the name of the enterprise to be East End Auto Sales, because I knew what the reaction of the police and general public would be to a used car business associated with me in any way, but John wouldn't have it. His whole motivation, after all, was to shove it up society's ass in any way he could, so he absolutely insisted that the name be Jake's Auto Sales. I had all I could do to talk him out of keeping my last name out of it.

"Oh, we had a real show going all the way, banners strung across the lot, all that, but the topper was the beautiful '68 two-tone green Chevy convertible we had sitting on the cor-ner out front, with a six-foot tall electrically powered me-chanical gorilla standing up on the front seat waving the people in. The first thing I'd do when people came in was walk up to them and get them excited about having their picture taken sitting in the driver's seat next to the gorilla, and once they were behind the wheel and we got to talking about cars, they were mine.

"Like I said before, the great thing about Jake's Auto Sales was that I was able to set a lot of people up with a nice car who would never have had any kind of ride otherwise. The truth of the matter, though, is that it was John's gener-osity and good will that made it all possible. He didn't give a damn whether or not we made money, his whole thing was comforting the afflicted while confounding the comfortable, or something like that.

"The other used car lots around town didn't like the fact the Jake's Auto Sales was giving people tremendous deals that they couldn't come near to matching, of course. They were all saying that I was selling hot cars, but they were dead wrong. We had proper documentation for every car we sold. The story was that a lot of the cars that we sold were ones that John bought from the dealers themselves on the up and up and brought to Jake's Auto Sales for resale. He got off on acquiring a car from a dealer, then selling it to a deserving member of the public for far less than what he paid the dealer for it. The dealers were stymied because, on the one hand, they liked it when John bought one of their cars, of course, but after a while the buying public knew that if they liked a car they saw on a lot anywhere in town, all they had to do was wait a while and it would show up on Jake's Auto Sales lot with a lower sticker price on it. John even took orders from friends of ours now and then. They'd see a car on some used car lot they liked, tell John or me about it, and there you go. John's methods weren't exactly the way business is usually done, we lost money just about every time we sold a car, actually, but we both enjoyed the hell out of upsetting our competitors and making the police and assorted city officials wonder what the hell we were up to.

"As a 100% American and a highly-decorated veteran himself, John was particularly eager to help down-and-out veterans anyway he could, and his generosity extended to more than just ensuring that they acquired the vehicle of their dreams. One of us would read in the paper that a veteran had died, for instance, and if there was no mention of a funeral, we'd contact the family and pay for a nice funeral. The personnel at the various funeral homes around town loved having me walk into their office and handing them a fat check and, of course, the families of the deceased were very grateful. Sad to say, three of the veterans we helped had committed suicide, so their families were very grateful that they would be buried with dignity in spite of their troubled lives.

"Jake's Auto Sales was kept under very close scrutiny by the police, of course, because I was a notorious car thief and four-time convicted felon, who was currently on parole from federal prison, no less, operating a used car business in their city, and that frosted their asses big time. But they couldn't get anything on us. We kept the business operating from 1985 to 1989, had a lot of fun, and helped out a lot of deserving people.

"All good things must end, though, and Jake's Auto Sales was history when John decided to return to Marblehead and resume his former life, and I decided I missed being with my Hell's Angels brothers and decided to go down to Lowell and live with them for a while."

Jake and friends at Jake's Auto Sales in 1985.

VOLUME TWO

MY 1979 TWO-TONE GREEN PLYMOUTH FURY

I just had to tell Jake something at this point. I couldn't hold back. I knew he wouldn't remember me, but I was one of the 'deserving veterans' who acquired a car from Jake's Auto Sales. Jake set me up with an immaculate, two-tone green 1979 Plymouth Fury at a time when I needed a good car very badly and didn't have a lot of money to make it happen. I was drawn in by the mechanical gorilla, and the rest is history.

"I bought a car from Jake's Auto Sales, Jake," I told him.

"Great! Did you like it?!"

"It was one of the best cars I've ever owned," I said, looking up from my notebook. "You saw me hanging around the lot and came out and started to give me your sales pitch, but after you found out that I didn't have enough money to be choosy, you stuck with me anyway. I've always appreciated that."

"Is that why you agreed to help me write my life story?"

"Partly, at first, maybe," I said.

"So, Jake," I said, looking to get back to the task at hand, "you ran Jake's Auto Sales for about four years, from 1985 to 1989, from age forty-seven to fifty-one, so I assume that's about the time you started to gear your activities down a bit, huh? The ravages of time, all that, the years take their toll on all of us, even Jake Sawyer." I said it with a straight face, knowing all the while that I was rattling his cage, big time.

"Calm down?!" he boomed. "That was more than thirty years ago, man, and I'm still living right straight friggin' out, no questions asked, no quarter given, so, what the hell do you mean by asking if I calmed down when I hit my fifties?! Haven't you been paying attention at all?! Don't you know that I'm never going to calm down?! Hell, I'm going to go on being exactly who I am for as long as I'm still striding the surface of the friggin' planet!!"

JAKE

"Let's get on with it then!!" I yelled, thrusting my arm in the air the way he does.

"Right on!! Here we go!!" he yelled back, shooting his arm up, causing us both to sit there laughing our asses off at whatever it was that we were laughing our asses off at.

Jake posing in 1990 with his Harley in front of a farmhouse some-where in southern Maine that he rented for a few years to stash the huge amounts of marijuana he was bringing into the state in his Chevy Malibu after closing Jake's Auto Sales. There were times when the pot was piled up to the ceiling in every room of the house, he says.

Jake went to New York City at that time to pick up a large load of marijuana, and thought he'd take a ride on the Wall Street bull while he was there.

JAKE

YOUNG LOVE

"During the time I owned Jake's Auto Sales I was introduced to the training facilities at USM and began working out there regularly, and that's where I met Mary, who was the most beautiful yoga and modern dance instructor in the universe. We ended up having a long-term relationship in spite of her being in her late twenties, which should have been a little old for me, but she had weathered the years well, though, so I made an exception. Mary had such an incredible female presence that every man with any testosterone count at all immediately fell in love with her. It's not often that one encounters a graceful dancer with, ah, substantial frontage, my friend, so she drew a lot of looks. The way to handle that kind of over-crowded situation, of course, is to be the one who doesn't look. Well, you look, but you don't keep looking. As I've told you, we used to get 'starers' in the fitness studios I managed, and I used to enjoy leading them out the door by the ear.

"Anyway, the gorgeous lady could see that I was there to work out in a very serious and professional manner, and she respected that. I saw her glancing over at me a few times, though, so I went over and asked her what was up. She said she'd been waiting for me to come over and talk to her. I took that as very good news, and we started sitting under the apple tree together, you know?

"I can hardly believe it myself, to tell you the truth, but I was true to her all the time we were together, which was for about two years. I was still running around town like a madman on steroids, raising all kinds of hell, just the same as ever, but I was no longer having sex with any lifted skirt that happened along.

"Well, that's not quite the truth, you know how it is. I did kind of stray when I was down in Lowell visiting my Hell's

Angels brothers, but that wasn't about the sex, of course, that was just about doing whatever fucking outrageous thing that came to my mind to do. Getting it on with a camp follower isn't cheating on your old lady, it's just what you do when you're with your brothers. It's just kind of a ritual that goes with the territory."

"Okay, I forgive you, Jake," I said, "but, now that you mention the Hell's Angels, we haven't talked about what was going on with you and them for a while. What was up with them?"

JAKE AND THE LOWELL HELL'S ANGELS

When I found the Hell's Angels I found my true family, and there was no way I was not going to keep in close contact over the years, you know?

"When I got out of San Quentin and returned to Portland in 1968, I knew that my parole restrictions weren't going to allow me to attend club meetings down in Lowell on a regular basis, and that I also would not be able to ride with my brothers on the required number of club runs per year, so I stopped wearing my colors at that time.

"That *Hell's Angels, Nomads Chapter* patch meant more to me than anything else ever has in my entire life. I am a Hell's Angel to the core of my being and taking off my colors was like I was hacking part of my body off, but I knew what I had to do. To represent myself as a patch-holding member of the Hell's Angel when I wasn't any longer would have been disrespectful of my Hell's Angels brothers, and I'd rather die than have that happen.

"Taking off my colors didn't stop me from spending time with my Hell's Angels brothers down in Lowell, though. Having former members show up from time to time to party and raise hell along with everybody else for a day or two hap-pened sometimes. I did kind of take things to extremes though, I guess.

"I'd been ramming down the 295 South on my Harley to Lowell in the early morning hours on a fairly regular basis for a number of years, and had bonded big time with the patch-holding members down there. But once in a while I'd get some shit about former members not really being mem-bers and hanging around too much, and that's when I knew a fight was about to happen. Fights were no big deal, though. When we ran out of other people to fight we'd fight each other, that was expected.

"The problem wasn't just that I was not a patch-holding member any longer, it was also that I was a lightning rod for trouble. I'd go to some local bar down there and raise holy hell, maybe bust up the place and knock some heads, usu-ally both, and the next day it would be in the papers that the Hell's Angels were at it again. I never identified myself as a member of the Hell's Angels at that time, but somehow or other the connection was always made.

"One Monday morning as I was stradling my bike getting ready to pull out of the clubhouse parking lot to head back to Portland, Irish Red yelled after me that the whole club was very pissed at me over all the shit I'd been pulling and that I'd better stop coming around. I was going to get beat up real bad if they ever saw me again, he said. Irish Red was a big jolly guy with a bushy red beard that everybody liked and listened to, so I knew that what he had said to me was real serious business.

"The message that Irish Red had delivered to me didn't make my ride home to Portland very pleasant. Having your heart ripped out of you is not the best way to start your week off. So, after spending the next day in Portland absolutely obsessed about the matter, I returned to Lowell the following day and rapped on the clubhouse door. No answer. A bunch of bikes were parked outside, so I knew a number of my brothers were inside, so I yelled to them that one of their brothers was outside so would they please open the fucking door. Still no answer, but then Irish Red came to the door and glared at me, like he was very pissed off that I didn't get the message from before. Of course, I wasn't about to turn tail and head back to Portland at that point, so I looked straight into his face and said: 'I'm here for two reasons, man. The first is that I love you, and the second is that nobody fucking tells me where I can and can't go.'

"Irish Red just kind of snorted and chuckled, like he admired me for saying what I did, but then he shrugged his shoulders, like he didn't have a choice in the matter, and said that if I didn't leave he was going to have Franny come out and fuck me up so bad I'd be lucky if I could make it back to Portland.

"Franny was six-feet, nine-inches tall, weighed over three-hundred and fifty pounds, and made his living wrestling bears at carnivals and county fairs. To make matters worse, he was a Hell's Angels prospect, which meant that he would do anything, and in absolutely any manner, that any patch-holding member told him to do.

"I told Irish Red that I wasn't going anywhere, and he just grinned and went back inside. Then Franny kind of lumbered through the door and started walking towards me with a very concerned look on his face, while a few other brothers stood on the porch watching. Franny and I were tight buddies, so the whole thing was very awkward, but he had his orders, and we both understood that. When he got to me, I reared back and punched him between the eyes as hard as I could. I've knocked guys clear across a barroom floor with that punch, but Franny hardly moved, and proceeded to beat the friggin' shit out of me. After he had punched me around with his massive damn fists, he wrapped his arms around me and squeezed so hard I knew for sure he fractured at least two of my ribs. I thought it was over at that point because Franny once told me that the fight was over at the carnivals and county fairs when he broke the bear's ribs. When he heard that tell-tale crack he knew that their spirit was broken, he said. I wasn't going to give up as fast as the bears did, though, so after he heard my ribs crack and I didn't give up, he threw me down on the ground and jumped onto my stomach, ass first. Three-hundred and fifty pounds of Hell's Angels prospect, ass first, man! It felt like my guts were going to come gushing out of my mouth!

"That's when the real rough stuff started. He pounded away at my face and whatever else he could get at, screaming at me over and over to give up. When I yelled, 'The fucking bears are smarter than you are!' he grabbed my head and started pulling my hair out in bunches. Franny was sorry it all had to happen, though, he truly was. He knew I was only kidding about the bear being smarter than him too, but he had to do what he had to do, and I understood that.

"He kept asking me over and over, 'You had enough?! You had enough?!' The thing to understand here is that every man there standing around watching knew that giving up would mean that I could never hang out with my Hell's Angels brothers again. Hell, they'd shoot me on sight if I came back after I gave up in a fight. So, after Franny realized that I'd never give up, no matter what, he got off me and threw up his hands and yelled, 'Jake, I love ya, brother! You are one bad ass brave motherfucker!'

"That was nice, but then Irish Red stepped up and said that it didn't matter whether I gave up or not, that I was going to get the same treatment every time I showed up, so I might as well just get on my bike and get the hell out of there and never come back.

"'Fuck you!' I yelled, 'Any one of you other bad boys want to take me on right now?! I'm having a great time!!'

"They all just looked around at each other and started guffawing amongst themselves. Here I was, this fifty-year old desperado, all beat to fuck, staggering around, blood and snot all over me, asking for more. They went into a little huddle, then Irish Red looked over at me with a big smile and said, 'Jake, how would you like to attend a party with us at the Salem chapter's clubhouse?'

"I was all for it! I didn't even go inside and get cleaned up, I just swung my leg onto my bike and yelled, 'Let's go!'

"Being invited to go a party with the club didn't necessarily mean that I was back tight with the them, though. They were just having fun with me, and I knew that. I was intimately familiar with the lifestyle of the Hell's Angels, so I knew that parties in other chapters' clubhouses often entailed fights between the two chapters. I also knew very well that the hit of the evening would be for the Lowell chapter to bring along an old, beat-up, trying to hang on, former member like me along who was willing to take on anyone, no matter how big and tough they were, at any time, for any reason.

"Anyway, that party was the wildest free-for-all, friggin' drunken bash I'd been to since I partied with my Hell's Angels brothers out in Oakland more than twenty years before. Somewhere in the course of the evening, just to get things riled up, one of my brothers from the Lowell chapter introduced me in a loud voice as the current arm wrestling champion of Maine. Of course, he knew exactly what he was doing, and right-off a guy from the Salem chapter yelled, 'Maine?! What the fuck is that?! A place where old bikers go to die?!'

"Well, as you might expect, one thing led to another and the guy who had made the remark and I got into it pretty good shortly after our little exchange. I was still standing, though, and the Salem chapter wasn't going to leave it at that, not by any means. I had to fight three more of them, one at a time. I got my licks in each time, without a doubt, but I got pretty well beat up myself. Beat all to shit is a better way to put it, actually. Hey, we're talking guys who were twenty-five years younger than I was. I didn't give up at any time, though. I might have been an old fuck, but I was still one ferocious maniac who was not at all into losing.

"What you have to understand here is that when Hell's Angels fight among themselves there are certain rules that are followed. No eye gouging. No kicking in the balls. Stuff like that. So, I knew that if I kept fighting, I'd survive, and I did. All in all, I got the fuck beat out of me, but at the end of the night I was still friggin' standing, and that's all you can ask of a man.

"Let me say, at this point, that from the time of those incidents to the present time, I have enjoyed the company of my Hell's Angel's brother's, both down in Lowell, and when I've hosted some of them up here in Portland. I am made to feel very welcome whenever I visit the Lowell chapter for a day or two of hell raising. I have clearly illustrated to them, once and for all, that I was a Hell's Angel to the core of my being for as long as I might live. They knew about the suicide charge I led in California, and they saw me be willing to die before I'd give up having the Hell's Angels in my life, and that was enough for them.

LIVING IN LOWELL

"It could well also be, my friend, that I took my brothers' concern with my behavior somewhat to heart and started acting a little more civilized, I don't know. My ties to my Hell's Angels brothers got so close over the years, actually, that I moved down to Lowell for a while in the late 80s and lived with my brother, George Carouso, who is currently the president of the Lowell chapter. George owned a small construction company and he bought a house in Lowell that no one else wanted to own because the former owner was a gambler who had been shot to death in the living room. George didn't give a shit about that either way, of course, but I kind of liked the idea myself.

"The back yard was very large and there was a rumor that the gambler had buried a big bag of money in it somewhere, and I kind of turned George on to the idea of locating it. We started by using a metal detector and digging little holes all over the place, but when all we came up with was bottle caps, George brought in a front-end loader, and within a day or two there were deep cavernous holes all around the back yard, and when we didn't find what we were after there we dug up the front lawn too. We never did find that big bag of money, but we had a good time looking for it!"

Jake says Big Vinnie, from the New York City Hell's Angels, visited him many times. "Big Vinnie and I met at Laconia and found out we had a lot in common," said Jake. "The broads loved him! Figure that one out!

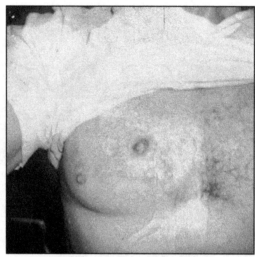

Jake says this is a picture of the bullet wound he received when his good friend Al Martin shot him in the chest in the year 1990. The story goes that Jake and Al and about a half-dozen outlaw-bikers were partying in the basement of Al's locksmith shop/whorehouse on Congress Street, near Longfellow Square, and there was a lot of the usual loud-mouthed bragging going on, so at one point Jake declared that he could take a bullet to the chest, no problem, and invited anyone who wanted to have a go at to step right up and fire away. Everybody immediately guffawed, of course, except for Al Martin. What Al did was immediately pull out his stub-nosed .22 caliber pistol and fire a .22 long bullet into Jake's chest, from about twelve feet away, and everybody was astounded when the bullet bounced off and fell onto the floor.

The thing is, though, that Jake was wearing a one-foot square Kevlar bulletproof patch under his tee shirt, which is why he made the brag, of course. I googled Kevlar bulletproof patches and vests and learned that they, like all "bulletproof" items, are actually "bullet resistant", which accounts for the wound and resultant scar the bullet made on Jake's chest. Jake says he was definitely jolted by the force of the bullet, that the area around the wound was quite painful for a few days, and that he had a very large bruise there for quite a long time that featured all the colors of the rainbow.

When Jake told me the story, it occurred to me that Al Martin undoubtedly wouldn't have hesitated to fire away even if he had had a larger caliber pistol, and the wound might well have been fatal. It also occurred to me that it was a good thing that the bullet struck where the patch was. I guess Jake's guardian angel was on the job again, I thought to myself.

JAKE

This is Doc, a long-time member of the Lowell chapter of the Hell's Angels, and the president of the chapter when Jake went down to live there in the late 80's and early 90's. "One night," Jake says, "Doc and I were barreling along some highway when all of a sudden Doc hit a dead deer lying in the road and he and his bike were launched high up into the air. I thought we were looking at a hell-uva disaster, but Doc maintained control of the bike and managed to land on an embankment with both wheels flat on the ground! What really astonished me, though, was that when he landed Doc didn't even change his expression!"

NINETEEN

When I arrived at his apartment for our next appoint-ment, I was shocked to find Jake with a very puffed up and severely bruised right hand, the same hand that had been slashed by a beer bottle in the fight at The Novelty Bar with the Devil's Disciples about fifty years earlier.

"I was walking on Congress Street the night before last, taking my after dinner constitutional," Jake said, "when all of a sudden, this very well-dressed big guy gets in my face and starts razzing me about what he'd been reading about me in *The Bollard*. He was very loud and ignorant sounding and kept saying things like he didn't believe anything I said about myself, that I had made everything up, and that all I was doing was bullshitting people.

"The guy appeared to be in his mid-thirties, and here I am an eighty-two-year-old gent strolling down the street, mind-ing my own business. I realize that I don't look like your av-erage old duffer, but it's pretty obvious that my Junior prom was more than a few years ago, if you know what I mean. And here's this surly young buck is, right in my face.

"My first reaction was to ignore him and just keep walking. I've had to deal with big mouths like him all my life, so I wasn't at all surprised to be accosted in such a way now that the story of my life has been coming out. I'd been anticipating it, as a matter of fact. There's a certain type of individual who deeply resents the way I am, and the only way they can deal with it is to call me a liar and a faker. As much as I like to fight, though, I don't get mad over petty ego shit like that. I have only been violent with other violent men who like to fight like I do, and know how to fight like a man. I try to avoid getting into confrontations with assholes like him who are out to prove to themselves and the rest of the world that they've got a set. Hey, if you've got anything at all hanging between your legs, you aren't always looking for ways to prove it to the world, you know?

"So, I just gave him a dirty look, like he wasn't worth even bothering with, and attempted to walk around him. That's when he gave me a little push, as if I was aggressing on him, which I definitely wasn't. But after the push, I definitely was. Full frontal assault is the way it might be described.

"Boom!"

"I threw a very hard overhand right that ended up with my fist planted right between his eyes. What a super-satisfying smacking sound it made!

"He didn't go down, but he looked to be unconscious standing up, so I didn't hit him again. As I was walking away, I looked back and saw him bent over, holding onto his face with both hands. He could have fallen over sometime after to that, I don't know, sometimes they do.

"I have not seen the guy since, but I have no doubt that he has two black eyes. That's what a punch delivered to that particular spot of the facial area is designed to result in, after all, and I think I employed the maneuver quite adeptly."

I didn't say anything. I just looked at his bruised and swollen hand and winced. But he was looking down at it, grinning.

"Geez, Jake," I said after a moment, "what did the guy find so objectionable? I mean, why all the bad feeling?"

"The individual didn't get specific as to what he found questionable about my story," Jake answered. "He just seemed to want to make the point that everything I've been telling you is nothing but bullshit. You have to understand that there is a breed out there who are not capable of standing out in any way themselves, so their whole thing is to bring other people down to their level. Guys like him have been dogging me for years. They worship average and hate exceptional, and they're everywhere."

I felt somewhat relieved after he said that. At least I knew the problem wasn't some particular thing that I wrote, but I realized at that point that neither of us had much appetite for conducting an interview that day, and we arranged to meet on another day.

As I walked home, I kept shaking my head as I thought of what had just occurred. I just couldn't believe that almost fifty years after having his hand slashed by a broken beer bottle in the bar fight he had in the Combat Zone on his way home to Portland from San Quentin, he'd injured the same hand again, as a result of yet another violent incident. A half-century later. I kept seeing his puffed-up hand with the fifty-year old scar across the top, just below the knuckles. The scar was more visible now, with the hand puffed up the way it was, and I couldn't help thinking that that puffed up hand with the fifty-year old scar on it amounts to a visual record of how he's lived his life.

Jake, showing his swollen hand, five days after punching a doubter in the street.

JAKE

ROCKY MOUNTAIN RECLUSE

Remembering that swollen hand and glint in his eye, the subject of age and the toll it normally takes was playing in the back of my mind the next time we met, so I asked him about how he felt about the big picture when he found himself in his fifties, after just having closed the door on Jake's Auto Sales.

"Maybe I was going through some kind of change of life, I don't know," he responded, in an uncharacteristically reflective way, "but around the time I came back to Portland, after living down in Lowell for a while, I began to feel the accumulative effect of all the tension I had created in my life and I just needed to get away from all the bullshit. The wonderful woman I told you about earlier had left me because she just couldn't take my right straight out wild and crazy ways anymore, and I was getting pretty tired of it myself. I needed some space to get my head straight, so I decided to sell all my possessions, except my custom-made-for-speed Harley, and head out for a year's mountaintop retreat in good ol' Ward, Colorado, where I had hidden out about a dozen years earlier right before going to Lewisburg Penitentiary.

"After gunning it across the country on my Harley in record time – damn, I covered more than 2000 miles in less than 48 hours – I arrived at Left Hand Canyon, outside Boulder, and rode the nineteen miles uphill to Ward. At that point, I decided that what I really needed was complete solitude, so I bought an old school bus that still ran well and drove it up to a grove of trees not far from the peak of a ten-thousand foot tall mountain about two miles from Ward. I lived in it all alone, with lots of animals and a fine selection of exquisitely-made throwing knives that I practiced with daily, for almost four years."

"What?!" I said, throwing down my pen and looking over

Jake at his campsite in the early 1990's proudly displaying his selection of throwing knives custom-made for him by Derrick "Mountain Man" Stevens, who was born in Ward, and owned a nearby campsite and forge. Jake says Derrick's two-pound knives can easily go clean through car doors. Derrick is quite a character. He used to fight all comers on the 4th of July in Ward. His father was a highly-decorated Veteran.

at him in disbelief. "Jake, did you just tell me that you lived ike a hermit on a mountaintop in Colorado for four years?"

"Yes, sir!" he bellowed, laughing. "Ol' Jakey boy's got one surprise after another for ya, huh?!"

"Ya sure do!" I yelled, eliciting a booming laugh from him.

"As I said, my original intent was to spend a year in Ward, to be with some of the most interesting people in the world," he continued, still chuckling to himself, "but once I got out there, I decided to live apart from civilization all together. I got accustomed to the peace and restfulness I was experiencing living in that old school bus all alone, and I just couldn't bring myself to leave. Part of that was due to the break I was getting from the excitement and danger I had always invited into my life, and part of it was due to the taste for being alone that I had developed during my various times in prison. Please keep in mind, my friend, that at that point I had spent more than ten years of my life in one lock-up or another, and at least three years of that time had been spent in solitary confinement. That's a lot of time spent in your own company, my friend.

"Now here I was living alone in the woods about 10,000 feet above sea level. On a clear day, I could see Denver, which was about sixty miles south of my campsite, but aside from that all I was looking at was fantastic mountain wilderness.

"I didn't' lack for activity, though. I really enjoyed climbing expeditions throughout the Rocky Mountains with my friends Tall Bob, Lex, Pete, Charlie, Howard and others whose names are lost to history. Other than that, I spent my hours in self-reflection, and perfecting my knife throwing abilities. Actually, I competed in axe and knife throwing competitions throughout the state of Colorado and did quite well.

"I built a fourteen foot by twenty foot wood shed attached to the back of the bus, and I had my domain. It wasn't as if I was entirely alone, though, not by any means. My campsite was regularly visited by bears, wild dogs and cats!

Jake at his mountaintop campsite, 1995.

King of the Rocky Mountains.

JAKE

Every year on the 4th of July, the residents of Ward, Colorado gather to have the annual town picture taken. In this 1993 picture Jake can be seen in the back row on the far right, proudly holding the American flag. On the far left in the back row holding the other flag is Derrick "The Mountainman" Stevens. He is in war paint in this picture. He was born in the woods and still lives in the woods! The legendary Hotel Columbia looms in the background. Old western outlaws stayed there from the 1880s to the 1930s, and Jake says he slept in the long-vacant hotel some nights and communed in his dreams with Jesse James, Cole Younger, and Billy the Kid.

"My closest companion through it all was my very handsome pure-white Pyrenees dog, Shawn, who had been mistreated and abandoned on the mountain. When I first took him in, he was very fearful of me, but as time went on, we became inseparable and were great company for each other. I'll never forget my old friend, Shawn, but he wasn't my only companion, not even close. I took in every living creature that happened by. Before long I had about half-dozen wild dogs, assorted squirrels and racoons, and even an eagle with a broken wing living with me. I've never had better friends in my life. I was as dependent on them as they were on me.

"The solitude I experienced camping out on that mountaintop was the most restful and enriching period of my life, but I don't I want to give you the impression that I did entirely without human company during that period of time. Over the course of the four years I was there, I ventured down the mountain on a number of occasions to go over and visit my neighbors in Ward, and we enjoyed many festive occasions together. I also made the trip across the great country of America a few times to visit my Hell's Angels buddies in Lowell and my friends up in Portland.

"Where ya been, Jake?" my friends in Portland all said to me when I made my appearance. Like they were going to believe that I'd been away to some mountaintop retreat and not locked up in some prison somewhere, you know? There are some questions you just can't answer in a way that people understand, so you just don't try, you know?

"Oh, and it wasn't as if I had no social contact at all at my campsite either. I actually had a number of visitors from Portland. One of them was Kristen, a beautiful former girlfriend of mine who showed up in Ward one summer day looking for me. My friends in town told her what was up with me and accompanied her up to my encampment. Kristen wanted so much to look good upon her arrival that she walked the two miles up the mountain in the bright, shiny green dress

and high heels she was wearing when she showed up in
Ward. She did look good, too, believe me. When she arrived,
it was as if a radiant goddess had appeared out of the sun.

"We had some wonderful days, the fine lady, my dog
Shawn, my various friends from the wild kingdom, and me.
Kristen had come to talk me down off the mountain, but
when she saw that there was a calmness and contentment
about me that she had never seen in me before, she abandoned that plan and we parted with big smiles and hugs, and
with me slapping her the ass and telling her to come back
soon.

Kristen seducing Jake at his campsite in Colorado.

Jake and Chris Chapman, Bob Seger's longtime bass player, and Jake, clowning for the camera at Chris's vacation home in Nederland, Colorado in 1994. Jake met Chris at the local health club and soon became his personal trainer.

JAKE

"I had another visitor to my campsite that you might like to hear about. One night when I was having a beer or two at the Pioneer Inn in Nederland – which is the Rocky Mountain town where Jimmy Hoffa is in a plaid sleeping bag in an abandoned gold mine – I met up with a guy by the name of Chris Chapman, who was Bob Seger's bass player for over thirty years. I invited Chris up to my campsite, where I introduced him to the fine art of knife throwing, along with a variety of other mountaintop recluse survival skills I had acquired. Chris had a vacation home in Nederland and I visited him there quite often and became his personal trainer.

"He said he really enjoyed the peace of mind he experienced at my campsite in the mountains after jetting from gig to gig around the world, hardly knowing where he was most of the time.

"I also remember Chris saying that he was married to three beautiful blondes at different times, and that they looked so much alike he had a hard time keeping them straight in his memory!

"My social activities also included accompanying mountain climbers up to tall peaks now and then, and that was something for a cloistered monk like me to look forward to. The picture I have provided you, my friend, is one such group, and I remember having a grand time with them. I was about thirty years older than any of them were, and they probably thought I was nuts to be climbing up tall mountains with them on my fifty-three year old beat-up legs. All I wore on my feet was a cheap pair of sandals, and halfway up the mountain I veered off to rougher terrain and told them I'd beat them to the top. They all said I wouldn't even make it, and when I arrived up there only ten minutes after they did, they were amazed. Damn, except for the thin air, I would've beaten them."

The other climbers were breathing different air? I wondered to myself.

Jake and friends at the top of 13,000 ft. Mt. Toll, 1995

JAKE

The Bowie knife embedded in the wall of Jake's dramatically conveys his passion for knife-throwing. He says he spent many hours at his camp throwing large knives custom-made for him by Derrick "The Blade" Stevens, a resident of Ward. Jake says that he did very well at the various knife-throwing competitions he entered throughout the state of Colorado, in spite of the very large age difference between him and the other competitors.

"Oh, I also had another visitor from Portland, and you might know him, my friend. His name is Steve Luttrell."

"Yes, of course," I said, "the publisher of the *Cafe Review* and a former poet laureate of Portland. Steve told me that he grew up in the same neighborhood as you did, in South Portland."

"Right! Well, Steve had come to Colorado for a poetry festival that was being held at the University of Colorado in Boulder, and he decided to visit me while he was there. We got to talking about the festival and when he mentioned that Allen Ginsberg would be there, I got excited and decided to go along with him to the festival to visit with my ol' pal Allen.

"You, of course, remember that I met Allen at Sonny Barger's house way back in 1966, when he and Neil Cassidy visited Sonny for the purpose of explaining to him that the hippies marching in the streets of Berkeley at the time loved America as much as the Hell's Angels did, and were just being patriotic by protesting the war in Vietnam. Sonny and the rest of us didn't buy that particular line at the time, but as time went on, our opinions changed. You will also remember that I encountered Allen again when I got out of San Quentin a few years after that and attended a hippie wedding in a field somewhere in New Mexico on my way across the country back to Portland, so I was excited to meet up with my ol' buddy Allen again.

"Jake!" he said when he saw me, "you still raising holy hell?!"

"Naw," I told him, "I've turned into a meek little ol' mountaintop mystic and all I want to do is sit around communing with my higher being and chasing after little boys in my spare time like you do, Allen!"

"That got a big laugh out of everybody, especially Allen, and when it came time for the poetry reading, he insisted that I get up and do something. I'm not one to shrink away from the limelight, of course, so I was happy to oblige. I can still recite the poem I made up for them if you'd like to hear it, my friend."

"Fire away," I said, motioning for him to take the floor the way he did that evening in Boulder. Sure enough, he got up from his chair and let fly:

"Zip-a- zam!
Zip-a- zam!
Rotten fish and stinking ham!
Son of a bitch!
Goddamn!
Holy fuck!
Here I am!
Hell's Angels forever!"

"They loved it! All of those renowned poets from all over the country gave me a standing ovation and it was the first poem I had ever composed!"

"Have you written any poetry since then?" I asked him.

"No!" he laughed. "Why take the chance of falling from the pinnacle of the poetry world?! The esteemed attendees that evening in Boulder will always hail my name as one of the greatest poets who ever lived! I'm up there with Shakespeare and Muhammad Ali! Why mess with that?!"

Photo taken at the Hell's Angels Bent Shoe Ranch of 'Big Al' Perryman and Jake, partying in 1993. Big Al was president of the Nomads chapter in 1966, when Jake became a member, and is featured in the movie "Hell's Angels Forever", which Jake says was made using real Hell's Angels...and is the greatest movie ever made!

TWENTY

That we'd meet at Jake's apartment, unless otherwise noted, was assumed at this point because we both felt more comfortable there and were inspired by the memorabilia all over the walls.

"After you moved back to Portland from your reclusive years in Ward, I'm sure you were a completely different person, huh, Jake?" I asked him, knowing what his reaction would be.

"No!" he roared, "but I will say that I was somewhat more subdued in my activities. I enjoyed the seclusion I experienced in Ward, but I sure as hell didn't want to experience the kind of forced retreat going back to prison would mean, you know? Living in a cell after having experienced the total freedom I did in Ward just wasn't going to happen. No way. So I kind of kept a lid on my natural instincts to raise hell, as difficult as that was for me."

STONE STREET GYM

"It should come as no surprise to you that I made my living after I moved back to Portland by training people. The difference between then and earlier in my life, though, was that I no longer had any interest in owning or managing any kind of health club. So I set up a gym in a friend's basement and was more than content to train select clientele that I had built up over the years at the various health clubs I had been associated with. The people I trained were all very successful in their chosen fields, and could have gone anywhere to train, but they chose me and the very musty

Flyer promoting the Stone Street Gym with, from left, Al
Martin, Jake, Bob Penney and a guy who shall remain
unidentified because "he turned out to be a fuckin' rat,"
Jake says.

JAKE

Jake in San Jose, Costa Rica, in the late 1990s, having flown there to deliver some survival money to an acquaintance living there on the lam. "He was riding an old white BMW when I met up with him," said Jake. "I gave him the money and off he went with a big smile on his face. That was about twenty years ago and as far as I know he is still running around Costa Rica leading a great life."

basement because of their earlier experiences with me, and also because they weren't into the social scene at the other health clubs around town.

"We were into getting healthier and stronger, not looking better and meeting hot babes. Well, even if we were into that kind of thing, when you're in your sixth decade, no matter how good a shape you're in, you didn't want to be showing your body off next to the college athletes that frequented the uptown state-of-the-art gyms, you know?"

"All this went along fine for a few years, and I was probably happier than I had ever been in my life. Well, more content and settled, anyway. Ol' Jakey boy had finally discovered the benefits of moderation, I guess. Who would'a thought? Now that I look back on it, I can see that my desire to turn others onto the benefits of physical fitness turned out to be my own salvation as well."

HEALTH AND FITNESS GURU ON
THE ISLAND OF TORTOLA

"I took a vacation and business trip in 1999 that I must tell you about, my friend. One of the very affluent friends I was training invited me to take a trip with him to the Island of Tortola, which is in the British Virgin Islands, out in the Atlantic Ocean, just south of Puerto Rico. Tortola turned out to be a tropical paradise that will live with me forever. Lush green landscape, ideal temperatures, and a laid-back way of life that I soon got very accustomed to. I kind of sunk into it, if you know what I mean. There was a buzz of good-will, kindness and natural joy about the place that made me feel restful and secure, like I didn't have anything to prove, I could just relax and be myself. After a few leisurely weeks, my friend was ready to return home, but I told him that I had decided to stay and might never leave. He didn't say anything, he just gave me a little smile, like he had seen the change that had come over me and wasn't at all surprised.

"Tortola is a relatively small island and you're bound to come into contact with each of the inhabitants before very long. The residents are made up of a few thousand of the native population, mixed with a number of well-heeled, part-time residents and tourists from around the world. I naturally gravitated to the native population, as you might suspect, but I also managed to form good friendships with many other people. Turns out that the affluent vacationers were intrigued at encountering a former Hell's Angel who had done time in well-known penitentiaries, but came from a background of privilege like they did.

"Prominent among the many fascinating people from around the world I met on the island was Dr. Robin Tattersall, a world-renowned British reconstructive surgeon – commonly known as a plastic surgeon – who had taken up permanent residence on the island and had established his practice there many years before. Dr. Tattersall was a very dynamic individual all around, actually. He had been a male model who appeared on the cover of *Vogue* magazine, and was also an extremely skilled yachtsman who had represented the Virgin Islands in a number of Summer Olympics sailing events. His wife, Jill, was also a very accomplished person who wrote a very well-known travel book entitled book *Memories of the Virgin Islands*. The native population was extremely fond of her because of her deep love of Tortola, and they were in awe of Dr. Tattersall because of all of his skills and accomplishments. The fact that he provided his medical services to them at no charge was the clincher. He was like a god that had descended from the Sun to make their lives even happier and more content than they already were.

"Shortly after my arrival on the island, I began training people at the Cutting Edge Gym, where Dr. Tattersall and his wife, Jill, worked out, and it wasn't long before I became the personal trainer to them and to another doctor and his wife who were friends of theirs. They were willing to train seriously, so we got along fine, and they paid me very well, which was also very nice, so all was good.

Jake (at left) with Dr. Robin Tattersall (right) gym owner at the Cutting Edge Gym on Tortola in 2000.

JAKE

"I trained quite an exclusive clientele at the Cutting Edge gym, including Hollywood movie stars and prominent politicians and jet setters from around the world. Dr. Tattersall was very clear about the absolute need for confidentiality in regards to the identity of people who received plastic surgery, so I am not at liberty to name names. I might have mentioned to you somewhere along the line here, my friend, that I am not a snitch. But, let me just say that when I turn on the TV today, I often see prominent entertainment personalities who don't look a day older than they did years ago when I met them on the Island of Tortola. Dr. Tattersall was extraordinarily good at what he did.

"As much as I enjoyed the company of people like Dr. Tattersall and the others, I've never been entirely comfortable in high society situations, so I ended up living out in the jungle with a group of about twenty Rastafarians. We knew we were kindred spirits the moment we encountered one another, and that was that. I was the only white guy in the group, but that mattered for absolutely nothing. What I had going with my Rastafarian brothers was the closest I've ever come to what I had experienced with my Hells Angels brothers, and I got to the point where I had to force myself to emerge from the jungle to train Dr. Tattersall and his friends.

"There is an aspect of life on Tortola which anyone who has been there will inevitably comment on, and that is the extraordinary beauty of the women there. Never had I experienced the likes of the great beauty and graciousness of Tortola women. My special friend while I was on the island was a vision of a woman who I named 'Tracy True Love,' who I knew loved me beyond question, and made me feel it in every way. I was sixty-two and she was about thirty-two, so we weren't going to elope or anything, you know, but I knew she loved me. She was obviously far too beautiful and full of life, though, to tie herself down with an old white guy – even me! Some nights, at about nine o'clock, I'd look around and she'd be gone. There wasn't any question of what she was up to, of course, so I started gently teasing her by calling her 'Tracy True Love.' She'd blush and giggle and tell me that she'd be true to me no matter what, but we both knew what was up.

"I might've stayed on the Island of Tortola for the rest of my life, but one day I got a call that my father was in the hospital and was very ill, so I immediately returned home and arrived in time for his funeral.

"As you know from what I've told you, my friend, my father and I were two very different individuals but, when all was said and done, I loved him. I was deeply saddened by his passing, and felt a lot of regret about the way things were between us. Funny, but on the trip home all I could think about was that time when I was six years old and gave that toy truck to the Salvation Army so they could melt it down to make into a bullet to shoot up Hitler's ass. I told you how confused my father was by the intensity he saw in me. That toy truck had been handed down to my father from his father and it hurt my father to think that I would part with it for any reason. So, there I was, feeling bad about something I did when I was six years old. Man, we live a long life, and every bit of it matters and is always part of who we are, you know?"

"Ah, ya," I said, looking over at him and nodding.

"Anyway, I left Tortola after almost a year of being there and never returned. Got involved in my life otherwise, I guess. But, hey, you never know, I might make it back there someday. Tracy True Love would still be thirty years younger than me, and I know damn well she's still absolutely beautiful, and I'm sure we could make arrangements similar to what we had before. So let's get this book done so I can get headed back to the Virgin Islands, Man!

"I do know that my pal 'Reo' is still living where he grew up there and has a popular band. He moved to New York City once and did not like it so he went home."

A MOTORCYCLE LAND-SPEED RECORD

"Well, there I was, back in Portland again, ready to resume the relatively quiet and uneventful life I had been leading before my trip to the lovely island of Tortola. That 'quiet and uneventful' is not to be taken for granted, sir, not by any means. It was more along the lines of a colossal achievement that was a lifetime in the making.

"I immediately resumed training the same select group of individuals that I was working with before I went to Tortola, so that meant that I was among long-time friends and also had a reliable source of income, so life was clicking along for me at a very reasonable pace.

"Oh, I just have to tell you about one off the wall antic I got involved in at that time, just so you won't think that my testosterone count had sunk completely out of sight."

"Okay, Jake," I said, "one last story. Wha' d'ya got?"

"This is something you've got to hear because it involves me setting a motorcycle unofficial land-speed record for secondary roads that I'm reasonably sure still stands, at least for the State of Maine, and maybe for someone in my age group anywhere on the planet, I don't know. It took place around the year 2008, when I was an exuberant sixty-six years old.

"A friend and I had attended a motorcycle show a few years before where I had acquired a Boss Hoss motorcycle that was one brutal piece of machinery. That Boss Hoss could wipe out any bike it came up against, including the most highly customized-for-speed Harleys, Indians, Japanese rice-burners, whatever. The Boss Hoss motorcycle is made in Kentucky, where I had spent time as a Kentucky rumrunner, as you will remember, so I knew those Kentucky boys knew something about speed. Basically, a Boss Hoss motorcycle is a Corvette engine on two wheels. When you sit on it, it's like you're straddling a tornado.

"The engine was 335HP and I decided to see how fast it would go on a long, flat section of road up on Rte. 113, just outside of Fryeburg, which is a town about forty or so miles west of Portland, Maine.

"I talked two friends of mine, who had years of experience timing the speed of cars, to join me. I can't use their names, because of the traffic laws we broke, so I'll refer to them as 'Ding' and 'Dong.'

"That section of road is quiet in the early morning, so I knew we'd have it pretty much to ourselves. I stationed Ding a mile and a half down the road from my starting point. When I passed him, he timed me at 163 miles per hour. I knew I could go faster than that, but the problem was that I had trouble keeping my grip on the handlebars at those speeds, so I told Dong to tape my wrists to the handlebars with Gorilla Tape. He was reluctant to do so because of the danger involved, but I insisted, so there you go.

"After the application of the Gorilla Tape, my grip was greatly imporved, and my confidence soared as I screamed down Rte. 113. The faster I went, the louder that V-8 engine between my legs roared.

"One of the things I discovered was that your field of vision gets narrower and narrower as you go faster and faster.

"When I passed him that second time, Ding timed me at 171 mph, a new (unofficial) motorcycle land-speed record for back roads! What a great and glorious morning that was on Rte. 113, just outside of good ol' Fryeburg, Maine!"

I sat there thinking that Jake was telling me this right after informing me that his life had quieted down around this time period.

"Okay, Jake," I said, shaking my head, "you're right! That was an amazing feat! The stories just keep coming and coming! You never let me down, man! Are you ready to get to those stories people have been telling me about you?"

"Let's go!" he yelled.

Jake on his Boss Hoss, 2001

VOLUME TWO

DAY TO DAY ROUTINE

Whenever I go to Jake's apartment now I encounter people in the halls or on the elevator who know why I'm there and want to tell me Jake Sawyer stories, sometimes from far in the past, sometimes from that morning. He prefers to stay home and avoid the limelight these days, but when he does step out there's fluttering and fanfare along the way sometimes, and it's obvious that he sure as hell enjoys it. He's content to stay home most of the time, though, and spends his time reading, mostly historical books, watching cable TV documentaries and, of course, working out. At present his routine is to work out on his Chuck Norris "Total Gym" that is constantly advertised on the TV documentaries he watches. Once when I arrived, he had just finished bicycling eleven miles up a steep incline on his stationary bike.

"For the last few miles my legs ached so bad I thought I was going to cry," he said, "but I had set my goal at eleven miles, man, and that was it. I made myself achieve my goal! Physical exercise empowers one's life, sir! That is the grand news I am attempting to introduce to the individuals in my building who attend the exercise classes I conduct in the rec room of our building. I get them moving around and laughing and it brings some light into their lives! I've seen it all through my life, with business execs, beauty queens, and lonely guys hidden away in prison cells – regular physical exercise, done in the proper way, gives us all a natural high that leads to all the good things in life!

"The health training that I provide for my friends in my building is not restricted to providing them with a certain amount of entertainment health training. I have been extremely fond of my friends and when I hear that one of them has become the victim of a bully, I search for the offending individual and deal with him. That's it. Period. I hate fucking bullies. Some people work out to feel better, some people work out because they want to look better, or maybe live longer, but with me it's so I can fight better and annihilate bullies and snitches. I've told you that all along the line, sir, and it's as true today as it ever was."

Sonny Barger and Jake at Sonny's place in Arizona nine years ago.

TWENTY-TWO

After we had finished chronicling his life to the present, and I was spending my time putting the book together, Jake and I didn't see one another for a while, then ran into each other on the street, not far from where he stopped me a few years ago to talk to me about writing his life story, actually. When I asked him what he'd been up to, he didn't say, "Oh, not too much, what's up with you?" like most people do, especially, let's face it, if they're eighty-two years old. Jake being Jake, of course, proceeded to tell me about his latest hair-raising adventure.

"Had a little fun up to Eastern Cemetery the other night," he said. "Eastern Cemetery was established in the year 1668 and is the oldest burial ground in the city. I sometimes wear my long, navy blue Revolutionary War lieutenant's dress coat and put on my tri-cornered Ethan Allen hat and go there in the evening to visit the graves of my ancestors, and those of other renowned Portland people from the past. When I'm there I feel like I'm walking on holy ground. I know I have told you that my ancestors were among the first settlers of this area. An ancestor of mine was the second person to own a plot of land in what became the town of York, and another ancestor of mine ran the first ferry between South Portland and Portland. You know, of course, that Sawyer Street, the longest street in South Portland, is named after him, so I won't bother to go over all that again.

"Anyway, there I am, wandering among the tombstones in the early moonlight, when I hear some kind of activity way down at the gate that turns out to be a nighttime guided tour of the cemetery. Nighttime cemetery tours tend to be more spooky than respectful, in my opinon, so right away I'm feeling a little antagonistic towards their presence. Anyway, I chose to ignore them and just kept wandering around, but the tour guide saw me and took a step towards me and yelled: 'You're not supposed to be here! The cemetery is closed! You've got to leave right now!'

"Fuck him, I said to myself, no stuffed shirt civilian tour guide, probably another rich asshole that just moved here, is going to tell me I can't visit the graves of my ancestors anytime I want to. So I yelled, 'Welcome to the Eastern Cemetery! I'm so happy to see so many of you this evening!'

"I took the guy's tour away! When the people saw me in my Revolutionary War get-up, they all brightened up and started to walk towards me! They thought I was part of the tour! The guide immediately set them straight, of course, then he yelled over to me, 'If you don't get out of here right now, I'm going to call the police!'

"Of course that scared the hell out of me. Ha! I just kept poking around the tombstones, and before long I hear sirens, then I see blue lights, and two black and whites pull up to the curb out in front of the cemetery, each of them with two police officers in them, and one of them with a dog in the backseat, all for an aged Revolutionary War veteran visiting the graves of his ancestors.

"Now, of course, a normal person would just walk over to the gate at this point, have a civil conversation with the nice police officers, and everything would be fine. So, here's what I do: I start bobbing up and down around the gravestones, like I'm trying to elude capture, which incited the police big time. Three of them started trotting after me, and the fourth one stayed behind with the dog to guard the gate so I couldn't circle around and make my escape. I loved it, and I'm sure my ancestors did too. One officer was coming right at me and the other two were approaching from the sides, so they thought they had me hemmed in, but I quickly disabused them of that mistaken notion. After standing at attention and giving them a snappy salute (I've always respected officers of the law, after all) I ran like mad for the four-foot tall stone wall that runs along the Mountfort Street side of the cemetery, vaulted up onto it, then jumped down onto the sidewalk and ran like a bastard across Mountfort Street into the Munjoy South housing complex.

"I could hear the dog barking his head off, so I knew the police weren't far behind me and were catching up fast. Hey, I lettered in track at Kents Hill, but, well, you know, that was then. Anyway, I knew they were going to be on me before long, so I ducked into a doorway, took off my Ethan Allen tri-cornered hat and my Revolutionary War lieutenant's coat, slung the coat over my arm with the hat tucked inside it, and calmly stepped back out into the pleasant night air. By this time my pursuers were only a couple of blocks away, and I knew damn well they saw me and knew I was the interloper they were after. To my great surprise, though, they just turned around and left. The dog kept barking, of course. He sounded confused and angry as hell, they had to kind of drag him away, actually, but I think the story was that when the police got a better look at me they realized that I was just an eccentric but harmless local character having some fun, and they decided that they had better things to do than apprehend me and have to listen to me go on and on about whatever I might go on and on about."

JAKE

As I stood there listening to him tell the story, I finally started to get it. All the drama and excitement that took place with the tour guide and the police at the Eastern Cemetery didn't have to happen. Just like he didn't have to lead the Hell's Angel's 'suicide charge' when he knew it was a very bad idea that would end up with everyone involved either dead, seriously wounded, or in prison. And like when he stole the marijuana from the Coast Guard base under the noses of the Feds, when he knew damn well he'd definitely be appended sooner rather than later. Or like when he dumped stolen cars off the end of Maine State Pier into Portland Harbor, when he knew it was an absolutely absurd thing to do because, of course, they'd be visible at low tide, and there'd be an immediate investigation.

It's all about the drama! Excitement for its own sake! When he approached me about writing his life story, Jake said, "I want to tell people what a life lived going right straight for the gusto every time looks like so they can apply the principle to their lives if they are so moved!"

"So, Jake," I said to him that day on the street, "you turned eighty-two years old on March 1, 2020, and you're still going for the gusto every damn time, just like always, huh?"

"Yes! I am an adrenaline junkie! I get off on pure excitement! That kind of thing never goes away! Hell, I could've handled the situation at Eastern Cemetery in a calm, mature manner, but what fun would that have been? It was all a charade created for my own benefit and amusement. The difference between the things I do now and the things I did in the past, though, is that the things I do now don't put my personal freedom in jeopardy. Even if the police had apprehended me that night, I know I could've sweet talked them out of arresting me. Hey, I hadn't assaulted anyone or stolen anything, I had just upset a tight-assed tour guide. There's no way I'd ever risk going back to living in a cell. I've definitely had enough of that. My living accommodations at the moment are just fine and dandy, thank you. I've got an extraordinary amount of living space, for someone who spent as much time in jail cells as I have – kitchen, living room, bedroom, weight room, my own bathroom – and I'm living like a damn prince. Throw in the fantastic view of downtown and Portland Harbor out my front window and I'm in heaven, man! Not to mention that I'm living in a building full of people that I know and love!"

I went to Jake's apartment a few days later to talk about how the book was progressing and, as usual, I encountered people in the halls and on the elevator who knew very well why I was there and wanted to tell me Jake Sawyer stories. Some of them wanted to tell me about incidents that took place years ago when they knew Jake from elsewhere, and some of the stories were about such things as seeing him walking down the street that morning. He's definitely a big celebrity to them.

WALL OF SHAME

The local newspaper would not print a Letter to the Editor that Jake sent them, so he is including it here in his biography, so it will be read by future generations!

JAKE

To the Editor-

*While Jogging up Munjoy Hill on my way home
from church last Sunday, I was looking around. It
is obvious to me and many others that our beautiful city of Portland is being raped by the rich.*

*Our 'City Fathers', etc. are out of their minds.
Ugly over-builiding has destroyed the quality of life
in Portland.*

I was born here more than eighty years ago.

*What we have going on here is some Mainers
selling out the majority of other Mainers that they
grew up with so that they can get richer and richer.*

*Local developers are now looking forward to
building a seven hundred car parking lot, etc., in a
crowded area on the waterfront with narrow
streets.*

*People that are destroying our way of life here
deserve to have their names carved into a large,
granite WALL OF SHAME!*

*Visualize a large granite WALL OF SHAME and
a large American flag flying over Fort Gorges coming to Portland soon.*

*Rev. Jonathan Parker Sawyer,
Sr.
Veteran Paratrooper*

P.S.: Bring back the draft!!

VOLUME TWO

JAKE'S EXERCISE CLASS

I decided to attend one of his exercise classes to see what they're all about. When I arrived at the rec room a little before Jake did, I encountered a group of sixteen people, nine men and seven women, some of them in wheelchairs, leaning on walkers, or on crutches. I immediately became aware of an expectant buzz in the room and wondered if anything was different from usual.

"What's up today, anything special going on?" I asked one of the men.

"Oh, yeah!" he said excitedly. "At the end of the last class Jake said that we're going to have a special celebrity guest today, and he told us that when we see who it is our minds are going to be completely blown! He said our lives will never be the same!"

Who knows who the guest might be? I thought. Jake has a network of friends and acquaintances that extends far and wide, after all. Could be Stephen King or someone of that stature. Stephen King is from Maine, has spent a lot of time in Portland over the years, and he and Jake could very well have met and bonded. Or, who knows, maybe it'll be Bob Dylan. Jake knew him in the 1960's, of course, when he was the bartender at the Luau Club and Dylan was a frequent customer for a while.

Or maybe it will be Barbara Streisand. Jake said a friend of his told him that a buddy of his knows a guy in Hollywood who said Barbara Streisand saw the *Bollard Magazine* online and said Jake's handsome as hell and she can't wait to meet him when he goes to Holywood to make the movie of his life.

We got our answer to the celebrity question when

JAKE

Jake arrived at the rec room carrying a life-size card-board cut-out of Marilyn Monroe wearing a slinky pink dress and a big, broad sexy smile.

"Ladies and gentlemen," Jake yelled as he positioned Marilyn up in front of the group, "as you can see, our special guest today needs no introduction! She has spent her life devoted to the fine art of physical fitness and you can see the results!"

We all cheered and applauded, probably more than we would have for either Stephen King or Bob Dylan in the flesh, actually. It was actually Jake we were applauding, of course – and I lined up with the others to be part of the fun.

"Okay, folks," Jake boomed, "the first thing we're going to do is loosen up a bit, so let's get to shakin' up our bodies like we're happy as hell to be here together right now, on the way to feeling better than we ever have in our entire lives! Let's shake, rattle and roll, my friends!"

I lined up to be part of the excitement, and shake, rattle and roll we all did, following Jake's lead as best we could. Neck, arm, and leg rotations came rapidly, one after the other, first one way and then the other, all to the accompaniment of Jake's non-stop chatter.

"That's it, Theresa!" he yelled at an older woman with a walker and wearing a bright ribbon in her hair. "Shake it up, baby! Oh, you're giving me something to think about when I wake up all alone in the middle of the night!"

Theresa's face, of course, flushed with delight, and everyone whooped and stomped their feet when she thrust her good leg out in front of her and rotated it alluringly.

"Yes! That's it!" Jake roared. "Let's all extend our legs and rotate them very sexually one at a time, first one way and then the other, but let's not forget our thumbs, my friends!" He extended his hands out in front of him and rotated his thumbs, first one way and then the other.

"You've got it, Mark!" he yelled. "You definitely are going to have the most handsome thumbs in Portland when I get through with you! You'll be walking down the street and the ladies you meet will be giggling about how handsome your thumbs are!"

Then, with all of us loosened up sufficiently, came the muscle-against-muscle exercises that would be the cause of the muscular pain we'd all feel later. First, palm against palm, pushing against each other to strengthen the arm and chest muscles.

"Imagine you've got hold of a good ol' Maine apple you're making into some of that famous Maine applesauce!" he yelled. "Then later on, when you're moaning about all the pain and discomfort you're going to feel because you've expanded and strengthened so many of your muscles, you'll at least you'll have something good to eat!"

Next came twenty-five counts of going up and down on our tip toes to strengthen the leg muscles, then it was the same thing, one leg at a time.

"Just do the best you can," he roared, "even if you've got only one leg, you want it to be the most beautiful, strongest leg the whole entire world has ever seen!"

The highlight of the day for me, and obviously for Jake too, was seeing a one-legged man on crutches convulse with laughter as he laid his crutches aside and commenced to rise up and down on his leg.

"That's it, Erwin! You are amazing, man!" Jake said breathlessly, obviously filled with astonishment and admiration at the man's efforts.

JAKE

"This is the best group I've ever worked with in my entire life," he said quietly as the man retrieved his crutches and stood there grinning happily, "and as I look around the room, I see some great advances. You're all looking much younger, unbelievably thinner, more energetic, and better in every way.

"Brian!" he yelled to a very overweight man, "you've lost about a hundred pounds since you started attending my classes, right?"

"No!" Brian said, laughing. "I've gained about ten pounds!"

"Only ten pounds!" Jake roared. "Imagine how much you would've gained over that period of time if you hadn't been working out like a mad man instead of spending your time sitting in front of the TV eating chocolate donuts like you were before!"

"I don't work out at all, and I still sit in front of the TV eating chocolate donuts like before," Brian answered with a loud guffaw, "but I feel thinner!"

"Great!" Jake exploded, "Feeling better about yourself is what we're after here!"

At the end of the class, I found out that having Marilyn Monroe with us wasn't the only special thing about the day. It was about a week before Christmas and the group had gotten together and bought Jake a present. I could see he was moved by the gesture, but he attempted to hide that by frowning and saying gruffly that it was probably a Dunkin' Donuts gift card, and he doesn't eat unhealthy-as-hell-for-you Dunkin' Donuts. When he opened the present, though, and saw that it was a super cool looking battery-operated miniature chopper motorcycle with a very outlaw-biker looking Santa Claus astride it, he was immediately delighted.

"Oh! How did you know?!" he exclaimed, clutching

it theatrically against his chest. "this is just what I asked Santa for!"

Then, with the assembled multitude laughing and cheering him anew, he threw his arm around Marilyn and they made their exit, with him talking to her in an intimate voice, just loud enough for us to hear: "Let's kick this hairy old coot off my motorcycle, dear, and we'll go for a long ride along the seashore, then we'll stop and get a dozen large chocolate donuts, and after we get home to my place we'll eat every one of them and spend the rest of the afternoon making mad, passionate love!"

As I watched Jake walk down the hall with that distinctive lurching gate of his, carrying the miniature motorcycle with Santa Claus riding it in one hand, and his other arm around a cardboard cut-out of Marilyn Monroe, it occurred to me it had been about fifty years since his right leg had been almost severed at the hip in a motorcycle accident, and the doctors said it would have to be taken off. I stood there thinking about all he went through with that, then I thought of what the one-legged man had done in the exercise class, and I had a pretty good idea of why Jake was so moved by seeing him do it.

THE MERRY CHRISTMAS THAT WASN'T

A few days before Christmas, I tried calling Jake a number of times to wish him a Merry Christmas and to talk about the progress of the book, but he never picked up, which was very odd because he had always been so readily accessible. I thought he might be spending the holiday with friends somewhere, but when I called the day after Christmas and he still didn't answer, I went to the Munjoy Hill Tavern to see if Stan knew what was up.

"Jake's in the hospital," Stan said, in a deeply troubled voice, then he lowered his head and said, "and he's not doing very well."

Damn! I said to myself, he was in the hospital that whole time I was trying to reach him!

"He called me last Sunday morning, two days before Christmas, to tell me that he wouldn't be coming in for a few days because he fell down a flight of stairs and fractured three ribs and he's in the hospital," Stan said. "I would have called you, but he made me promise not to tell anyone because he didn't want to spoil Christmas for his friends."

I was alarmed, of course, because I knew what fracturing three ribs could mean for someone who was going to be eighty-one years old in a couple of months, even if they are Jake Sawyer. An event like that can cause a downward spiral of the type that I didn't want to think about at the moment. Neither did I like the sound of Stan's "and he's not doing very well."

"How the hell did it happen?" I asked Stan.

"You should go up to the hospital and talk to Jake," he answered, averting his eyes, the way men like Jake and Stan do when anyone asks them anything about a friend, even when it's a mutual friend doing the asking.

Right away, I assumed Jake had been doing some holiday partying, got a little tipsy and, bang, here come the stairs, one after the other. The fact that he wears a built-up orthopedic shoe might have played a part too, I thought. Whatever the cause of the mishap, I knew for sure that he was in for a very long and painful recovery period. I fractured a couple of ribs on a fall on the ice a few years previous and couldn't move for a month or so without experiencing sharp, twist-ing, spasms of pain that haunt me still.

I doubted that Jake had been hospitalized for just fractured ribs, though. I found out when I had my ep-isode that there's nothing they can do for fractured ribs but prescribe pain pills and send you home to heal on your own. So, on my way to the hospital, I was worried that one of the fractured ribs might have punctured an internal organ, and I was just hoping that it hadn't caused serious damage.

When the nurses station buzzed Jake to tell him that he had a visitor and gave him my name, I could hear him yell back, "Who the hell is that?!"

Okay, he's still with us, and he's still who he was, I thought to myself, smiling and shaking my head as one of the nurses grinned and pointed me to his room.

He didn't look pretty. It immediately struck me that in all the time I'd met with him over the past few years, I'd never seen him be anything but bubbling over with energy, clean-shaven, with his hair carefully combed, and very meticulously, even artfully, dressed. Now here he was, looking drained and troubled, unshaven, matted hair, connected up to various pieces of medical equipment, tubes coming in and out of everywhere and, somehow most alarming of all, wearing a stand-ard issue hospital johnny.

Somehow or other, I knew that any kind of expres-sion of sympathy on my part would be met with un-mitigated scorn, so I said, "Well, Jake, I hope you had a good Christmas!"

"What?!" he roared. "Did you come up here to say that to me?! Nurse! Come and throw this character the hell out of here!"

Not a peep from the nurses' station, of course, each

of them having become very accustomed to Mr. Sawyer's antics by this time.

"Alright, Jake," I drawled, "what happened? The last time I saw you we were planning to finish up a book and get it out there, and now you're laying around in bed doing nothing. So what the hell gives? C'mon, you can tell me anything, let it all out."

"Okay, here ya go," he said, as if reluctantly giving in to my excessive demands. "I've got a confession to make. This was all my fault. Somehow or other, I got it into my head to return to my old habits for just one night, and it sure as hell turned out to be a very bad idea. I looked out my window and saw all those Christmas lights twinkling in the night, though, and I just had to be part of all the friggin' merriment, just one more time! Just like the old days! I just had to get drunk and drugged out of my mind, get into a few fights, pick up two or three babes and have an orgy, you know, here we go! Man, I couldn't wait to get out there in the middle of all that fun and excitement and do some very heavy partying! Just one more time!"

I knew it, I said to myself.

"So, I put my best party clothes on," he continued, "including my very cool Santa Claus hat, and went out and got drunk as hell at some wild-ass, hell-raisin' den of iniquity that's been the ruin of many a poor boy, now including me! The situation is that the men's room of the establishment is located on the second floor, at the head of a very old rickety wooden staircase, and after I'd made a visit to the men's room and was going down the stairs, some weightlifter asshole, you know how they are, was showing off for the two young women sitting at my table by shaking the friggin' staircase with me on it, so there goes ol' Jakie boy tumbling down the stairs and crashing at the bottom.

VOLUME TWO

As soon as I hit the floor I immediately sprung up and punched the guy's lights out, then picked him up over my head and carried him over to the door and threw him out it, without opening it beforehand, you understand. Picking him up and carrying him like that, then heaving him out the closed door is evidently what caused all the damage to my ribs. Most weightlifters tend to be very heavy and awkward to handle."

He's still doing the same stupid stuff at eighty that he did when he was a Hell's Angel, I sat there thinking, and I guess it showed on my face.

"No!!! No!!!" he yelled, waving his hand at me dismissively. "Don't you know when I'm pulling your leg, yet? You've got a long ways to go, young man!"

"Yeah, yeah, I guess I do," I said.

"Okay, here ya go," he said, grinning over at me and launching into the real story. "The exciting adventure in question took place on Saturday, December 22, at about nine o'clock in the morning, when I was completely sober and not feeling the effects of any recreational drugs, which is exactly the way I have been at all hours of the day, every day, for the last number of years. I was definitely not out on the town friggin' partying, looking to get into fights and pick up loose women, as you were so ready to believe I was!

"The story is simply that after finishing up at the Munjoy Hill Tavern that Saturday morning I drove to a good friend's house to deliver some Christmas presents for him and his wife. We had a very pleasant gift exchanging thing around their Christmas tree, followed by a nice brunch, but as I was going down the long flight of stairs that leads from their living quarters, with my arms full of Christmas presents and assorted goodies, I missed a step, and you see where that little piece of action got me. It was a long ways

down and I hit every stair. I really couldn't do much
to help myself but, thanks to the seven-point landing
technique that was drilled into me during my paratrooper training, I did manage to avoid hitting the floor
head first. I landed directly on the left side of my chest
with such force that my rib cage got crushed, though,
the result being three severely fractured ribs, and here
we are!"

"Wow, so now you're in a world of hurt," I said. "I
know what you're going through. They don't usually
keep you in the hospital for fractured ribs, though,
because there's nothing they can do for you. The only
thing they can do is prescribe some pain pills and
send you home to heal. So what are you doing still
laying around in bed, and what are all these tubes and
wires and stuff all about?"

"Have I ever let you down, sir?" he asked, looking
over at me in frustration. "Has any story I ever told
you been boring as hell? Have any of the adventures
I've related to you been simple, like, you know, one-
dimensional? Do you actually think that the whole
story here is that I fell down a flight of stairs, fractured
three ribs, and that's it? Is that a story even worth
telling?"

"Ah, no, I guess not," I said.

"Ya, you guess not," he scoffed. "Well, here ya go
with the *rest* of the story: When they were assessing
the damage to my ribs, a very observant young female
doctor noticed something very odd about my stomach,
something entirely unrelated to the ribs situation, a
bulge in an odd place or something, so they did an x-
ray and found that I had a seriously perforated ulcer
on the lining of my stomach that was about to burst
and spew poison throughout my system! If they hadn't
opened my stomach up and cut the damn perforated

ulcer out, ol' Jakie boy would have been enjoying the company of his famous ancestors in a matter of days!

"The story behind the frigging' story, my friend, is that if I hadn't fallen down those stairs and fractured my ribs, the frigging' perforated ulcer wouldn't have been discovered and I would have been gonzo. God saved my crazy ass once again! He figured he'd better find a way to get a message to me real fast, so down the damn stairs I go!"

Wow. He'd spoken of his guardian angel intervening and saving his bacon on a number of occasions, but he'd never mentioned God. I didn't know what to make of that, so I took a deep breath and asked him point blank if he actually meant that God had directly intervened in his life, or was he referring to his guardian angel.

He just looked over at me with a blank expression, like he didn't really know himself why he had said "God" and not "guardian angel" the way he always had before.

Then, after a moment, he said: "Well, ah, where do you think guardian angels come from? Like, they don't have a home, or a boss to please, or anything like that?"

I didn't know what to say, so I just shrugged my shoulders.

THE PROGNOSIS

On my way out I asked at the nurses' station about Jake's prognosis and they said that it was definitely a good thing that the perforated ulcer was discovered because, like Jake said, he most likely would've been dead in a matter of days otherwise. They also added that Jake was still a very sick man, that things could go either way in the next few days, and that even if things went as hoped, he was without question facing a long and challenging period of recovery.

"He's going to be with us for two weeks or more before he goes to a nursing facility," one of the nurses said, rolling her eyes and laughing, "but, don't worry, we'll survive!"

She was obviously pleased at how hard I laughed at that one, and we kind of bonded after we chuckled together a bit about Jake's antics, so when I asked her exactly what we were looking at with him, she gave it to me straight.

"There's no question that falling down the stairs saved his life. The perforated ulcer we found was so large and near to bursting that it created a protrusion in his stomach that one of our doctors spotted and knew wasn't related to the injury to his ribs. Good thing the doctor acted on her hunch, because Jake would have died a very painful death shortly thereafter otherwise."

I just there stood there looking at her wide-eyed as she went on to tell me that after a couple of weeks at the hospital Jake would either go to a nursing facility or have live-in care at home for a period of time. Living at home alone was a long ways off for him, she said, if it ever happens at all. She could see I was very alarmed at that prospect so, by way of making me feel better, she said for me not to worry, that from her experience she knew that as time went on, a soon to be eighty-one year old man who's had a serious stomach operation, and who's also recovering from three fractured ribs, would end up being very grateful for the care he'd receive at a nursing facility, and living at home alone would be far from his thoughts.

"Most people in Jake's situation hate the thought of not living home alone at first," she said, "but when you're in constant pain and discomfort you start to look at things very differently. What was at first unthinkable to you becomes very desirable, you know?"

No, I didn't know. Somehow I couldn't put Jake Sawyer and Oceanside Manor together, no matter how hard I tried.

TWENTY-THREE

There wasn't much else I could do for Jake besides keep working on getting the book together, so I busied myself with that, trying the best I could to get my mind off what the nurse had told me about his prognosis. After getting to know him, I knew that his personal freedom means everything to him, and that he loves living alone in his very well-ordered and taste-fully decorated apartment with his cat. I knew that he would definitely have an explosive reaction to even the hint of his going into a nursing facility, even for a short period of time. When he called me three or four days after my visit he was in a chipper mood, though, so I figured everything was fine. I really wanted to know how he was feeling, how things were going, of course, but Jake's not one for small talk.

"You wouldn't believe what happened!" he began. "One of my nurses walked into my room and as soon as she saw me she yelled: 'Oh, no! You're Jake Sawyer! You're the one who punched my husband in the mouth about forty years ago and knocked all his front teeth out!'

"Naturally, right away I thought, oh well, I'm in for some serious payback here. It's not good when one of your caretakers has it in for you. She didn't seem to be holding a grudge, though. Actually, she seemed to be very amused by the whole thing. I'd even say she was a little giddy over it, and she very much enjoyed filling me in on the details of the episode in question.

"Even after she told me his name I didn't remember him or the incident, which didn't surprise me at all, because such incidents have taken place on a fairly

regular basis throughout my life. If you haven't noticed, my friend, every day of my life has featured multiple adventures, each of a different nature, so I often
don't recall this or that one when I'm asked about
them, as you know."

I nodded my head over at him in affirmation of what
I knew to be very true.

"Okay, so I didn't remember her husband or the incident, but the one thing I knew for certain was that I
hadn't beaten on the guy for no reason. I've never bul-
lied anyone in my life, as I have told you many times.
I've never pounded on anyone just because I could, in
other words. So I told her in a very quiet, sympathetic
voice that if it is true that I punched her husband's
front teeth out years ago, he must have deserved it.

"'He says he did!' she laughed, 'he says he had a
little too much to drink and was picking a fight with a
guy smaller than he is, you jumped in, he got mouthy,
and you plastered him! He laughs like hell about it
now and says he learned a valuable lesson! I wish I
had a quarter for every time I've heard him tell that
story!'"

The thought of her being all excited about going
home and telling her husband that she's got Jake
Sawyer as one of her patients cracked both of us up.
Especially because we're talking forty years after the
fact here.

"So now you'll have some old guy with false front
teeth coming through the door with a big smile wanting to shake your hand for growing him up!" I said.

"Yes," he laughed, "that's the kind of thing that
happens when you've been as active around town as I
have been for such a long period of time," he said, still
chuckling. "This is a small town and you can't escape
your past."

"Okay, Jake," I said, "other than that, how are you feeling?"

"Terrible!" he roared. "I've got three severely fractured ribs and fourteen staples holding my stomach together! I haven't been able to eat a normal meal or practice my regular workout for days! How the hell do you think I feel?!"

I sympathized a bit and said that at least he was getting good care and would eventually heal up, that sort of stuff, you know; I was trying to be upbeat. Then I asked him when he thought he might be transferred to a nursing facility.

"Do you know something I don't?" he asked in a lowered, suspicious voice. "Is a crew of star-spangled medics going to be showing up at any time now to put me on a stretcher and wheel me down the hall into the elevator? Then when we hit the ground floor they're going to roll me from my apartment building out to the curb, and then they'll load me into an ambulance that will transport me to the nursing facility where I'll live in heavenly bliss from now to eternity, right? Are you the one in charge of my affairs now and you've set it all up?"

"From your apartment?" I said, "What the hell are you talking about?"

"I cut out of the hospital yesterday!' he yelled, "I just couldn't take laying around in a bed anymore! I'd been there for two and a half days!"

I didn't say a thing.

"Do not get the idea that I wasn't a good patient while I was there," he went on. "I was very grateful for the highly professional and compassionate care I received, and I co-operated with the program in every way. I didn't make incessant demands like I heard other patients doing, and I remained respectful of my caregivers at all times. After two days in bed, though, I was going absolutely bat shit, and became obsessed with getting up out of that damn bed and maybe strolling around a bit with the aid of a walker. The nurses said that I wasn't really ready to get up and take a walk, though, because at that point any sudden movement could further damage my fractured ribs, and could also tear open the nine-inch long incision in my stomach they had made to operate on my perforated ulcer. They also said that the various pieces of medical apparatus that I was hooked up to would have to travel with me, and that was going to be difficult, so to just relax and be patient. I tried to talk them out of that negative attitude, of course, but they put me off by saying that they were too busy to help me get up and take a walk even if they wanted to.

"Alright, so I waited until about three in the morning, when everything was quiet, and called the nurses station and asked if someone would please come and help me get out of bed so I could take a little stroll. They had the same doubts the day shift staff had about me getting up and taking a walk so soon, but they said that if I really thought I was up to it they'd provide me with the necessary assistance to at least get me sitting up on the side of the bed, and before long a very pretty young nurse's aide showed up to help me out.

"Well, having a pretty young lady on the scene probably made me act a lot more confident about my ability to pull the whole thing off than I actually was, because I damn well was in a world of hurt, but we kept at it and before long, with her capable and gracious assistance, I was out of bed leaning on my walker, then slowly, painfully, but happily, nonetheless, making my way down the hallway.

JAKE

"Things went very well as we progressed down the hallway and both the young lady and I felt very encouraged. I was managing to drag one foot after the other and make some sort of forward progress, and my lady friend had figured out how to bring the pieces of medical apparatus along with us, so before long we were moving along very nicely, having a very pleasant conversation about what she liked to do for fun on her days off. As we went along, though, I found myself gradually picking up the pace, because my natural tendency is to do so, I guess. Then, out of nowhere, I felt a surge of exhilaration and started to open 'er up!

"'Mr. Sawyer! Mr. Sawyer!' the young lady whispered excitedly in my ear, because she didn't want to alert the rest of the staff, 'Please slow down! I can't keep up! I can't keep up!'

"I couldn't help myself, though! I was laughing like hell at her struggling to keep the equipment erect, and she started laughing too, but the rest of the staff weren't too amused when they saw me rampaging down the hall with my johnny flying open and all of the medical apparatus bouncing around.

"'Mr. Sawyer,' one of the nurses said, very calmly and professionally, 'you are in no condition to be acting this way. Any sudden movement could interfere with your ribs healing, and you could easily tear out the staples that are holding your stomach together. So, please, Mr. Sawyer, let's get you back to bed and I promise we'll be getting you up regularly from now on.'

"I knew she was trying to be reasonable, but I just couldn't bring myself to slow down quite yet. To make matters worse, a fat out-of-shape male nurse's aide showed up and positioned himself in the hallway directly in my path! What the hell is a fat, out-of-shape nurse's aide standing in his way mean to a man who's ridden in formation with the Hell's Angels doing ninety-miles per hour weaving in and out of traffic on a crowded California freeway! The guy had no idea who he was up against! You should have seen the look on his face when I hooted my head off and headed my walker straight for him! He was able to stop me with his fat stomach, no problem, of course, c'mon, look at the handicaps I had, but I did back him up against the wall! He outranked me, obviously, so I backed off, but I saw some momentary fear in his eyes, that's for sure!

"Shortly thereafter, I quieted down and we got me put back to bed okay, but I had had the outing I was looking for, and then some. What you have to understand here is that this all went down in a spirit of good humor. I wasn't terrorizing anybody. Everyone knew I was just letting off pent-up steam and they enjoyed my raising a rcukus as much as I did. The only damage was to myself, actually. Seeing that guy's eyes bulge like that when I backed him up to the wall got me to laughing so hard I thought I was going to die from the friggin' pain it was causing me!

"Hey, none of this was anything new, I was just being me, so wha' d'ya gonna do? You remember me getting naked and having sex with women in bars and other public places around town, right?"

"Yeah, yeah, I remember," I said.

"Well, the deal at the hospital was the same thing. It's all in how you go about it. I didn't hurt anybody in any way, or gross anybody out, I just went to certain extremes and made everybody laugh, that's all.

"Okay, so the next morning the head nurse comes into my room and gives me a gentle scolding about what had taken place the night before and, because I'm not good at handling anything that sounds even slightly like a reprimand, and also because I knew that there were other and even more dramatic scenes yet to come if I remained a patient at their facility, I decided to check myself out. The hospital staff was extremely alarmed, of course, and they all tried to talk me out of it, but I knew I had to do what was best for all concerned."

HOME, HOME AT LAST

So, there he was, at home, when he should've been in the hospital for a couple of weeks, at least, then transferred to a nursing facility for who knows how long. I had gained an appreciation of what it means to have someone living with you providing care and comfort when I fractured my ribs falling on the ice – I really don't know how I would have gotten through the recovery period without my loving wife, Leslie – so I was extremely concerned about Jake's being at home alone, considering that he had fractured three ribs, not two like I had, and had undergone a serious stomach operation as well. That he's also about thirty years older than I was when I had my accident was on my mind too. I knew by this time, though, that Jake is an exception to many rules, and I also knew that it's never a good idea to crowd him in any way, so I waited a couple of weeks before I gave him a call. Truthfully, I half-expected that he'd be back in the hospital to get his stomach sewn back up or something, or maybe he'd still be home, but not able to get to the phone.

He picked up on the first ring and barked: "Hey, wha' d'ya know, you're still with us!"

"Of course!" I answered. "Just wanted you to know

that the book's on the way to getting done, and I also wanted to find out how things are going with you."

"Well, all my friends are getting older and more boring every day, and I'm not getting much in the way of sexual gratification, but other than that, I can't complain," he answered.

"C'mon, Jake," I said, "how's it going, how are you feeling?" I said.

"Okay, you want to know the truth?" he said in a sincere, subdued voice. "I'm feeling worse than I ever have in my life. I'm in severe pain throughout the day and night. I can't take a breath without my ribs hurting like hell. The perforated stomach ulcer they operated on causes me excruciating pain if I even take a small drink of water, and I have constant, sharp shooting pains from each of the fourteen places they put staples in to hold my stomach muscles together. I also haven't slept for more than two consecutive hours in a couple of weeks, and even then, I don't really go to sleep, it's more that I pass out from exhaustion. I haven't eaten a proper meal in about two weeks either, even though I'm hungry as hell. Two weeks ago, I weighed one-hundred and fifty-three pounds, and I'm now down to one-hundred and thirty-two pounds. Please remember that in my prime I weighed two-hundred and ten pounds, by the way. The worst part of all this nonsense I'm going through now, though, is that I haven't been able to work-out on my Total Gym for more than an hour or so at a time since I fell down the stairs, so obviously I'm feeling very weak physically."

"Jake, are you telling me that even though you're in serious pain, exhausted from lack of sleep, and feeling weak from hunger, that you're still able to get yourself out of bed on your own and climb on the stationary bike and work out for an hour every morning?"

"No!' he yelled, "That's not what I'm telling you! I didn't think I'd even have to mention that I've been working-out! That should be assumed! Regular exercise is central to my being! Hell, I was on that damn bike the first morning I was back from the hospital! What I'm bitching about here is that I'm still not able to spend more than an hour working-out on it and it's been almost three weeks since my accident!"

And I was thinking two weeks or so longer in the hospital, then Oceanside Manor for who knows how long.

"I didn't do much that first day home but pedal the stationary bicycle a little," he continued, "and even that caused severe pain in my stomach and rib cage. I tried to get my right hand up to the bar that lifts the weights, but I just couldn't do it. I made a little progress every day, though, just like I've been telling people I've trained over the years: keep at it, keep at it, push yourself, don't forget to smile, and you will see results. So, there you go, after a few days I got up to pedaling a mile on a level grade, and I was able to get my right hand up onto the bar and pull it down with thirty pounds of weight on it. Before the accident, I was up to seventy-five pounds with my right arm, but that was then. This morning I pedaled two miles on a slight grade and lifted fifty pounds of weight with my right arm. Still can't get that left arm up there, between the fractured ribs and the damn staples in my stomach, but I'll get there."

"Damn, Jake," I said, "I can't believe you're even getting out of bed on your own, to tell you the truth. So you're still getting up out of bed at six, like you did before the accident, then you work out, huh?"

"No, my friend, not quite," he answered, "I do roll out of bed at six, but I don't get back home until about nine, and that's when I commence my daily work-out."

I was confused and told him so.

"What, did you think I retired from my cleaning job I started at the Munjoy Hill Tavern?" he asked me, incredulously. "No way, my friend, I'm not ready to lay down in the pasture yet. On my second day home from the hospital I got up at six, got dressed, which is always a friggin' nightmare these days, managed to stagger down the hall and just about fall into the elevator, rode down to the ground floor leaning on the wall of the elevator, more or less friggin' crawled out to the sidewalk, then managed by some miracle to make it to my van on the top floor of the parking garage, plopped myself down in front of the steering wheel, and proceeded to motor merrily, though not without excruciating pain, up to the Munjoy Hill Tavern to attend to my usual morning duties."

Okay, he went back to work on the second morning after he checked himself out of the hospital. I knew he had taken a job cleaning the Tavern, just because he likes Stan and wanted to help him out, but I assumed he had taken some time off.

"Our good friend Stan was absolutely amazed to see me. Right away he started assuring me that I didn't have to come in to work so soon, that he'd pay me anyway, you know, even though he knows I really don't do it for the money, I do it to remain active, and for something to get dressed for and go to in the morning, you know?. Anyway, he felt very bad about me showing up, and did just about all the cleaning work himself. Well, he'd always been there in the morning when I showed up even before my accident anyway. We're good buddies, and he's always willing to help me with the cleaning, but after my accident he tried to do everything. I wouldn't let him, though, except for mopping the floor, which I did have a go at. Pushing that heavy mop out in front of me like that, then pulling it back full of water and rinsing it out put terrible pressure on my mid-section and caused me so much pain that I begged Stan to take over. Of, course we laughed our asses off over that one because all he'd ever done was beg me to let him help me!"

"Sounds like you're on the mend, Jake," I said, chuckling. "Can't keep a good man down."

"Please spare me the tired cliches," he said. "I've been through enough pain for the past three weeks. The worst of it is over, though. I've started to eat solid meals, and I've gained a little weight, and I feel like I'm going to make a complete recovery, and then some. Hell, this whole damn episode was all about getting me off my lazy ass and getting me stronger than ever. I will tell you, though, that I hope I'll never have to go through something like this again. When you're in your eighties, like I am, you develop aches and pains in parts of your body you didn't know existed, but this falling down stairs and fracturing three friggin ribs, then getting your stomach sawed open to cut out a perforated ulcer, forget it. Hey, normal suffering I don't mind, but this extracurricular stuff is just too much. Well, at least I'm on top of it. The worst is over. Let the games begin!"

"You got it, Jake," I said, "after what you've been through, you deserve a nice smooth ride from here on in. Let's have a little justice for Jake Sawyer!" I yelled.

"Yeah, man, you've got that right!" he yelled back.

VOLUME TWO

DAMN IT, MORE HURT

After that telephone conversation, I left Jake alone for
a week or so again, because when you're hurting like
I knew he was, you like your privacy, and it wasn't as
though he was dependent on my help in any way. I
was very pleased to see his number come up on my
cell phone early one afternoon, though. I anticipated
a very positive update on his progress, of course, like
he was up to pedaling ten miles on a steep incline on
the stationary bike, was lifting one-hundred and fifty
pounds with the right arm, had managed to get the
left arm up to the bar and was lifting at least one-hundred pounds of weight with it, and had gained all his
body weight back, and then some. That sort of thing.

No. He sounded more despondent than I'd ever
heard him, as though the spirit had been drained out
of him.

"I'm back in the hospital and I've never been in
more pain in my life," he said. "I know I said that a
couple of weeks ago, but now I know that no matter
how bad things are, they can get worse, and they sure
as hell did."

My immediate assumption was that he had over-
done it with the getting up at six in the morning to go
to work, then coming home and working out vigorously for an hour or more, so I knew this set back was
his own damn fault, but I felt very sorry for him anyway. When you're the sort of low-key, kind of on the
periphery of things person I am, you spend a lot of
time in your shell, and I'd come to look forward to
Jake's rapping on mine now and then. He's the kind
of guy who gets you out of yourself, you know, standing up square-shouldered and looking at the world

straight on. Now here he was, sounding subdued and withdrawn himself, and somehow that made me feel very sad.

"So, Jake," I said sympathetically, "your ribs and the insides of your stomach are not healing up the way they should be and you're still in a lot of pain, so you decided to spend some time in the hospital after all, huh?"

"No, my friend," he said in a low voice, with a slight air of exasperation, "once again you have leaped ahead on your own and made a grossly unwarranted assumption. What's going on with me now has nothing whatsoever to do with my recent injuries, as far as anyone can tell. Yes, my ribs and stomach continue to give me a great deal of pain, but the medical staff here and myself are satisfied that they are healing at a satisfactory pace.

"This new affliction from hell is a whole other thing, though. It's called 'crystals' and it's an infection that attacked my right wrist yesterday afternoon around this time. You would not believe the terrible, indescribable pain I have been in since that time. It feels like I have dozens of bees inside my wrist that are stinging me over and over again, and the pain of each sting goes all the way though my wrist and arm. It's scary as hell, and it goes on and on and on. I was afraid I was going to go crazy with the pain, so I checked myself into the hospital last night to get some help.

"As soon as I described my symptoms to the extremely competent medical staff, they knew I had this crystals friggin' thing, and they hooked me up to a bottle of some kind of liquid that continually flows through my wrist and washes out the crystals. I'm still in a lot of pain from it, but the flushing does seem to help and they tell me that the pain will be entirely gone in a few days."

I quickly googled "medical term for crystals in humans" and found that what Jake had is an infection called "Hydrogenation Crystal Disease", which is as severely painful and frightening as he described it as being, has no known cause, and appears not to be related to other conditions in the body. In other words, it appears out of nowhere, I guess. The good news, though, is that it's treatable by the flushing method Jake described, and the pain normally goes away in a relatively short period of time.

"Damn, Jake!" I yelled. "What the hell? There you are, laying in bed all day again when we've got a book to put together! I've got some more questions to ask you. I want to be sure of some stuff here and there, you know! So, give me a call from your apartment when you feel like getting up off your ass and we'll set up a time for me to come by and we'll get this thing done!"

"Yes, sir!" he boomed, "If I could raise my right arm, I'd salute you!"

We sat there chortling over the phone about that one for a while, because we both knew that he'd been entirely focused on getting the book out, and had always been as cooperative with me as he could possibly be. This latest malady was just about the only kind of thing that could derail him from getting the project done, and we both knew it.

We also both knew that there was a time, and it was not so long ago, that I would not have been able to address him in the tone I just had, even in jest, and that's what we were laughing at the hardest.

Ah-h-h ... progress.

TWENTY-FOUR

Jake checked himself out of the hospital a couple of hours after our telephone conversation, surprise, surprise, and as soon as he got home he called me to set up a time for me to go to his apartment to do the editing I wanted to get done. When I arrived the next morning and found his door ajar, the way it has been for all of our appointments, I chuckled to myself, thinking of the apprehension I felt seeing it that way the morning of our first interview. When I rapped once and stepped inside and he boomed: "Enter, Sir! The troops are standing in formation awaiting your inspection!" it hit me that I was really going to miss our little get-togethers.

Anyone else would've looked haggard and shell-shocked after what he'd been through over the past two months, but by this time, truthfully, it didn't even occur to me that that would be the case with Jake, and it was not. Oh, he'd lost a considerable amount of weight, so he looked a little tired and worn out — he went from 153 to 132 in two months, after all — but he didn't look weak and exhausted, the way you'd expect for someone who'd lost that much weight in such a short period of time. Not only was he looking good physically, given the circumstances, but it was also obvious that he had gone out of his way to make himself presentable for my visit, the way he always did for anyone, being the considerate host that he is.

Today it was a form-fitting blue denim shirt, blue jeans, and shiny black western-style boots. The only way to describe the scene is to say that he looked and acted like Jake Sawyer, only about twenty pounds lighter.

"Gee, Jake," I said, "you're not looking bad, considering, you know ..."

"Considering what?" he said in his usual barking way. "Considering that next week, on March 1, 2019, I'll be eighty-one years old, or considering that I've been to hell and back with this body over the last couple of months, or maybe it's a combination of both those items, huh?!"

"I, ah, I ah ..." I said, "hey, c'mon," I stammered, "when I fractured two ribs falling on the ice a few years ago I was in constant pain and was confined to an easy chair for about two months, and here you are up and dancin' around the flagpole two months after the fractured ribs and stomach surgery, not to mention the crystals! You've got to be in a lot of pain, man!"

"A lot of pain?" he asked. "Yeah, I'm in a lot of pain, but I'm not going to let it get to me because if I did, then I'd be afraid of it, and when you're afraid of something is when you suffer, and that I wouldn't like. It wouldn't be me. It's the ol' pain is necessary, suffering is optional thing, you know? What you have to understand here is that I've incorporated that particular concept so completely into the core of my being that it's become a reflexive reaction with me to ignore pain to the extent that I'm able to, and get on with things. I feel pain just like anyone else does, believe me, but I don't wallow in it, I don't let it get to me. I've banged myself up on a fairly regular basis over the course of my life and each time I've gotten a little stronger inside.

"So, here we go! One more time! This time it was three severely busted ribs, a seriously perforated stomach ulcer, and friggin' crystals from hell in my wrist! If I gave into shit like that, though, I'd be checking out in no time at all, either that or living the same life of quiet desperation I see just about everyone else on the planet living. No way! Not for me, not today, tomorrow or ever! Onward and upward!"

"Right on!" I yelled, raising my right arm and giving a close-fisted salute, while not even looking up from my notebook.

"When we first started talking," he went on, after a little chuckle, "I told you that I made a decision at a very early age that I'd head right straight for the gusto every damn time throughout my life, no matter what the circumstances, and I don't believe I've indicated to you at any time, that I set any time limit on that approach to living my life. This moment we are in right now is just as precious and bursting with potential as any moment we've ever experienced throughout our lives! Everything we've ever done or experienced was getting ready for right now! So let's go, man! Bring it on!"

Alright, then, no quarter asked for, no quarter given. I worked him hard for about three hours filling in gaps and providing detail here and there relative to all he'd related to me throughout the interview process, and he was right with me all the way. I kept going on and on, and he didn't show the slightest sign of tiring, nor was there any mental fog to contend with. There wasn't even a nuance of difference between what he said about his various experiences that day under questioning, and what he had originally told me about them. Which, truth be told, is a lot to be said for anyone, much less someone in their eighties, especially one who has led the exceedingly raucous and event-filled life Jake Sawyer has.

He did take what he called a "weight-gaining break" about half way through the session, though, and when I asked him what that was all about he answered that his regimen is to consume five meals a day, and that he wasn't going to interfere with that, no matter what was going on. He had gone about six weeks with little sustenance of any kind, he said, but over the past two weeks he had worked his way up to his current five meals a day in order to 'maximize his daily nutritional intake', as he put it. The five meals, he said, consist of three solid protein-based meals, supplemented by two high-protein drinks between meals that are each the nutritional equivalent of a meal in themselves.

"Before I leave for the Munjoy Hill Tavern at six in the morning," he said, thereby confirming for me what I had suspected, that was getting up at 5:30 in the morning to go to his job like before, "I eat the same breakfast I've had for years and years: a simple bowl of oatmeal, with a handful of raisins thrown in. I don't know why it works, but it does."

At that, I told him, after all this time, that once, years ago, before I actually knew him, I had overheard him say that very thing to a friend he was with one morning at the Porthole Restaurant, and have had oatmeal with a handful of raisins for breakfast ever since. I don't quite know why I had never mentioned that to him, but I guess I was waiting for just the right moment.

"Ha! Wha' d'ya know!" he roared when I told him. "That's why you've been able to keep up with me all this time!"

We both laughed heartily at that because we both knew there were many times in the course of the interview process when I had to hang on for dear life. I'm accustomed to taking life in smaller doses than Jake does, after all, and, for some reason, the notion that the oatmeal and raisins for breakfast routine he unwittingly turned me onto years ago gave me the wherewithal to keep up with him amused the hell out of both of us.

"As beneficial as it is, my friend," he went on, "oatmeal and raisins for breakfast is only a part of my weight-gaining program. There's also the wholesome and nutritious food that our good friend Stan from the Munjoy Hill Tavern provides me with, which is often given to him by friends of his from down around the Portland waterfront and beyond who have taken an interest in my welfare as well. It's looks like getting ol' Jakie boy to good health has become a community project. Today I will have baked scallops for lunch, directly off a fishing boat that was docked in Portland Harbor this morning, for instance, and later in the day I'll have a small piece of filet mignon steak that another one of Stan's friends in the food business gave him to pass on to me. I am gaining weight before your very eyes, my friend!

"Then, of course, there's my two very special high-protein drinks per day, which are each the equivalent to a meal in itself. You, of course, remember me telling you about California Hi-Protein, the magic elixir I first developed as a prisoner at San Quentin, then later produced and promoted at the various health clubs I've managed in Portland, Boston and beyond, I'm sure. The only difference today is that I've somehow misplaced the smock I wore when I prepared it in those days, but I, of course, remember the ingredients exactly: twenty grams of specially-formulated protein powder, containing all of the amino acids, and the whites of two eggs, all mixed into a large glass of fresh whole milk, and you have the nutritional equivalent of a complete meal. Two of those babies a day, along with oatmeal and raisins for breakfast, the high-protein meals Stan and his friends provide me with, and it won't be long before I'll be too obese to get out the door!"

I recalled that when Jake told me about the high-protein drinks he prepared, he stressed that the all-important "secret ingredient" was the absolute belief instilled in the individual consuming the product that it would work, that drinking it would make them get bigger and stronger, and I knew, beyond any doubt, that that ingredient was not lacking in his own case at the moment.

"So, Jake," I said, "you're kind of taking it easy with the exercising so you'll gain some weight and allow your body to heal, huh? You've been through a lot. You need to give your body a rest, huh?" I said.

"What?!" he roared, "there is never a time when exercising won't get you where you want to go, including gaining weight! I get on my stationary bike and pedal uphill for an hour immediately after I arrive home from work at the Munjoy Hill Tavern in the morning, then work out on my Total Gym. The whole-body workout I engage in every day gets the blood pumping through my system, which makes the creation of muscle possible. I'm into gaining muscle! I am exercising at the present time to get bigger and *stronger* just like I have every day of my life!"

After the three hours of editing we'd done, and after listening to him talk about what he puts himself through every day, I told him I was feeling a bit weary and had had enough for the day. As I closed my notebook and got up to leave, though, I happened to remark that it was too bad he had to stop conducting the exercise classes for the people in his building because I knew how much the people looked forward to them.

"Yes, you're right," he said, regretfully, "we've had

about a two-month hiatus in our exercise class, and that's not good. After managing to get myself out of bed and get dressed in the morning — oh, what a friggin' ordeal that is — then going to clean the Munjoy Hill Tavern and coming home from that and working out vigorously for two hours, I just didn't have enough gas left by afternoon to do much else but read and watch TV documentaries. Considering what was going on with my body, I didn't look forward to getting up in front of an exercise class and demonstrating all those stretching and muscle against muscle exercises. That's about an hour and a half of that stuff, man, with three fractured ribs, my stomach still healing from the fourteen staples being pulled out. Man, that hurt! The nurse who did it was chatty as hell, she'd stop to tell me about things like the day of the week she has to put her trash out, stuff like that! Oh, man!

"That stuff's all in the past, though, we're on to a new day," he said as I was walking out the door, "I trust you'll be joining us in the rec room next Tuesday afternoon at one o'clock?"

TUESDAYS WITH JAKE

I wouldn't have missed the class for anything, actually. Whenever I'd run into someone from his building around town over the past few weeks they'd pepper me with questions about how Jake was doing, and if he was still going to do the exercise class, so I was looking forward to witnessing the warm reception I was sure he'd receive upon getting back at it. I anticipated that they'd be protective of him, urging him not to extend himself for their sakes, that sort of thing. No way, though. Nothing like that. Neither his present condition, nor what he had gone through over the previous two months, were alluded to in any way, by Jake, or by any of the attendees.

The story is that the people all had encountered Jake in the hallways of the building since his series of medical incidents and had gotten the message loud and clear from him that he was up and running at pretty much full-speed and didn't need their condolences or sympathy, thank you. I could just hear him barking them off the subject, actually, so I knew very well what the story was, but I was still amazed – yeah, that's the word for it - *amazed* – as I sat there watching him up in front of the group leading them in stretching and muscle against muscle exercises, with no indication whatsoever that he was feeling any pain or discomfort, and with not a word said by him or anyone in attendance about what had transpired with him over the past three months. It was as if nothing had even taken place. The only difference between this class and the one I had attended before Christmas, the one right before Jake fell down the stairs, is that that class numbered sixteen attendees, nine men and seven women, and this class was up to twenty, and was evenly split between the genders, some people with walkers, some not able to fully stand, but all one-hundred percent in tune with Jake. It was exceedingly obvious that his classes starting up again was a very big deal to them.

"Welcome everyone to the world of better living brought to you through the miracle of exercise!" Jake announced. "Today we will continue with our advanced commando training in preparation for that great and glorious day when we take over the world!"

Then came a series of leg lifts, arm rotations, deep

JAKE

Jake's exercise class with Lynelle, Program Coordinator, on the far left, and Jake on the far right. "My class is even larger now," said Jake. "Now that's a class of characters! I tell them that they are helping me as much as I am helping them. Everybody wins and I love it!"

Commando Training 101. Leg rotations, 13 times one way, then 13 times the other way. (both photos on this page by Dave Wade)

Jake leading bends and stretches a few weeks after fracturing three ribs and having a perforated ulcer removed.

Getting ready to row their boats in Portsmouth Harbor. The big guy with his arms crossed is a former Russian professional boxer who does not speak English yet. This was his first class.(both photos on this page by Dave Wade)

JAKE

Jake with Commando "Chaplain" Theresa, loved by the whole class. Jake was still recovering from surgery when this picture was taken. (photo by Dave Wade)

knee bends, standing push-ups leaning over the back of chairs, toe touches, and cross-toe touches, with each movement being executed thirteen times, for two sets. Yes, he did each routine thirteen times. The stretching cross-the-body toe touches is the exercise that really got to me. When I saw him up there bending over at the waist and touching each hand to the opposite foot thirteen times each, I was sure I'd spot some sign of a grimace. Some indication that he had severely fractured three ribs just two months before, then had his stomach cut open and sewed back up with fourteen staples, then, just about a week ago, had that excruciating experience of crystals in his right wrist. But, nope. No grimace. No indication of a sudden stabs of pain. Nothing.

"Why do we do each exercise thirteen times, Jake?" a guy yelled out between sips of orange juice.

"Because thirteen is one more than twelve, and twelve is all weaklings can do!" Jake yelled. "We are not weaklings, though! We are the cream of the crop! We are the one percent the other ninety-nine percent worry about!" he bellowed.

"Let's row a boat!" he yelled, pulling on imaginary oars. "We're going to take a trip around Portland Harbor! Oh! We're going by Ft. Gorges! A very historic military installation that has been guarding the harbor from invasion by the enemies of America since before the Civil War! There should be an immense American flag – a garrison flag! – proudly waving in front of the historic walls of Ft. Gorges to express our undying gratitude for a job well done!"

Needless to say, the crowd signaled their approval of the idea with hoots and hollers as they rowed by Ft. Georges.

"Back to shore!" he yelled, then, and everyone had

clamored out of the boat and were standing on the shore: "Now we've got to loosen up from our time of sitting down! Sitting down is the absolute worst thing you can do to your body! We are meant to be up and around and getting the most out of life we can! Okay, now, thirteen right leg kicks!" Kicking his right leg out to the side and counting off the thirteen times, then, after repeating the process with the left leg, "Now both legs at once!" acting confused and frustrated because he couldn't do it, flapping his arms comically and yelling: "Yeah man! That's it! Let's fly! I've always wanted to fly! Just picture yourself up there with the seagulls, gliding, soaring, masters of all you survey! My friends the seagulls are noble creatures and so are each and every one of you!"

The group erupted with laughter, of course, and everyone started flapping their arms, trying to kick both legs out to the side at the same time. One older man with a cane was trying so hard to do it, while laughing his head off, that Jake had to calm him down.

"Irwin!" Jake yelled, "get hold of yourself! We haven't got to the part yet where we're going to actually take off flying! We'll get there, though! Flying is happening next month! The world and all we survey will soon be ours! Just hang in there a while longer!"

Then there was the attractive, heavily-rouged and perfumed woman who had extended her leg out and rotated it alluringly in the previous class and gotten Jake so excited. This time she was wearing a very provocative, not-really-meant-for-working-out dress, and had a large pretty ribbon in her hair, and Jake yelled out: "Theresa's getting in shape for her week-end job as an exotic dancer at a nearby strip club!"

"No-o-o!" she yelled back, "I dance on the weekend,

but it's on Sunday morning at my church! We dance in praise of the Lord!"

"Hallelujah!" Jake yelled, inspiring everyone else to yell "Hallelujah! Hallelujah!" too, which inspired the woman to step forward and do a little dance for the group, which elicited enthusiastic cheers and whistling from everyone, including me. It was impossible not to get caught up in the excitement, you know?

Then Jake gave them a short break, during which the troops had their choice of a variety of citrus juices, or some 'good ol' "Adam's Ale' as Jake referred to the large glass of water he gulped down.

Jake had told me that he was well aware of the fact that most of the people he trained in his building wouldn't ever get in tip-top shape or lose much weight, but he wasn't concerned with that because the main purpose of the exercise classes was to get them feeling better about themselves, not to make them into Olympic athletes, and as I watched the people from his class disperse, with a lilt in their steps and a smile on their faces, I knew he had indeed done just that.

We had well-known Portland photographer Dave Wade with us that day taking pictures of Jake and the class, and when he gathered the class at the end for a group photo, I thought of other group photos with him in them that Jake had shown me in the course of our interviews: The one of him and his two pals when they were five years old, a group of friends at Kents Hill Prep School, the weight-lifting team he started at San Quentin, the body-builder friends he trained in Portland, in the barber chair with buddies around him at Maine State Prison, with a group of hikers in the Rocky Mountains, and then there's the one of him with the Wayside Ministry softball team he managed. And in every one of those photos he's smiling the same delighted, proud, gleefully happy smile he was smiling as he posed with his exercise class that day.

Okay, now, I was thinking, here's a guy who's obviously fiercely individualistic, and who says he's most comfortable when he's alone, having spent years in prison cells, a good deal of that time in solitary confinement, and also having spent four and a half years living alone in an abandoned bus off in the woods in the Rocky Mountains. Yet there's these various group photos taken over the course of his life that tell a very different story about him. So what's up with that?

To tell you the truth, I don't know.

WE HIT THE HEIGHTS

Jake gave me a call one morning a couple of days later and asked me if I was up for a little excursion, to sort of mark the completion of our little project, he said. Sure, why not, I said, although I had no idea what he had in mind.

"I've got it in mind to climb Mt. Washington!" he said excitedly. "It's as high as you can get in this part of the world and I feel like getting high!"

High, indeed. Mt. Washington, which is about ninety miles northwest of Portland, is the highest peak in the Northeastern United States, at 6,288 feet, or 1.2 miles high. Part of the Appalachian Mountain chain, which begins in Georgia and ends in central Maine, Mt. Washington experiences some of the most extreme weather conditions on earth. Featuring hurricane force winds 110 days of the year, the summit of the mountain, until quite recently, held the world's wind speed record of 231 mph, along with one of the world's lowest recorded temperatures, at minus fifty degrees

Fahrenheit. The Appalachian Hiking Trail crosses the summit of Mt. Washington, so one is well advised to choose the season wisely and check the weather forecast very carefully before starting out on that particular part of the 2,190 mile, five to seven months-long hike.

I had never been to the top of Mt. Washington and definitely had a few reservations. Warm weather had arrived at the time Jake proposed the trip, though, and a quick google search assured me that hurricane winds weren't predicted for the summit. But there was still the part about driving the ninety miles back and forth with Jake at the wheel to worry about.

I whined to my wife, Leslie: "C'mon, he's an eighty-one year old former Hell's Angel driving a vintage Lincoln Town Car with its rear-end lowered the way they do with hot rods and race cars. We'll be going over the same piece of road outside of Fryeburg that he set the land speed record on, so what's to say he won't get inspired to go after a new one on this trip? Also, please keep in mind that he's had medical procedures in the past few months that would have landed anyone else in a nursing home for life. What if he gets an excruciating pain in his side just when we're whooshing by a line of cars, trying to beat the red light ahead? Hey, I'm going to be riding one-hundred and eighty miles with him! And there's no way out of it! After all we've been through over the past few years, how the hell can I tell him that I'm scared shitless to ride with him?!"

"Has he ever let you down in any way before now?" she asked.

I immediately got her point and shut up.

Travelog says the ninety mile trip from Portland takes one hour and thirty minutes, but it seemed like six hours to me, even though we left Portland at nine in the morning and arrived at ground zero at ten-fifteen, a mere fifteen minutes shorter than the estimated travel time. Fast, too fast, but not maniacally so, and with no close calls. I had anticipated a worse scenario, of course, and Jake knew it by the way I kept my eyes glued on the road ahead the whole time.

"You can relax now," he said when we arrived at the base of the mountain, "from here to the top is a breeze."

Actually, I was hoping beyond hope that we'd leave the winged chariot at the bottom and ride the Mt. Washington cog railway to the summit, but, naturally, it was the Auto Road all the way.

The Mt. Washington Auto Road is 7.6 miles long, and is an extremely steep, narrow, two lane, winding mountain road without guardrails. The road overlooks deep rocky ravines that, of course, get deeper as one ascends to the top, so one wrong move and there you go. Jake was all business, though, and for that I was very grateful. No glancing down into the ravines or anything like that. Truthfully, I didn't glance down into the ravines either, on the theory that looking straight ahead and holding your breath would keep you safe.

"There, you can start breathing again," he said when we pulled into the parking lot just below the summit.

Well, not really. The air is very thin that high up and breathing can be difficult. In any event, though, we were there, the weather was warm and sunny, and the view was grand. I actually felt a certain elation, as though we had conquered something or other.

"I've been coming up here all my life," Jake said as we climbed the wooden staircase to the summit. And then, as we stood at the edge of a precipice looking out across miles and miles of picturesque New England forests, fields, and meandering streams and rivers, he said: "As you well know, I tend to gravitate to extremes, and this place is as extreme as you can get around here. I've always felt quite at home up here."

So did I. Damn it, so did I.

OUT OF NOWHERE
THE SON I DIDN'T KNOW HE HAD

I was somewhat mesmerized by the experience, truthfully, and wandered off on my own a bit for some quiet reflection. Jake was completely understanding of that, of course, and left me alone, but after a little while I started looking around for him but couldn't locate him. I figured he'd had enough and had gone back down to the car, and when I stood at the top of the staircase and looked down at the car, there he was, standing next to it talking to some middle-aged guy in a leather jacket straddling a Harley, and the guy was waving his arms the same way Jake does when he's talking about something he's excited about.

When I got down to them, Jake said: "This is my son, Jonathan Sawyer Jr., he's called Jon. He just rode halfway across the State of Maine to meet us up here."

I was kind of slack-jawed because, after all the ground we'd covered over the past few years, Jake had never mentioned that he had a son. But he does, and not only does he look and act a lot like Jake, he also rides a customized Harley Davidson motorcycle.

After we shook hands and chatted a bit, I discovered that Jon's a very articulate, intelligent guy and I ached to get him alone to find out what he might have to say about this individual I'd been dogging for so long. Jake, being the perceptive character that he is, saw what was on my mind and said: "I'm going back up to the top to do some quiet reflecting, you guys are on your own."

Jon and I laughed heartily at the "quiet reflecting," then when we were alone, I asked him how he happened to be there just when Jake and I were.

"My father called me this morning and told me he was going to Mt. Washington with his writer and if I wanted to meet him at the top, great. Well, I had a full day planned, but you know how that goes. I'm a painting contractor and I'm lucky enough to have a bunch of very loyal employees, so I get to play hooky when the occasion calls for it. I don't get to see my dad that often, so when he called, I wolfed down my breakfast, quickly got some stuff I had to attend to out of the way, then jumped on my Harley and lit out."

"Oh, I guess seeing you must be the reason Jake wanted to travel to this part of the state," I said, "you must live fairly locally, right?"

"Not exactly!" he laughed. "I live in Waldoboro, which is about one-hundred and thirty miles west of here! I've been barreling across the state on my motorcycle for about an hour and a half!"

An hour and a half. That means he averaged well over eighty miles an hour.

"Jon," I said, "it's becoming apparent to me that your father and you might have some things in common ..."

Truthfully, I kind of assumed that Jon, like his father, has kind of, well, lived his life on the edge.

"Well, yes, I guess my father and I do have a few things in common," he said, chuckling, "like our loyalty to our friends, our dedication to helping the underdog whenever we can, and our love of Harley motorcycles, but our lives have been very different in some major respects. I own a very successful business, I'm a very happily married family man, and my life is dedicated to serving Jesus. So there you go."

Wha' d'ya know.

When I asked Jon for his favorite story about his father and him he didn't have to think long to come up with it.

"I served on an aircraft carrier when I was in the Navy, about twenty-five years ago or so, and when we returned from our tour of duty in the Mid-East during operation Desert Storm we docked in Ft. Lauderdale, Florida. I didn't expect my father to be there, since Portland is so far from Ft. Lauderdale, but as we were nearing the shore I spotted him, and because I had been telling my shipmates all about my father all through the tour, I called a bunch of guys over and pointed him out. They actually gave a little cheer! There he was, wearing a U.S. Army Airborne tee shirt and Tony Lama boots with red flames on them, looking every bit as cool as I had been telling the guys he was. When we got ashore and I made eye contact with him, he punched his right arm in the air and yelled: "Aw-w-w-right!!" I'll never forget that moment.

"The main event the Navy had planned for us was a welcome home cruise on the carrier from Ft. Lauderdale to Norfolk, and various dignitaries, along with the families of crew members, were invited to join us. There were a lot of people aboard, the carrier had a five-thousand-person crew, after all, but my father definitely stood out and was a big hit with everybody. The top enlisted man aboard took a special liking to him, and he got us invited to a special dinner in the captain's quarters. I had never even seen the inside of the captain's quarters before, but there we were!"

When Jake returned, he immediately gave Jon the high sign without saying anything, Jon revved up his Harley, Jake and I jumped into the Lincoln Town Car, and the two Jonathan Sawyers and I were off down the side of the mountain.

WHAT THE HELL COMES NEXT?

I was preoccupied with putting the finishing touches on the book for a couple of weeks after the trip to Mt. Washington, so Jake and I didn't get together, but I had told him as we parted company that day, that after I got the rest of the book together, I'd like to end it by writing about what he thought he might like to do with the rest of his life. Like, what's the plan?

"Plan?" he had asked, with his face shriveled up in confusion, "that's an excellent idea! I've always wanted to have a plan! The only problem is that every day of my life has been filled with one adventure after the other, and they happen without any *planning* or intention on my part! They just jump out at me! Wham! That's it! Deal with it! So, let me ask you, do you have reason to think that the rest of my life is going to be any different?"

"No! I mean I don't know!" I yelled back at him as I got out of the car, "just give it some thought and see what you come up with!"

Okay, so when we got together in his apartment the next time, he opened with: "I've given a lot of thought to what I'd like to do with the rest of my life and I've come up with a plan. I've decided that I want to become a dentist. I want to go to a dental college that has a very good volleyball team, though. I've always wanted to play volleyball competitively and I've never gotten the chance. So wha' d'ya think?"

"I think it's a wonderful plan, Jake," I said, "except for the volleyball part. I think you're going to have trouble finding a dental college with a good volleyball team."

"Forget the whole thing then!" he roared. "See what I told you? Planning doesn't work for me!"

We sat there musing over the matter for a while, with both of us smiling and shaking our heads. Somehow or other, after all the grand adventures he had related to me over the course of our interviews, the thought of him going to dental college at eighty-one and playing on the volleyball team was very amusing to us. You had to be there, I guess.

"Aw-w-w, c'mon, Jake," I said after a bit, "you didn't get where you are, and do what you've done in your illustrious life, without a good deal of planning, so what's up, what are ya' gonna do with your life now that your guardian angel intervened once again and gave it back to you on a silver platter?"

"Damn straight! If she hadn't made me fall down those stairs and break a few ribs so I'd go to the hospital where they'd discover that damn perforated ulcer, I'd be tooling around outlaw-biker heaven or hell now! So, okay, you go to it. I'm going to give you the lay of the land as we move forward here.

"Of course, both our lives will be impacted quite soon by the avalanche of money and fame that the proceeds from our upcoming book and movie will cause, my friend, so a little planning for that inevitability might be in order.

JAKE

"The first thing I'm going to do when this block-buster book and movie we're working on takes off is add a great deal of do-re-me to the coffers of the recreation department of my building so that my friends can enjoy trips to various cultural and sporting events, have many wild and crazy pizza parties in the rec room, and maybe have enough left over to purchase a large video screen to add to the festivities that will, at that point, start to happen on a more regular basis.

"After that's taken care of, who knows. I don't have many material desires to speak of, and neither do I have any desire to travel anywhere. Well, maybe except for purchasing a small late-model RV camper, and driving across this great country to visit my good friends in Ward, Colorado.

"You know, of course, that Ward is the small, remote mountaintop town in the Rocky Mountains where I spent a few months hiding out in the late seventies, then returned to for four-and-a-half years of rest and recuperation in the early nineties. Because it's up so high and there are no roads leading to it, Ward has always made an excellent outlaw hideout. Jesse James, Cole Younger, Patty Hearst, and Jake Sawyer are known to have spent time there!"

"Famous outlaws all!" I yelled, thrusting my arm up in the air and giving him a clenched fisted salute.

"Well, thanks for the recognition, even though it is a little late in coming, but what you have to understand here is that not only was I the least known famous outlaw to hide out in Ward, I was also the *last* outlaw to do so. The FBI has got you covered wherever you go in the country today, even in remote mountaintop towns, so outlaws tend to flee to mountaintops in little-known and distant undeveloped countries.

VOLUME TWO

There's only a few dozen people living in Ward now, and I don't think anyone of them even ran a red light before they came to town. In other words, they're not running away from the law. They went to Ward to escape the stress of modern life, which is exactly why I returned there in the early nineties and lived in a cabin in the woods for four and-a-half years, all alone, with the company of only my beautiful pure white dog Shawn, and all my animals from the forest, who I still miss to this day.

"Remember I told you about Fuzzy, the town cop who was the first to greet me when I first went to Ward in the late seventies? He's still there! He lives in an abandoned mining shack and spends all day alone playing his guitar. When I was there in the 70s, and 90s, sometimes I'd stand outside his bus at night listening to him play. In all that time I never knocked on his door, though. We liked each other a lot, but everybody in Ward respects each other's privacy and that's it.

"And then there's Tall Bob. He's lived in Ward for just about as long as Fuzzy has, off by himself alone in the woods, and he's one of the people in town who I've maintained regular contact with over the years. Tall Bob was a sixties flower child who was never going to turn into a straight world nine-to-fiver, no matter what, so he headed for Ward, because it was the remotest part of the world he could ride his bike . He set up housekeeping in an abandoned shack deep in the woods. He's been living in that shack since the year 1969, and he says that he's never paid rent and doesn't even know who the owner of the shack is. Tall Bob is a master jewelry craftsman, by the way, and his only contact with the outside world is when he walks down off the mountain and hitchhikes to Boulder to deliver the jewelry he makes to a store there.

"Wait! Oh yeah! See this belt buckle?!" he yelled, all excited, "I called Tall Bob a couple of weeks ago to tell him I might be visiting soon, and I got this belt buckle right here in the mail from him the day before yesterday! It's pure silver! The etchings of marijuana leaves on each side of the HDMC is one helluva reminder of the good times I've had in Ward! This item you see right here," he said, tapping his finger lightly on the belt buckle, "became one of my most valuable possessions the instant I laid eyes on it!"

"I can't figure out what the HDMC stands for," I said.

"I thought you were a writer! Good with words, you know?! And you can't friggin' figure out that HDMC stands for *HARLEY DAVIDSON MOTORCYCLE CLUB?!*"

Hey, what can I say.

"Yeah, Tall Bob's a good friend," he said, after he composed himself, "talking with him on the phone is like being back in Ward for me. It's a very interesting thing, actually. It's like people in Ward are frozen in time. They say the same things they've always said, over and over, but everyone acts like they're hearing what the person is saying for the first time. It's kind of a favor they do for each other, or something like that. When I talked to Tall Bob on the phone last time – and, oh, by the way, he does like to be called Tall Bob, not Bob, for some reason – he said that he's thinking about getting a car, so he won't have to hitchhike to Denver to deliver his jewelry, and that's the very same thing he's been saying, in the same words, for over fifty years. The thing is, though, I never get tired of hearing him say it. I actually look forward to it. It feels like family, you know? The people in Ward are like family to me, and that's the way it is in close-knit families.

"There's something else I want to add here about Tall Bob," he said. "The last time we talked, he said he was still quite happy with life in Ward, but that he's started to think that there might be something missing. After all these years, he's talking about finding the love of his life and having her come to live with him. He's a very gentle, responsible, good looking guy, and he's had girlfriends over the years, but he's never made any kind of commitment. Now maybe it's time for the big one, he says. So who knows, maybe an exceptionally loving, gem of a woman will read this and get some ideas. For interested ladies, and anyone who appreciates finely crafted, customized-by-request, distinctive jewelry of any type, Tall Bob Murray can be reached by that name at P.O. Box 321, Ward, Colorado, 80481. Any lady who responds has to like 'em tall, though, because Tall Bob is six-foot, five-inches in height."

And I was sure he was eventually going to say Tall Bob was maybe four-feet, nine-inches tall or something.

"Then there's Rebecca, a good friend of mine, and the wife of a good friend of mine," Jake continued, "she's one of these women who's everybody's mama. I love her to bits. Oh! You want a piece of banana bread?! Rebecca gave Tall Bob a freshly baked loaf to send to me along with this fantastic belt buckle. I'll get some for you!"

Normally I wouldn't partake, you know. Banana bread in the middle of the day, out of nowhere, forget it. Especially because it had traveled across the country from a small town in the Rocky Mountains in the same package as a silver belt buckle made in a cabin out in the woods. He kind of forced the banana bread on me, though. It was good. Very good. It tasted like it was made on a mountaintop in Colorado by a big-hearted woman. Maybe that was all in my mind, who knows. Somehow or other, though, I was genuinely touched by the idea of Jake being sent a loaf of banana bread by a big-hearted woman from a small town high in the Rocky Mountains that he lived in years ago and wants to go back and visit after the book comes out.

Photo/ The Fuge

VOLUME TWO

LET'S GET THIS SHOW ON THE ROAD

"Well, Jake," I said, "it sounds like you've got some plans after all. You're going to make sure the people in your building are taken care of, then you're going to buy a super-duper RV and head for Ward. So, there you go. That should take care of your immediate future, I guess."

"Well, it's good that you're happy with my plans, my friend," he said, "but you should know that you have a very incomplete picture at this point of what I see contained in my future."

"Oh, you haven't given up on going to dental school and playing on the volleyball team thing yet, huh?" I said.

"Actually, I have given up on that plan. You're probably right, it's going to be hard to find a dental school with a good volleyball team. So, I've decided to go to hairdressing school instead, but it has to be one with a touch-football team, and it doesn't even have to be a good one."

"That sounds more like it," I said.

"Okay, okay, enough of that horseshit," he moaned, "what I'm trying to get at here is that I have a major activity in mind for my future that I haven't told you about. A very major activity. It could be the thing I've spent my life preparing for, and what God had in store for me all along."

He had my interest.

"My intention is to devote my life to helping deserving veterans in any and all ways that I am able to, particularly those honored veterans who are struggling with Post Traumatic Stress Disorder, which is commonly known as PTSD.

"My good friend Steve Sawtelle put a bug in my ear about helping deserving veterans and now I'm all over it. There are a large number of Vietnam, Iraq, Afghanistan and other veterans who are continuing to struggle with adjusting to life as it is now being lived in this great country, after having suffered trauma worse than the rest of us can imagine.

"Steve and I are currently working out the details, but mainly it will involve bringing our song and dance routine to veterans centers around the country. As you know, Steve is a combat veteran himself and is dedicated to sharing the coping skills he's learned with his fellow veterans. In May of 2019, Steve had the honor of riding in the front formation of tens of thousands of participants in the "Rolling Thunder" motorcycle ride through the streets of Washington, D.C. to raise money to help our deserving veterans, and to raise awareness of the suffering currently being endured by American prisoners of war in hostile countries around the world. 2019 was the last year "Rolling Thunder" was held in Washington D.C., but the thirty-two-year tradition will continue on a state-by-state basis around the country. I encourage motorcyclists everywhere to take part, and sincerely hope that patriotic Americans across our great country continue to support their most worthy cause.

"You, of course, know that I have never had the honor of engaging in mortal combat with enemies of America myself, so I have not experienced the kind of trauma the people did who I'll be visiting at the veterans centers, but let's just say I can relate to their experiences to some small degree. The various shrinks I've come into contact with over the years have all said that the trauma I suffered over the years due to the extreme situations I have found myself in in has resulted in my developing a clear case of PTSD myself.

"Like, try being a prep school kid from South Portland, Maine, who got his leg almost severed in a motorcycle accident at age twenty-five, then became a Hell's Angel four years later, then found himself incarcerated in San Quentin prison with criminally insane killers shortly afterwards. Then there was Maine State Prison, Lewisberg Federal Penitentiary, and the New York City Metropolitan Correctional Center. I have presented my stay at such places in a rose-colored way to you, but the truth is that I suffered a great deal in every one of them. I have experienced times of dread and desperation that have left their mark, and I struggle to this day to stand up and face the world with a smile, but I do it, damn it, I do it!"

Reminiscent of the way he handled his recent physical ordeals, I was thinking. He didn't deny that he was in pain, but he didn't let it get to him. Dwelling on pain isn't what he's about. Not even for a little while.

"And that's what I want to help our honored veterans do!" he continued. "Stand up and face the world with a smile! It's a great and glorious day *today* and every one of us deserves to get out into it and make the absolute most of it we can! Front and center! Here we go! Our future awaits us!"

A DAY IN THE LIFE OF AND
A PARTING MESSAGE

A few weeks later, with all of the book but this last chapter ready to go to the printer, I gave Jake a call just to see what he was up to, but the reception wasn't very good and I could barely here him.

"What you're hearing in the background, my friend, is the North Atlantic winds," I heard him say. "I am up here on the Eastern Promenade enjoying the wonderful Spring sunshine and the robust winds blowing across the ocean. Won't you come out and join me?"

So I did, of course. Anyone familiar with Portland, Maine, knows what a special place the Eastern Promenade is at any time of the year, but especially in early summer, after the long cold, hard winter is beginning to become a memory and luscious green grass abounds. And there Jake was, sitting about half-way down the slope, taking in the one-hundred-and-eighty-degree view of expansive oceanscape the Eastern Promenade affords, eating an Italian Sandwich. An Italian Sandwich. Here's a guy who should, by all rights, be still recuperating in a nursing home and on a mostly liquid diet, sitting on the grass on the Eastern Promenade eating an Italian Sandwich.

"The Italian Sandwich was originated in Portland, you know," he said as I sat down next to him.

"Yes! Of course it was!" I yelled, even though I know that sandwiches virtually identical to it were made elsewhere at the same time, and that in those other places they're called Submarines, Hoagies, or Poor Boys. Well, maybe it's true that Portland's the only place where it's called an Italian Sandwich, and more importantly, it could be the only city that actually cares where the sandwich originated.

After Jake unsheathed the fine looking Bowie knife he had strapped to his side that day and cut his sandwich in half to share with me, we just sat there eating and taking in the view for a while. Seagulls, of course, know when there is anything organic within a quarter mile or so of their peruse, and they employ a very effective web of communication between themselves as well, so it wasn't long before one or two, then ten, of them were circling above us, screeching away.

"I always save a little bit for them, so they recognize me," Jake said, "sometimes I have a grand ol' time time coming up here and throwing those little round, day-old donuts up in the air for them. I give 'em a hell of a work-out! Exercise is good for *every body* I yell at them."

We sat eating in silence for a while, then from somewhere behind us we heard what sounded like a group of people jogging to a military-type cadence call.

"Attention!" Jake yelled as he jumped to his feet and stood at military attention, saluting the squadron of Portland Police recruits jogging by up on the street. I, naturally, joined him, feeling a bit awkward because I hadn't stood at attention and saluted anyone or anything since my Army days, about fifty years previous, but there you go.

After we had held our salute for a respectful period of time, we raised our right arms with clenched fists, and Jake yelled: "Hooray for the Portland Police! You men and women are becoming part of the best police department on the planet! Thank you for your service!"

I swear, every one of those young Portland Police recruits immediately turned their heads and smiled broadly at us, obviously pleased and gratified at receiving such enthusiastic public recognition. Hey, the experience could well stick in their minds throughout their careers, you know? You never know what comes from what.

"I've always respected the police," Jake said, as we tossed the bits of our sandwiches we had saved for the seagulls over our shoulders and walked up the grass to the sidewalk. "I've never resented anything about the criminal justice system, in any way, actually. I've gotten arrested and incarcerated a number of times, but I've never complained about it. I've always known I deserved it, if not for what they got me for, then for something else I did that they didn't get me for. I've always been perfectly willing to take responsibility for anything I've ever done. The police were just doing their jobs, just like I was just being me. You've got to be who you are, right to the end, you know?"

When we got up to the sidewalk and it was time to go our separate ways, I told him that I was finishing up with this last chapter that day and asked him if there was anything he might like to add.

"No," he said, "there's a lot more I could say, but we've got to call a halt to it somewhere, right? I mean, every day of my life features one or more grand adventures, so we could go on forever."

"Right," I said, "but I thought you might have one final thing to say to the people."

"Alright, alright," he said, barely pausing to reflect, "tell 'em that only the strong survive! But the good news is that each and every one of us has the absolute ability to be as strong as we decide to be! This is a great and glorious life we're involved in here and we need to go for the gusto every time and make ourselves and everyone around us as happy as we can possibly become! That's what God intended for us and we can't disappoint Him!"

I didn't say anything. What could I say? I just lowered my head and walked quietly away. I stopped after a bit, though, and looked back at him walking the other way with that familiar lurching gait of is, and yelled: "Jake!" And then when he turned and saw my broad smile, we both thrust our right arms with clenched fists up into the air with great manly vigor and yelled:

"HELL'S ANGELS FOREVER!"

JAKE SAWYER STORIES

From the time we started serializing Jake's life story in the Bollard magazine, everyone I run into has had a Jake Sawyer story. I've heard a lot of very enthusiastically told yarns, and made a lot of notes, so it was hard to decide what to include here. When I asked Jake for some help deciding, most of the time he either didn't remember the person or the story they told me about him, or said he did kind of know what they were talking about, but the person had it all so garbled it that it doesn't resemble any reality he's familiar with.

"Bullshit stories about me abound," he said, "remember that stupid story you said you thought was true about me dropping a wad of money on the sidewalk just to see if some ape I want to recruit for a friend will pick it up and tell me about it or not?"

"Yes, I do," I said, quietly, without looking up at him.

"The best thing for you to do is not pay any attention to people who come up to you with half-assed stories about me. The woods are filled with 'em, what you need to do is talk to people who actually know what they're talking about. That's always a good idea, ya know?"

VOLUME TWO

RON DAMON

A retired, much respected and highly decorated South Portland police lieutenant who Jake trained at Al Martin's Health Club starting in the early seventies, Ron Damon was a well-known body-builder and power lifter, and also had a stellar military career before and during his career in law enforcement. The remarkable thing, though, is that after his discharge from what later became known as the Nave Seals, he reenlisted into the Army Reserves at age forty-two, around the age that most people retire from military service, and trained to become a member of the Army's Special Forces. An incredible feat at that age, as anyone with knowledge of what it takes to become a member of the Army Special Forces knows.

Sadly, Ron passed away as Jake's story was being written, but I was happy to have had the opportunity to talk with him. When I called him, I truly didn't know what to expect. I knew that he and Jake had known one another for a long time, of course, but Ron was a very well-known South Portland police lieutenant and Jake is a high-profile repeat-offender felon, so I was a little skeptical about them actually being friends. Ron had occasion to witness Jake in action on more than one occasion, after all. He was the officer the police sent for the night they stopped Jake's car on the suspicion of his just having virtually destroyed the clubhouse and motorcycles of the original Iron Horsemen; and he was the officer in charge when the police went into the Griffin Club to find Jake after he set his car on fire out in the parking lot. Jake referred to Ron as a friend, though, and I know full well that Jake doesn't just toss the word 'friend' around.

JAKE

When I told him what I was calling about, right away Ron said that he didn't want to talk about Jake over the phone, so I gave him my address and before long he pulled up in front of my house in a gleaming white, late-model Chrysler Continental, tooted his horn, just once, and sat there in the street with the motor running. I quickly ran out clutching my notebook and jumped in the passenger seat, we shook hands, and Ron got into the subject at hand with no preliminaries whatsoever.

"I got a lot of guff from my fellow police officers about associating with Jake," he began, "hey, the guy has done time in major prisons for multiple felonies and he was openly involved in what everyone knew to be illegal activities all the time I knew him. I sure as hell didn't condone anything he did, but he was wise enough not to discuss any of his illegal activities in my presence, and I counted him as my friend.

"I can tell you, from sometimes very exasperating personal experience, that Jake Sawyer has never, and absolutely would never, rat on his accomplices, or on anyone else, for any reason or incentive whatsoever.

"One time I was at a bar drinking with a bunch of my fellow officers and they started razzing on me over my friendship with Jake Sawyer. 'There's one thing I know for damn sure about Jake Sawyer,' I said to them, 'and that is that he will never, ever let a friend down. The man has got your back, period. When anybody else would be pissing their pants and running the other way, Jake will be out there right behind you! That I know for sure! There's absolutely no doubt about it! I'd trust Jake Sawyer more than I would any police officer or military man I've ever served with!'"

Damn, I thought, he was an honored veteran and a much-respected police lieutenant and he told a group of other cops in no uncertain terms that a notorious ex-con had more guts and integrity than they, or military man he ever served with, did. Wow.

BOB PENNEY

Another one of the men Jake trained at Martin's Health Club, Bob Penney is the founder of Abby Lane Taxi, a very successful local company, and is known for his encyclopedic knowledge of the city and the people who have lived in it over the last half-century or so.

"There never was before, nor will there ever be, anyone like Jake Sawyer to ever hit the planet again!" Bob laughed, "he could sell snow in January and after it melted they'd be happy that they had it for as long as they did!

"Seriously, though," he continued, "a lot of people think of violence and all the crazy-assed things Jake has done, but when I think of him I think of what he meant to me in my formative years. I was kind of a loner as a kid, and I started lifting weights as a way to become somebody. At first my increased strength made me start to feel good about myself, but after I was at it for a while I hit a wall where I couldn't seem to get any stronger and my old feelings of inferiority and depression started to return. Just in time, though, someone told me about Al Martin's Health Club and how great Jake Sawyer was. I was a little hesitant at first, because of the talk about Jake being in and out of jail, and his reputation for violence, but I needed something or someone very badly, so I gave it a shot.

JAKE

"Right away, Jake could see my weak self-image and was all over me to do something about it. My confidence immediately sky-rocketed just knowing that he believed in me and was going to stick by me all the way. Man, he worked me hard, but it was always in a very purposeful way. He know's a lot about the human body, the way it operates and how to get the most out of it.

"That's only part of what Martin's Health Club was for me, though. It was huge I was also accepted into a group of men where I had never known such camaraderie ever existed. Jake was the spark plug of it all, though. He saw that I was sorely in need of friendship and help, and his kindness and friendship has always meant a great deal to me.

"What is to be understood here is that Jake revolutionized the health and fitness business in Maine. He brought exercising out of the sweaty gym era and made it fashionable. He also brought a degree of professionalism to it that had been unknown here. He taught us how to lift properly, including positioning yourself before the bar, proper breathing, all that. And he also kept us motivated. His enthusiasm was contagious. Truthfully, I personally was in heaven when I discovered Martin's Health Club. It changed my life, and I'm still using what I learned from Jake almost fifty years ago when I work out today."

The attendees at Marty Joyce's annual party for the men who worked out together at Martin's Health Club fifty years ago! The bald man second from the left in the back row with a goatee is Bill Hogan, a highly decorated Portland Police officer and the holder of many power lifting records. On his left is Bruce Chambers, who was Jake's long-time training partner and set many power-lifting records. The man with the bandana in the second row is Sonny Day, a retired dentist and well-known power lifter and part-time stripper; next to him smiling in the back row is Ronnie Damon, a retired South Portland Police Lieutenant. In the front row in white shorts is Marty Joyce, the host of the party, and, pound for pound, one of the strongest men in the world in his prime, Jake says; next to him in the sunglasses is "Skippy Cup" Robinson, who was an outstanding power lifter and the holder of many body-builder titles, including Mr. World!

Jake is the tall guy in the back row standing beside his pal Ron Damon, who had to arrest Jake once in a while.

JAKE

MARTY JOYCE

Another friend of Jake's from the Martin's Health Club days, Marty Joyce, is a very successful financial advisor who hosts a lawn party at his home every August for a group of guys from the Martin's Health Club days. Okay, now, Martin's Heath Club was started in 1972 and it's 2020 now, so that's forty-eight years.

"It would be hard to exaggerate what Jake meant to us at the time," Marty said. "I was a college student with no money, I had nothing but a great desire to work out and develop my body, but that was enough for Jake. The bond that developed between the group of us at that time still exists to this day, and there's no question that it's due in very large part to Jake. I've been very involved in the business world over the years since, and have been around quite a bit otherwise as well, but I would have to say that Jake Sawyer is the most intriguing individual I have ever met in my life."

BARBARA

I got a very interesting and well-written email from a woman named Barbara, a long-ago girlfriend of Jake's, who asked me not to use her last name.

"I dated Jake for a while back in my outlaw days," Barbara wrote, "before I got my act together and went to law school, and ol' Jakey boy left an impression on me that's still with me to this day. At the time we were dating he drove a black antique Merc hot rod around Portland that, he claimed, was in the movie *Rebel*

Without A Cause. Who knows if it really was or not, but it looked like it was, and the car became part of the Jake Sawyer legend. There was no other car around like it. The cops would see it and issue a 'Jake Sawyer alert', but unless he did something really outrageous, they left him alone because they were kind of afraid of him.

"Jake was an outlaw, an outlaw's outlaw," Barbara continued, "but he was not a dumb criminal. He came from a classy background that he was rebelling against, evidently, and has a near Mensa IQ. He definitely did not fall into the outlaw life because he was a dumb shit who had no other options. He chose the life he lived, and he loved living it."

The Merc hot-rod that Jake claims was
used in the movie Rebel Without A Cause.

JAKE

TOM WATSON

An email long-time Portland resident Tom Watson sent me describes in graphic detail a typical Jake Sawyer scene.

"Some buddies of mine and myself were out for a night of drinking sometime in the early seventies, when we saw a Harley with a six-pack hanging off the handlebars out in front of a bar. I was more familiar with the local scene than my buddies were, and I knew it was most likely a trap set up by Jake Sawyer, so I told my buddies that they sure as hell should leave the damn six-pack alone, and luckily they did. We could hear a band playing inside the bar, and when we went in, there was Jake, sitting up front with his legs spread eagle and his boots plopped up onto the stage. He had his arms around two women, one on each side, and every so often he'd tilt his head back a little and they would take turns giving him a drink of beer. When the band finished playing a song, Jake jumped to his feet and yelled: 'You guys are fucking great!', after which he turned around and faced the crowd and yelled: 'Everybody start clapping right now!' Everybody else spontaneously complied, but some guys at a table behind us just sat there smirking, and when one of them yelled: 'Sit down, you fucking drunk bastard!' Jake got a very amused look about him, like he couldn't believe his good fortune, then, after getting another swig of beer from one of the ladies, he walked over to the guy's table very calmly and picked him up from around the waist from behind and threw him up into the air so high that when he came down ass-first he bounced off the floor a few times and got the place cheering and laughing like hell. After Jake glanced over at the other guys at the table, they started to clap for the band with a great deal of enthusiasm."

RANDEL PHILLIPS

I'd known that Randell Phillips, a well-known and highly respected chef in some of Portland's finest restaurants, was good friends with Jake, but I didn't know the extent of it until I saw them together one day when Jake was visiting Randel at his volunteer crossing guard job and I talked to Randel later about his relationship with Jake.

"I came to Portland from St. Louis a number of years ago," he said, "and I can tell you that when you were a black man in Maine back then things weren't always easy for you. People tried to be friendly, but they just didn't' know how to act around me, you know? Besides being a black man, I'm also a very big and strong guy, and sometimes people get intimidated by that. I'm actually a very gentle soul – except on the football field! – but the only one who could see that was Jake. Right from the beginning, there wasn't any kind of tension or pretense between us. We'd kid around about which one of us is stronger, you know, but we both knew that really didn't mean a damn thing to either one of us, that it's what's in your heart that matters. When I met Jake, I knew I had a friend who understood me and would stick by me under any circumstance, right to the end. To him I wasn't a big black man from St. Louis, I was his friend, and when Jake Sawyer's your friend, you've got a friend for life, end of story."

*Jake and his pal Randel Philips
hanging out in Portland, Maine.*

VOLUME TWO

JOHN DOE

I'd say the ratio of comments I've gotten would be about 20-1, pro-Jake, but there's always that one. Here's an email I got from an anonymous John Doe: "This guy Jake Sawyer that you're writing about has never been anything more than a self-centered narcissistic menace to society; a sociopath who felt above the law and selfishly decided to become a burden on society, rather than contribute to it. He's just another common criminal and your making a hero out of him is ludicrous."

Well, there you go. Thank you, Mr. Doe. All I can say is that there's another guy who has a much different view of Jake. His name is John Webster, and he contacted me a while ago and gave me a great picture of Jake and him together in the early 1990's, and he had quite a story to with it.

JOHN WEBSTER

"After my father was killed in a car accident in the late 1980's, Jake was like a father to me, man," John said, "he saved me from a life of crime and made me into somebody, and I'll always be grateful to him for it. I started hanging around a neighborhood garage where a bunch of tough guys worked on their cars, and it didn't take long before I had some very unsavory friends. Jake hung around there now and then, and he could see that I headed down the wrong path, and, without a doubt, would be end up in a cell sometime in the near future. So one day he came up to me and said: 'So, kid, you think you're tough, huh?'

JAKE

"Of course, I was nothing but a mouthy little punk at the time, so I asked him what the hell it was to him. All he said was: 'Shut up and get in my car. I'm going to take you to a place where you're going to find out how to fight, who to fight, and when to fight them.' So, I got in his car and he took me to the gym that was set up in the basement of the Griffin Club, in South Portland, and that was the day my education began. There were two very rugged black guys from Brunswick Naval Air Station who boxed in Eddie's gym, and when I put on the gloves against them they proceeded to beat the shit out of me one at a time. I kept coming back to the gym and they'd pound on me every time. After they saw that I had the necessary desire and motivation, though, they started to ease off and teach me a thing or two, and the rest is history.

"I turned pro in 1992 with Jake in my corner cheering me on. He didn't know much about boxing technique, which he acknowledged right away, but he sure as hell knew how to motivate people. He'd get me so pumped up I'd feel like I couldn't lose, and even if I did lose I'd know damn well that I'd put every ounce of energy I had in my body into it. I fought all through the rest of the 1990's and complied a very respectable record, then in 2004 I fought in Germany for the International Super Middle-Weight title. I got knocked out in the first round, but that's how it goes. I had given it my best shot, and win or lose, thanks to the way Jake turned my life around when I was a teenager, I was somebody."

*Jake (at right) with boxer John Webster
and Webster's manager Steve Cardilli in the 1990s.*

JAKE

STEVE SAWTELLE

Out of nowhere, a man by the name of Steve Sawtelle showed up at Marty Joyce's house for the annual summer get-together of men Jake trained and worked-out with at Martin's Health Club. No one recognized Steve at first, because he's in his sixties now and they hadn't seen him since he was nineteen, when he left Portland to go into the Army. As soon as he identified himself, though, the others remembered him very well and pumped him for stories of those long-ago days. After about fifty years of hearing each others memories over and over again, they were understandably eager for some fresh input, I guess. All were much entertained by Steve's recollections, from what I've heard, so I was eager to talk to him, and after doing an internet search on him, I was even more so.

Turns out that Stephen B. Sawtelle is a very successful Wall Street financier whose picture was once featured on the cover of *Wall Street Week* magazine. In the accompanying story, the editors refer to him as one of the sharpest and most successful financial traders in the country. Evidently Steve did alright for himself after he left Portland. After serving seven years in the Army as an elite Green Beret and 82nd Airborne Ranger, and achieving the rank of Captain in the course of an eventful seven-year stint, during which he was part of numerous hazardous and mostly clandestine operations around the world, Steve left the Army and entered the field of financial investment. Before long, he became a division manager of one of the country's largest mutual mutual funds and financial firms, then started an investment firm of his own, by the name of SBS Star Incorporated.

Okay, so Steve is a busy man. I didn't realize the extent of it, though, until we exchanged emails and we ascertained that the only way I could talk to him before my publishing deadline would be to somehow connect with him during the month-long motorcycle tour he and his wife go on together every year. His instructions were for me to install What's App on my iPhone, and to expect a call from him on an agreed upon Sunday afternoon at precisely 3:00 PM.

Steve had told me that his wife and he were touring Europe this time around, and I was aware that Europe was experiencing the hottest summer in recorded history, so the first thing I said when the phone rang, at precisely 3:00 PM, was that I hoped his wife and him were standing the heat okay.

"Go to your email and access the photo I just sent you," he said.

I did, and it was of Steve and his motorcycle, with patches of snow on the ground all around.

"My wife and I are doing the motorcycle Tour de France and we rode into a blizzard in the Swiss Alps," he explained, "we've been holed up at Goddard Pass for the last four hours, so things worked out well for calling you."

So here I was on a quiet Sunday afternoon in Maine, about to talk about Jake Sawyer to a guy on a motorcycle trip holed up with his wife in a mountain pass in the Swiss Alps. When Jake confronted me on the sidewalk in front of the library that day and informed me that I was going to be writing his life story, and that I was in for one helluva ride, I had no idea of how right he was.

"I have a hunch concerning where your interest in motorcycles comes from, Steve," I said with a laugh.

JAKE

Steve Sawtelle

"Yes, your hunch is right on," he laughed, "my passion for motorcycles started when I was fifteen years old and met Jake. I never did get the chance to ride with him, but I was truly inspired when I watched him ride. He looked so wild and free when he was on his bike that I knew immediately that motorcycles would always be a big part of my life too. Jake was also heavily into the motorcycle mechanics, and I've also taken a great deal of interest in the construction and design of motorcycles myself. Over the years, I've invested in the work Shawn Lezotte and Scot Doane, of Connecticut Custom Cycles, have done with custom designing and improving the operation and utility of motorcycles. My wife and I have taken motorcycle tours all over the world, including to Australia and New Zealand, and Thailand. Now here we are in the Swiss Alps. An added little bonus to all the fun and adventure my wife and I have is reporting to Shawn and Scot on how my bike had performed in various climates and altitudes. So, yeah, motorcycles are a big part of my life, and Jake was sort of the catalyst for it."

"Okay, Steve," I said, but from what the guys who attend Marty Joyce's annual parties have told me, your connection to Jake goes a lot deeper than just your mutual interest in riding and designing motorcycles."

"That's correct," he answered, here's the picture: I was a five-foot, three-inch, one-hundred and thirty-pound fifteen year old, with a burning desire to play on the Deering High School football team. I had made the team, but it looked like I was never going to make it off the bench. Then one day I spotted Jake's health club not far from where I lived, and the rest is history. Jake immediately took a great interest in me and my goals, and that was it.

"Everything was going just great, I was feeling stronger and was gaining some weight," Steve continued, "but then disaster struck. Jake's club burned down and I figured that that was it for me and my goals. But then there was Jake, standing next to me on the sidewalk as I was staring forlornly at the burnt building, telling me that my membership and the dues I had paid in advance would be honored at a new health club that his friend Al Martin had just opened in the Old Port. That was it. When I found Martin's Health Club, I had found a new home. Right from the beginning, Jake, Al Martin, Marty Joyce, Ron Damon, Bob Penney and the other guys who worked out there treated me with respect and made me feel that I was was the equal of any man at the club, or anywhere else, even though I was a young teenager and very unsure of myself.

"I'd have to say that my greatest benefactor at that time was Marty Joyce. He took me under his wing and made me his special project, and I'll always be grateful to him for that. Before long, with the help of Marty and Jake and the other guys, I developed some serious muscle and started to put on the body weight I was after. Even more than that, though, was that I was experiencing a degree of self-confidence and sense of well-being that I hadn't even known existed.

"I looked at Jake with a kind of awe, to tell you the truth. I called him "Mr. Sawyer," of course. Hey, he was about fifteen years older than I was, and had been an Army Airborne Paratrooper and a Hell's Angel. He was also very imposing physically. He had the biggest biceps I have ever seen on a man in my life. He's not that big of a man in terms of overall body size, but he could curl one-hundred pound dumbbells in each hand for ten reps. If you know anything about weight-lifting, you know how absolutely amazing that is, for a man of any size and weight. I was also fascinated by some of the unorthodox training techniques he employed. He'd stand on his head with his legs straight up for long periods of time, for instance. Man, he was light years ahead of his time. He was mixing weight-lifting with yoga way back in the early seventies! Back then, only sissies did yoga, and only slow-witted apes lifted weights, but here was Jake Sawyer combining the two, and he was anything but a slow-witted sissy!"

"Anyway, the upshot of it all was that not only did I end up starting for my high school football team, but I became something of a stand-out. When the coach got up to the mic at the team banquet at the end of my Senior year he said that because there was a huge snowstorm on the day of the big Thanksgiving day game between Deering High and Portland High, the people who were to choose the winner of the Fitzpatrick Trophy as the outstanding player of the game couldn't stay around to do so, but they had informed him of their decision later, and he had decided to wait for the banquet to announce that I was the recipient. What a feeling that was! I was the shortest guy on the team and the coach just announced that I won the Fitzpatrick Trophy! That wasn't all of it, though. The coach also said that he considered me to be the MVP of the team for the entire season!

"Those accolades were terrific, believe me, but I'd have to say that an equally as memorable thrill was when Jake and Marty Joyce, along with a few other guys from Martin's Health Club attended a Deering High football game just to see me play.

JAKE

"My athletic career included more than just football, though. I entered the Maine State Power-Lifting championships when I was seventeen, and even though I was the youngest lifter in the competition, I won the trophy for my weight class. I also became interested in competitive wrestling at that time, but Deering High didn't have a wrestling team, so I worked at it on my own and later did some wrestling in college. After high school, I enrolled at the University of Maine at Presque Isle, and in my Freshman year I won the New England power-lifting championship in my weight category, then in my Sophomore year I was awarded a wrestling scholarship."

It took Steve and I a while to get all of this straight, during which time I learned that he has an obsessive devotion to the truth. After one of our telephone conversations, I'd record bits of information I thought were accurate, but when Steve read them he'd invariably say "not quite." I guess he suspected that I thought he was being too nitpicking, so at one point he informed me that his approach to getting the copy about him right was the same as his approach to his investment counseling business, which he said involves three rules he never deviates from: One, always treat your clients as you wish to be treated; two, always invest their money as you would your own; and three, always be honest with your clients, down to the smallest detail.

"So there you have it," Steve said that summer Sunday afternoon from a snow-covered mountain pass in the Swiss Alps, "I can honestly say that Jake was one of the most influential people in my life. He's definitely one of a kind, and has done a lot of good things for a lot of people. I know he's done a lot of highly questionable things here and there as well, but, you know, I don't want to think of what my life would've been like without Jake and Marty Joyce and the other guys from Martin's Health Club."

MARK

When I ran into Mark, from Jake's exercise class, on the street, I couldn't believe how bright and bouncy he looked, and when I saw he was wearing a Planet Fitness t-shirt, I said: "Hello, Mark, you're looking great! Especially your thumbs! They look handsome as hell, just like Jake said they would! Hey, where did you get that fantastic t-shirt?"

After a big laugh and rotating his thumbs for me, like Jake taught the class to do, Mark was eager to fill me in on what had been happening in his life.

"Well, I got to feeling so good doing the exercises Jake taught us, I wanted to do more, so I went and joined Planet Fitness! I always wanted to go there, but I was afraid of the people, you know what I mean, but Jake told us to go right for what you want, and that's just what I did! I've got so much confidence you wouldn't believe it! I made friends with everybody there and they even gave me a job!"

"A job?!" I exclaimed.

"Yes!" he said, "I've got a part-time job there as a part-time assistant janitor! I was feeling so good about myself I went right up to the manager and told her that someone told me that she was looking for a part-time assistant janitor and I wanted the job! And she gave it to me! So now I keep all the machines rubbed down and so sparkly clean you wouldn't believe it! And

JAKE

I get paid one-hundred dollars a week! It's the first job I've ever had and I love it!"

Enough said.

Jake and Mark

VOLUME TWO

CAROL OF THE MOUNTAINS

When I called Jake to tell him that I was ready to send volume two off to the publisher, but that he could still make minor edits if he cared to, he asked me if I thought his recently having had his entire life upended might be worthy of mention in the book.

Okay, I have to acknowledge that my first thought was that, considering his age and the tumultuous way he'd lived his life, he had been given some sort of diagnosis. The possibility landed hard on me, because over the course of the interview process Jake and I had become friends, so I was almost afraid to ask him what he was talking about.

"Do you remember my telling you at one point that every day of my life features a new adventure?" he began. "Well, there ya go. The take-away from that, my friend, is that the longer you delay getting volume two to the publisher, the more stories there's going to be. So I do suggest that this be the last time you contact me before you ship out the stupendous pile of words you've been putting together, okay?"

"Yup, it's a deal," I said, "but, wha'd'ya got this time?"

"Alright," he began, "as you know, I am in regular contact with various friends of mine in Ward, Colorado, most often with my old friend Tall Bob, and he recently told me about an encounter he had with a very special acquaintance of mine from the last time I was in Ward, in the early 1990s. Bob said he was on one of the casual walks he likes to take on nearby mountain trails and met up with a woman named Carol, who he knew I had a thing for back then.

"Tall Bob said that when he mentioned to Carol that

he is in regular contact with me, and that volume one of my life story had been published, and that volume two would be out soon, she gasped and cupped her hands over her mouth in disbelief. Then after a bit she told Tall Bob that she had heard that I was killed in a bank robbery years ago! You have been made aware, sir, of the rumors about me that abound, so there you go!

"Here's the story with Carol: When I was living at my campsite in the early 1990s I applied for a part-time job as kitchen help at The Millsite Inn, which is located on the Peak to Peak Highway, a little higher up on the mountain from my campsite. I really enjoyed the work I did there helping out in the kitchen, and I especially liked that I got to bring home a lot of juicy steak bones for my dog Shawn. As time went on, though, the best part of my being at the restaurant got to be spending time in the kitchen with the owner's wife, who was the Carol we're talking about here. Carol and I got along great right from the beginning. She taught me a lot about food preparation and a number of other things, and I provided her with some insights into parts of life that she had never come close to experiencing. Let's just say that we had a mutually enjoyable relationship, and that as time went on I found that she was constantly on my mind.

"The problem, as is obvious, was that she was another man's wife, and that he was a friend of mine. It was a wrenching decision, believe me, but at one point I decided that the only way to handle the situation was for me to leave Colorado and head back to Portland. Saying good-bye to Carol was one of the hardeer things I've ever done in my life, believe me, and it was made even harder by the fact that I wasn't free to tell her how I felt about her. I knew she had certain feelings for me too, but that she just had too much character to express them while she was married to another man.

"After Tall Bob had gotten my instant approval for him to do so, he gave Carol my number and she gave me a call. So, what do you think was the first thing we said to one each other after all these years?"

"Hi, how ya doin'?" I answered.

"That's just what we said! How did you know that?!" he roared.

"I don't know," I said, "I just had a feeling, but what did you say next?"

Carol of the mountains, 2017

JAKE

"Well, since you're so curious, I'll tell you," he said.

"She knew a lot about what I'd been up to because she had read volume one of my life story, so we kind of had fun batting a few things around. Then when I asked her what her life had been like since we last saw one another, she told me that she had continued to be happy in her marriage, but that her husband had passed away a couple of years ago, and that lately she had been feeling somewhat lonely and depressed.

"To cut to the quick, my friend, let me tell you that Carol and I have been talking on the phone on almost a daily basis since out initial conversation, and both of us have been very much into it. She's told me that our little talks have lifted her spirits as well. She said she had been depressed since her husband died, and that our little talks were helping a lot with that. At one point I came up with what proved to be a great idea for her: after she expressed a desire to expand her horizons, and mentioned that, for some reason, she had always wanted to visit Deadwood, South Dakota, I talked her into doing just that. Actually, she had never taken a trip all by herself, she loved the experience, and told me that she's definitely going to continue to do such things.

"Great!" I exclaimed. "So what's next? Maybe a rendezvous in Paris?"

"I've got an even better scenario than that for you! I'm sure you remember the story of Mystique Figure Wrap, the business I had in Portland in the early seventies catering to the comforts of society women who wanted to be able to fit into a particular dress for that special occasion, and maybe even experience a bit of sensual gratification in the process. You might also remember that I've had a secret desire to revive the business someday, both to be of service to the ladies, and to provide some added income for myself. So, okay, here's the story: Carol has a very close friend who is a successful businessman in the Fiji Islands, and when she sent him the serialization of my life story that appeared in the *Bollard* magazine, he was totally captivated by the part about Mystique Figure Wrap, and he wants to open up a chain of Mystique Figure Wrap salons throughout the Fiji Islands, with Carol and me managing the entire enterprise!"

"So the two of you are going to pack up and go to the Fiji Islands to operate a chain of Mystique Figure Wrap salons, huh?" I said.

"Yeah, you've got it, that is the plan, man" he answered, chuckling to himself, "after I visit the veterans centers with my friend Steve Sawtelle, which I've told you about, Carol and I are headed for the Fiji Islands.

"I do suggest, though," he added "that you wrap up volume two of our little project here before another major event pops up my life that you can't resist writing about. I mean, you know, we have to call a halt to things and get the mission accomplished at some point. I'm only eighty-two, after all, so obviously many more great adventures will be taking place in my life. As I have told you, my friend, every day of my life features another new and exciting adventure."

"Okay, I get it, Jake," I said. "It's taken a while, but I finally get it."

JAKE

APPENDIX: JAKE'S ANCESTRY

Jake's first ancestor to arrive in America was Walter Norton. He was a soldier of fortune hired by Sir Ferdinando Gorges to protect members of the Gorges company which arrived at Wessagusset (Weymouth), Mass., in September 1623. He returned to England in 1625.

Norton retired as a Lt. Colonel and emigrated to New England on the ship *Katherine* with his wife. They joined John Winthrop in Charlestown in 1630.

In 1632 he built the second home in what became York, Maine. In 1634 Captain Norton was in a battle with Pequin Indians near the mouth of the Connecticut River that summer while sailing in that area. In a later report Governor Bradford of Massachusetts tells us that "Captain Norton defended himself a long time against many Indians in the cook's room of the ship, until by accident the gunpowder took fire which for readiness he had set in the open before him, which did so burn and scald him and blind his eyes as he could make no longer resistance, but was slain by the Indians though they much commended his valor."

Another of Jake's relatives ran a fishing business on Richmond Island, Maine, for a couple of years starting in 1632.

This genealogical research material can become very interesting as many, many paths are tracked back through the generations.

At one point, researchers found one line of Jake's ancestors linked to William the Conqueror (King of England after he led the Norman conquest of 1066) and another to Lady Godiva, a relative Jake says he can really relate to.

VOLUME TWO

Continuing back from William the Conqueror, Jake's lineage can be traced all the way to Rollo, a leader of a band of Viking warriors banished from Norway in the 850s A.D. for being too violent.

Rollo and his men later settled in what became Normandy in France.

Jake looks forward to meeting Rollo again when he gets to Valhalla!!

ACKNOWLEDGMENTS

Many people provided support and encouragement in the writing of Jake's life story, and they all deserve acknowledgment, but Jake wants to extend special thanks to all of those people who shared their personal memories of him; to Stanley Dobson, Jake's friend and owner of the Munjoy Hill Tavern; and to Angela Ronan, Jake's executive secretary and personal assistant. Jake would also like to extend a special thanks to Linette, the activities director of his building, who has been good at supporting and encouraging his exercise class. Additionally, we would both like to thank Tom Holbrook, of Piscataqua Press and RiverRun Bookstore, for his guidance and patience; and Chris Busby, the publisher of the *Bollard* magazine, now the *Mainer* magazine, for introducing us to the idea of using the "interstitial" literary method of the writing in this book, whereby the writer makes themselves a part of the narrative. My heartfelt thanks also go to Leslie Bailey, my first reader and grammar guru, for smoothing the road, and my brow, when I need it.

VOLUME TWO

9 781950 381340